Sex &
Money

Commerce and Mass Culture Series
Justin Wyatt, Editor

Sex and Money: Feminism and Political Economy in the Media
Eileen R. Meehan and Ellen Riordan, Editors

Directed by Allen Smithee
Jeremy Braddock and Stephen Hock, Editors

Sure Seaters: The Emergence of Art House Cinema
Barbara Wilinsky

Walter Wanger, Hollywood Independent
Matthew Bernstein

Hollywood Goes Shopping
David Desser and Garth S. Jowett, Editors

Screen Style: Fashion and Femininity in 1930s Hollywood
Sarah Berry

Active Radio: Pacifica's Brash Experiment
Jeff Land

Sex & Money

Feminism and
Political Economy
in the Media

Eileen R. Meehan
Ellen Riordan
Editors

Commerce and Mass Culture Series
University of Minnesota Press
Minneapolis / London

Published by the University of Minnesota Press
111 Third Avenue South, Suite 290
Minneapolis, MN 55401-2520
http://www.upress.umn.edu

Library of Congress Cataloging-in-Publication Data

    Sex and money : feminism and political economy in the media / Eileen R. Meehan and Ellen Riordan, editors.
      p. cm. — (Commerce and mass culture series)
    Includes bibliographical references and index.
    ISBN 0-8166-3787-3 — ISBN 0-8166-3788-1 (pbk.)
    1. Feminism and mass media.   2. Mass media—Economic aspects.
3. Mass media and technology.   I. Meehan, Eileen R., 1951–   II. Riordan, Ellen.   III. Series.
    P96.F46 S49 2001
    302.23'082—dc21

                                            2001004672

12 11 10 09 08 07 06 05 04 03 02   10 9 8 7 6 5 4 3 2 1

Contents

Acknowledgments

The editors wish to acknowledge the University of Arizona for travel support to the IAMCR conference in Glasgow, Scotland, UDC and ICA in San Francisco, and the University of Oregon School of Journalism and Communication for providing research and travel funds.

This project would not have been possible without the help and support of many colleagues and friends, including Caren Deming and Adele Barker at the University of Arizona, and Janet Wasko, Randy Nichols, and everybody else at the University of Oregon who provided much needed summer fun!

Special thanks to Chris Demaske at the University of Washington, Tacoma, for summer fun in Oregon (we hope she'll let us come and visit her new place!), and to Al Babbitt and Angie Record—persons extraordinaire!

We would also like to thank Justin Wyatt and the gang at the University of Minnesota Press for getting us through the process, and to Elizabeth J. Silas at Miami University, Ohio, for her discerning eye when proofreading.

Thanks to Vincent Mosco for his enthusiastic support for this project since the beginning.

And, finally, much appreciation goes out to all of our contributors not only for sticking with deadlines but also for being très cool!

Introduction
Ellen Riordan and Eileen R. Meehan

Controversies over gender and economics have produced some remarkable sights in the past twenty years: antiabortion fundamentalists
joining with prochoice feminists to picket movie theaters showing
pornographic films; fundamentalist Republicans calling for federal intervention in the private lives of gay Republicans; fiscal conservatives
decrying public funding of abortions for poor women and female sol-
diers, yet arguing passionately that their own rights to abortion be protected; white, middle-class men attacking affirmative action for giving
jobs to white, middle-class women.

These are but a few examples in which allegiances that seem easy
become difficult, in which oppositions that appear unchangeable shift
dramatically. At root, we believe, is the participants' answer to this
question: should social hierarchy be built on gender or on economic
status? If gender is selected, then an issue is seen in terms of gendered
privilege. If economic status, then the question is seen as a matter of
money. Consider how our understanding of pornography changes
when concerns about graphic sexual acts, objectification of women,
and role models are replaced by a concern about profits and pay scales,
about the working conditions and health benefits of sex workers appearing in films. Each lens brings different elements of an issue into
sharp focus. By using both lenses, thus metaphorically approximating
stereoscopic vision, we see that pornography as a phenomenon is rooted
in both sex and money, that is, in the intertwining hierarchy of patriarchy and capitalism. This book explores how gendered and moneyed
privilege play out in media-saturated, industrialized countries grap-
pling with the effects of corporate and governmental policies that promote the convergence of the media, computing, and telecommunications industries. The project began, however, with a simple question
about employment in an academic specialty.

Our field is communications research, particularly media studies,
and, like most people, we have a tendency to "talk shop" during otherwise social occasions. In 1996, over dinner, we were chatting about the
divide between scholars who study media texts and those who study

media corporations. We could easily assemble long lists of feminist textual scholars or of political economists, but we struggled to do the same for feminist political economists. Something that began as a question—"Where are all the women?"—now comes full circle in this book. We emerge with many answers to that question, posed by feminist political economists both male and female. As this collection illustrates, feminist scholars do research the political economy of communications and political economists of communications do take a feminist perspective. Perhaps this accounts for our relative invisibility, at least in the United States, where the academy marginalizes both feminist and political-economic research. *Sex and Money* serves as one corrective to this double marginalization.

Underneath their disparate research foci, feminist scholars and political economists share an interest in power: what social group controls the greatest portion of a society's resources and how does that group justify its privileges? Feminism focuses on the gendered system of privilege, political economy on privilege rooted in economic control. For the United States and the emerging global economy, sex plus money equals power. Addressing this equation in media studies requires the integration of feminism and political economy. This integrative approach is not simply a matter of adding one to the other. Rather, we argue that all media structures, agents, processes, and expressions find their raison d'être in relationships shaped by sex and money.

We have three goals for this edited collection. First, we want to encourage a rethinking of ontological and epistemological assumptions by feminists and political economists in order to understand communication at the personal, experiential, institutional, and structural levels. Next we want to break down the dichotomy between public and private by examining how women's obligations in the private sphere and societal assumptions about women's domestic obligations shape employment opportunities, work patterns, policy debates, and legislation regarding women in the workplace. Last, we wish to dismantle the notion that time spent using media or shopping for goods is a matter of leisure, of personal whimsy and individual taste. Just as gender roles shape one's work life, so too do vested economic interests shape one's leisure and personal identity. Under the pressures of patriarchy and capitalism, the barrier between one's private life and public life dissolves.

To achieve these goals, the collection begins with Ellen Riordan setting the framework for a feminist political economy in communication research. Contextualizing this in terms of traditional divisions between political economy and feminism, Leslie Steeves and Janet Wasko examine ways in which the two approaches could move toward a "friendly alliance." Further benefits of convivial relations are suggested by Lisa McLaughlin, who sees feminism as a means of resolving the often bitter debate between political economy and cultural studies. Overall, these essays work together to lay out the rationale for integrating the two approaches, for emphasizing theory building rather than critique, and for research that practices a respectful caution regarding historically structured differences but promotes the transformation of knowledge into praxis.

These essays are solid foundations from which specific research projects can be built, as the second and third sections of the collection demonstrate. These sections are devoted to case studies examining some particular interplay of patriarchy and capitalism in either the public or private sphere. We select this dichotomy of public/private in order to question its accuracy in describing human experience. We address the public sphere via case studies focused on women's employment, connections to new technology, experiences of violence, and news reportage on these matters.

Michèle Martin opens the second section, examining the claim that technologies are gendered such that they are hostile to women. Arguing that technologies must be understood in terms of social and economic context, Martin reconceptualizes technology as deployed in the interest of capital and patriarchy but with the possibility of progressive appropriation of such technologies by women. To get at the economic contexts of women working with new technologies, Ellen Balka analyzes telecommunications systems in Atlantic Canada, economic globalization, and employment, demonstrating how deregulation, mergers, and corporate deployment of new technology combine to deskill and destabilize women workers. Expanding the focus to all information sector jobs, Stana Martin examines the impact of child rearing, elder care, and other forms of domestic labor on women's participation in the information workforce. She traces the effect of a patriarchal division of domestic labor on women's and men's opportunities for advanced training and stable employment required by the "golden"-collar jobs. These three essays work together to theorize relationships between technology and work, and then to demonstrate how patriarchy and capitalism intertwine to define women's work in telecommunications as both highly technological and utterly unskilled.

Complementing this research are four essays focused on cultural and legal implications of women's work and of mediated representations of that work. Nancy Hauserman examines public discourse about women workers who were sexually harassed by corporate executives, comparing accounts of the Astra case in Sweden and in the United States. Roopali Mukherjee explores connections between news reportage, gender, and reactionary politics in a referendum campaign against affirmative action in California media. Moving to England, Karen Ross argues that the news establishment treats female politicians and voters as either mothers or fashion models, while sexualizing and underpaying female journalists. Carolyn M. Byerly supplements these discussions of women's work and women's rights by asking why systematic violence against women is not framed by journalists as a violation of human rights.

In their various integrations of feminism and political economy, the seven authors reveal how traditionally private concerns of domesticity, identity, and consumption intertwine with public concerns of employment, technology, and law in the media. The third section of the collection reverses that process by explicating how public concerns operate within the private sphere through case studies involving entertainment, identity, and consumption.

Justin Wyatt begins by tracing the career and marketing of actress Shelley Duvall to discern how the gendered division of actress/director labor connected with second wave feminism and shifts in the fashion industry's idealized body type to support the reimaging of liberated women as ultra-thin bodies with empty heads. Similarly, Amy Beer illuminates the economic dynamics that construct "Latinas" as female consumers in the United States whose families may be connected to any of the nations of Central and Latin America. In another example of market/identity creation, Angela R. Record explains how the "teenage girl market," generated by advertisers and media, actively encouraged teenage women to regard themselves as future wives and mothers whose current (and future) purchases were essential to their security. Fred Fejes explores advertisers' version of homosexual identity as niche markets made up of gay men who spend lavishly and lesbians who spend less. Fejes questions the value of being targeted as a consumer while being denied basic civil rights. He also demonstrates how capitalism uses patriarchy to differentiate and rank homosexuals by gender such that gay men are ranked higher and accorded more privilege than lesbians. This integration of feminism and political economy suggests that the dialogues between feminist scholarship and gay/lesbian/queer scholarship would benefit from a political economy of discrimination.

Focusing on how consumers are identified, Eileen R. Meehan identifies structural contradictions in the markets for television ratings, audiences, and programs that encourage television networks, advertisers, and producers to target a narrow and unrepresentative viewership. Robin Andersen shifts focus from the targets of advertising to the ads themselves, exploring advertising's disconnection of sexual desire from fulfillment, its projection of sexual fulfillment onto consumption, and its use of postmodernist irony to frame as hip images that are sexist, misogynist, and violent. Finally, Ramona Curry and Angharad N. Valdivia demonstrate how the work practices and assumptions used by television producers in the United States limit importation or adaptation of non-U.S. programming. For the Brazilian producer of *Xuxa,* this meant redesigning a worldwide hit to conform to U.S. commercial expectations regarding gender, race, and nationality as well as production values.

As these eight authors demonstrate, a feminist political economy illuminates how corporate practices and governmental policies limit the menu of personal choices and put pressure on people to make the "right" personal choice. Taken together, the book's three sections demonstrate the wealth of insights that can be had from syntheses of feminist and political-economic theories, methods, and research. The authors' rigorous integration of multiple methodologies affirms the power of interdisciplinary scholarship to unlock complex relationships between highly abstract concepts—patriarchy and capitalism—that have a very real and oppressive effect in the everyday lives of women and men.

I

Theorizing the Connections: Sex, Money, Media

1. Intersections and New Directions: On Feminism and Political Economy
Ellen Riordan

The current state of media and entertainment megamergers demands a closer analysis of the economic aspects organizing the logic of global communication industries. Political economists who analyze communications and media have suggested this for years (Golding and Murdock 1991; Garnham 1979); industry scholars have suggested this, too (Bagdikian 1997; Compaine 1982). Feminist media scholars, however, have been more reticent to venture into the field of media economics, industry analysis, and political economy; rarely do these studies examine capitalism, labor, and class as shaping women's experiences (McLaughlin 1997). And yet much feminist communications research is critical in orientation, looking to free women from oppressive and exploitative structures.[1] While feminist sociologists continue to make contributions by theorizing economic structures affecting women's lives (Acker 1999; Edin and Lein 1997), feminist communications scholars tend to gravitate more toward issues of representation and identity, concerns usually theorized within cultural studies analyses.

Perhaps one reason that feminist communications scholars have abandoned political-economic issues is that historically women have been unwelcome in overt political and economic domains (this also extends from the public sphere of law and politics into the realm of academia). Even though in almost every country women have the right to vote, are active leaders and heads of state in several nations, and have increased representation in local and national governments, the majority of women around the world do not acknowledge themselves as political beings because they do not directly work for the state or actively participate in policy discussions. Despite some limitations, second-wave feminism stressed that we should value the day-to-day moments and the private sphere of women's lives as political and economic. According to this standpoint, women's actions are political and economic (therefore valuable), whether or not they hold a public office, engage in legislation, or act as household wage earners.[2] While second-wave feminism emphasized that the personal is political, feminist cultural scholars have found it difficult, and often unnecessary, to connect the everyday moments of women's lives back to the structural level of capitalism. Indeed, this is one of the reasons why many feminist communications scholars choose to ignore political-economic concerns. However, avoiding the political-economic context of daily life can be detrimental to women, for it oversimplifies the complex interlocking forms of oppression to which women are subjected.[3] For example, even though a working-class woman comes home at the end of her day and finds pleasure in identifying with a character on a popular television show, she is not freed from patriarchal and capitalist ideologies that affect her work, family, and personal relations. While women as audience members can and do feel empowered by certain fictional characters and popular culture icons (and therefore we should acknowledge these moments as something very real and meaningful for women), feminist communications scholars cannot stop our quest for ideological meaning in those instances of empowerment, for restrictive structures remain intact, unquestioned, and often masked by these moments of reprieve. Feminist analyses that look for meaning, yet are void of any historical and political-economic context, may serve to validate women's experiences as real, something undeservedly neglected throughout time, but rarely do they change life opportunities for women. Women's experiences must not be dismissed, even when they contradict the apparent structural realities of patriarchy and capitalism, but feminist praxis will be misguided if we do not situate women's experiences in the context of material conditions.[4]

In this essay I suggest a movement toward a feminist political economy in communications. What I mean by this is that political-economic analyses begin to reconceptualize the economic and broaden the objects of study to include individual experiences rather than focus primarily on macro-level, institutional, and structural analyses. Women, as well as other marginalized groups, need to understand their lives as gendered and economic and shaped by both capitalism and patriarchy. In order to make this link, scholars must explicate how economics and gender are sutured into our smallest day-to-day actions. If communications scholars fail to elucidate the connections between the day-to-day lived experience of people and the structures of capitalism and patriarchy, then we will continue to participate uncritically in their reproduction.

As Acker (1999) suggests for Marxist sociologists, reconceptualizing political economy may mean rethinking class and its significance to a contemporary critique of capitalism. Perhaps such a reconceptualization means more theoretical self-reflexivity that allows political economists to address issues of epistemology. The scope of this essay does not allow for an elaboration on these theoretical points. Instead, this essay is an attempt to think through some of these issues at a fundamental level, questioning how best to proceed without eschewing core tenets of political economy, which would reduce our studies to industry analyses. Thinking through the meaning of a feminist political economy is the beginning of a lifelong theoretical project, whereby I seek to elucidate how social relations are always already gendered and economic, as well as intrinsic to one another. As a feminist political economist, I hope not only to bring more people to an understanding of how their lives are shaped by gender and economics, but also to push toward an understanding of how patriarchy and capitalism continually reproduce social injustices that must be eliminated. In this essay, I briefly discuss political economy and feminism in the context of communications studies, and I work toward defining a vision for feminist political economy.

Political Economy in Communications

Political economy is an approach to social analysis that explicates the nature and function of capitalism. Not all political-economic inquiries are critical in orientation;[5] however, a critique of capitalism needs to be at the core of feminist political economy, as I will theorize in the subsequent section. In *Capital,* Marx (1976) explicated the capitalist system and stressed the importance of labor as a major focal point for analysis. The traditional Marxist view of political economy argues that capitalism, comprising capital/wage-labor relationships, leads to a growing mechanization of labor, the concentration and centralization of capital, and periodic crises in which a distinct tendency for overproduction exists (Mosco 1996, 45). Marxist analysis, especially political economy, offers a significant break from the idealist Hegelian philosophy that preceded it, claiming that social relations can be empirically observed in the historical material conditions of a given society.[6]

Political economy of communications usually refers to the study of economic structures of mass media industries. Smythe (1960) defines it as the allocation of scarce resources for the production and distribution of media products. As Mosco (1996) suggests, political economists address consumption by looking at business growth as a structural response to the economic crisis of overproduction, and as a social response to the political crisis. Political economists often analyze patterns of ownership and control, to understand how they structure and constrain cultural production (Wasko 1994). As these definitions suggest, political economists concern themselves less with consumption practices of individuals and more with production issues of cultural artifacts. I argue that in order to further understand capitalism, and its relationship to the daily lives of people, political economists must focus on the meaning of consumption, not only as it results from a crisis of overproduction, but also as it stems from the "pleasure" many politically, economically, and socially disenfranchised groups derive from consuming. Understanding wants and desires as experienced by individuals and groups of people, as well as how this pathos combines with the crisis of overproduction, opens the way to changing social consciousness. Consumption is an integral part of the reproduction of capitalism, class inequalities, and women's oppression. The meaning and status conferred upon consumption practices, although wildly varied across different groups and communities classified by race, class, sexuality, religious background, ethnicity, dis/ability, age, etc., should be used as a means to understand how subjectivities are both economic and gendered. Cultural studies often take consumption practices as an entry point (particularly for feminist analyses), but rather than conceptualize consumption as an economic practice, it is most often theorized as a cultural practice. While capitalism *is* a cultural practice, it must be understood in terms of its economic implications as well as its cultural significance.

Feminism in Communications

Across disciplines and around the globe, feminist scholars find it nearly impossible to come up with a single definition of feminism. Even when one divides up the various camps—liberal, radical, Marxist/social, psychoanalytic, poststructural, postmodern, ecofeminist, womanist, and postfeminist—this does not account for all feminists, and this does not do justice to the blurring and complexity of feminist thought that does not fit neatly into one of these boxes.[7] As with political economy, there are branches of feminism that are not critical in orientation, meaning they do not find fault with social structures. For example, liberal feminists fail to critique the overarching structures of patriarchy and capitalism, even though they critique practices within these structures. Since theorizing a feminist political economy is critical in orientation, this section will focus mainly on critical forms of feminism (although as I suggest later in this essay, feminist political economists may gain insight into understanding the lives of women by incorporating information from noncritical analyses).

Most feminists explicitly working in the area of political economy have been Marxist or socialist feminists. Working from within these paradigms, feminists reject the liberal claim that human nature is defined by rationality. Instead, Marxists emphasize that human nature is defined by our labor or a need to produce our means of subsistence (Tong 1997, 39). While historical materialism offers an analysis of labor relations, class position, and exploitation, socialist feminists (as well as others) argue that Marxism does not adequately theorize gender relations (Hartman 1981). For Marxists, the exploitation of workers under the system of capitalism is privileged over the oppression of women under patriarchy. Subsequently, feminist critiques of Marxism point to a major theoretical problem that assumes the concept of class is gender neutral, when in fact it has a masculine bias (Acker 1999).[8]

The work of Marxist, neo-Marxist, and socialist feminists in communications research can be linked to critical cultural studies and political economy. These types of feminist approaches look at the structural ways in which patriarchy and capitalism come together to constrain women. Steeves (1987) argues that different assumptions about class, race, and gender shape different perspectives within a socialist feminist framework. Moreover, socialist feminists "assume the relative autonomy of ideological expressions in mass culture" (Steeves 1987, 106). This suggests that the economic base does not solely determine social practice. Instead, ideology expressed in political, economic, and social practices acts to produce and reproduce women's social status. As this suggests, gender is a complex construction of deep-rooted social factors including race, class, sexuality, religious background, ethnicity, dis/ability, age, etc. Thus, an analysis that seeks to isolate gender as a discrete variable may work to identify manifest differences in gender roles, but it fails to explicate the nature of these roles particularly since gender is linked to other social factors.

Feminist Political Economy in Communications

A feminist political economy presents ways to move away from conceptualizing political economy as only looking at labor or class relations in order to broaden our understanding of accumulation and the reproduction of capitalism. In *Capital,* Marx (1976) established that commodity production constitutes a social relationship between producers, and out of this interdependence arises a contradiction, or what

Marx described as commodity fetishism. The idea of commodity fetishism points to the ways in which the economic forms of capitalism conceal social relations because the products of human labor appear independent from those who created them. Marx's theory of the commodity is important because it establishes the idea that appearance may conceal reality. I would argue that for feminists it is not sufficient to examine only the mode of production, but that we must investigate the social relations arising from patterns of commodity consumption, not just as a cultural phenomenon but as an economic practice shaping women's lives. Even though both production and consumption are inextricably linked, feminist scholars and political economists tend to focus primarily on only one of these processes. Political economists tend to cut off their analyses when they reach consumption practices, and many feminists ignore production contexts of cultural artifacts. On a global level, communications industries produce a vast array of cultural artifacts in the form of entertainment, media, and cybernetic technologies, and feminist political economists must rigorously challenge both production and consumption practices detrimental to women, which these industries set into place. For example, it is not sufficient to look only at how corporations limit and constrain cultural representations; we must also interrogate the consumption of these ideological images by groups of people who are in turn sold to advertisers as a niche market. Examining both production and consumption as integral parts of capitalist accumulation provides a way to theorize subjectivity from a cultural materialist perspective.

Feminist political economy is different from socialist feminism, political economy, and cultural studies approaches. Whereas socialist feminism looks primarily to macroeconomic organizations structuring women's lives, a feminist political economy also looks to the meso- and microlevels of capitalism as they shape women's day-to-day interactions. While cultural studies legitimized women's private lives as political, it did so at the expense of a social-historical context of capitalism. Cultural studies research offers much toward an understanding of ways in which women know, experience, and relate to their worlds (Ang 1991; McRobbie 1978a, 1978b, 1980). Yet taken out of the social-historical context of capitalism, cultural studies has limitations in terms of praxis. This is not to suggest that feminist political economy is without limitations. However, feminist political economists must attempt to bridge theory with practice, arguably an important task for all communications scholars.

Much of political-economic research in communications excludes women's experiences, because it assumes a binary relationship of man/ woman in which women's ways of knowing are understood in relationship to men's and as a category within a masculine-biased system. Perhaps this is one reason why more women chose to utilize cultural studies approaches over political economic theories. A feminist political economy interrogates issues many women relate to, such as identity, subjectivity, pleasure, consumption, as well as visible and invisible labor, and looks at them through the lens of capitalism, gendered as androcentric or male-centered. Feminist political economists point out how capitalism naturalizes male bias because it values traditionally masculine ways of organization and knowing (Waring 1988; 1999). This androcentric structure shapes our way of knowing and how we conceptualize questions. In essence, political-economic research is much the same, as it often ignores the gendered nature of capitalism, and fails to ask research questions that investigate the naturalized androcentric social relations embodied in the mode of production. This is not to suggest that political-economic research that does not call attention to gender is in any way misguided or less theoretically informed. Rather, I suggest that acknowledging an inherent androcentric structure in the mode of inquiry opens up political economy to a feminist epistemology[9] that would allow for endless possibilities in understanding and critiquing capitalism, thereby allowing further opportunity for praxis.

By suggesting there be a feminist mode of inquiry, I am asking that we start to rethink the goals of our research—history, social totality, moral philosophy, and praxis (Meehan et al. 1994)—and how each of these areas may be enhanced. What feminism calls to our attention is that our own subjectivity informs our research. While most critical scholars deny the idea of objective research, this does not mean that we abandon standards and guidelines for sound and informed analysis. Most of us try to do ethical work that is politically informed. Moreover, feminist scholars do not expect everyone to look at life through a gendered lens.[10] Just as many feminist scholars make certain choices and commitments to understanding how the world works for women, and then piece that into a larger social totality of all humans, we would expect nonfeminist scholars to focus on other issues to figure out more pieces of the puzzle. Those within certain marginalized groups offer the strength of understanding social and cultural phenomena from an outsider's perspective (Collins 1990). Inviting women and other marginalized groups to explain how economics manifests in their daily lives only furthers our understanding of the way in which capitalism works.

In terms of method, feminist political economy is interdisciplinary, with critical self-reflection. Interdisciplinary work fits with a feminist sensibility that understands being located in multiple subjectivities. I am not a feminist in one moment and a political economist in another. I am not a consumer of sexist music in one moment and a social activist in another. Because I am a feminist does not mean that I automatically and uncategorically do not find pleasure in sexist music. Because I am a political economist and social activist does not mean that I always purchase products from corporations that have fair labor practices.[11] Because of our multiple subjectivities, there are levels of negotiation we each navigate through on a day-to-day basis. This affects women in particular, who along with children comprise the largest economically disadvantaged group worldwide and who do not always have the choice of taking action against the hand that feeds us—whether it be a sexually harassing teacher, an abusive husband, or an exploitative employer. Because in any one instance we all have multiple subjectivities that require levels of negotiation, there is a need for interdisciplinary research to understand the different forces that inform our decisions. A feminist political economy aims to understand these negotiations and contradictions and how they relate to capitalism and patriarchy. Crossing disciplinary boundaries reveals contradictions and assumptions, forcing researchers to confront their blind spots. Marxist philosophy of dialectical materialism holds this continued challenge, in that through the conflict of opposites or contradictions we will come closer to understanding reality.

Feminist political economy is not pluralistic, although it looks to accommodate difference and multiple standpoints. All theories are not created equal. Depending on the research problem and questions, different theories should be employed. Pluralism, particularly its manifestation in postmodern research[12] and its lack of critical engagement, divides feminists, as well as other communications scholars. Although many postmodern analyses suggest an apolitical stance, they are actually quite political and very noncritical and not self-reflexive. Yet all postmodern approaches should not be dismissed—not even the uncritical ones, because we can learn from them. All political economists would not agree on this point, however (Meehan et al. 1994). Feminist postmoderism inquiries emphasize women's resistance and work to break down modernist hierarchical notions of power. Postmodern feminists have challenged many of us to rethink totalizing assumptions that limit our theories to conceptualizing women as "passive objects of monolithic systems of oppression" (Fisher and Davis 1993, 6). Still, I argue that there are limitations not only to our understanding of women's experience, but also to the feminist political-economic goal of praxis if we focus solely on resistance and not on the injustice that many women face daily.

Because of opposing assumptions, a postmodern approach by itself can never constitute a feminist political economy. However, I suggest that when asking questions about how we derive pleasure from consumption, an intrinsic part of capitalist accumulation and reproduction, postmodern inquiries allow scholars to understand this action distinct from capitalism.[13] Since pleasure—at least types of it derived from globally mediated artifacts—is always and already economic, scholars can use this information and tie it back to the logic of capital accumulation. The information garnered from these inquiries does shed light, if only to further illuminate some of the contradictions in women's ways of knowing and understanding the world and their relationship to it. Postmodern inquiries also reveal how many women continuously participate in the reproduction of capitalism, which, in turn, reproduces social injustices. However, since our participation in capitalism is so naturalized, it is invisible to most of us. Even when our participation can be theorized as resistance, this often serves to mask other types of power relations.

A feminist political economy is committed to praxis, which includes dialogue across disciplinary boundaries. Feminist political economy is a critical form of scholarship, materialist in conception. Even though I fully believe this to be the most fruitful area of research because of my background, values, and interests, I do not believe one truth is knowable.[14] Abandoning the notion that one Truth is knowable and instead accepting the possibility that multiple truths can coexist does not mean that we stop our pursuit for knowledge. Rather, it opens up our inquiries to expanded possibilities for understanding lived experience and social reality from a political-economic perspective. In order for scholars to do our best work, we must resonate with a particular approach—no doubt my working-class background informs my inquiries. For a feminist political economist committed to praxis, understanding women's wants, desires, and needs is crucial. While in the end these feelings may be driven by capitalism and informed by cultural practices, what does it mean if groups of women have no understanding of their relationship to, participation in, and exploitation by capitalism? How do we work toward understanding resistance without dismissing it as subsumed under totalizing systems of patriarchy and capitalism, or without celebrating it while ignoring the historical material conditions that allow for it? As a feminist political economist one must be committed to understanding and respecting difference and individual positions. Theoretical connections such as understanding how pleasure and resistance can be simultaneously and contradictorily limiting, instead of only beneficial, will not be well received if there is no empathy for women's lived experiences. A commitment to empathy for all women, respect for scholarly difference, and the use of various theories does not mean the same thing as pluralism.

The effects of capitalism are ubiquitous, and its organization naturalized. The lives and experiences of women have often been relegated to the private sphere. For this reason, women tend not to think of themselves as political. Political economy has not been the terrain for many women scholars because many women do not resonate with the object under study: structural capitalism—which means overt politics, policies, institutions, organizations, laws, regulations, and an understanding of economics. Expanding the object of study from structure to day-to-day activities allows an entry point for women to pursue their interests and understand the many ways that we relate to capitalism. Feminist political economists should be concerned with demystifying political economy and making it resonate with women, which means looking to personalized and privatized capitalist moments in addition to looking at institutions, the state, and labor.

Conclusion

Understanding global capitalism is imperative, and discerning how this impacts women's lives as producers and consumers is a part of the process. Why is it that information about the exploitation of women workers in developing nations is not made more available to women around the world, many of whom purchase most of the domestic goods? Why is it that the concept of feminism continues to be used to pit women against women, as well as men against women? Why is it that many critical scholars who can look so closely at structural inequalities of class dismiss, rather than interrogate, feminist issues? Support from our nonfeminist colleagues who do not necessarily understand women's oppression will build solidarity through an empathetic understanding of injustice as it is evidenced in exploitation.

I have the distinct generational advantage (or perhaps naiveté) of wanting all critical scholars to be united in solidarity, trying to make visible exploitative and oppressive social relations. While we must know and understand the assumptions of the paradigms in which we chose to work and the stakes when we chose to cross disciplines, this does not mean we should rigidly guard and protect our paradigm as the only way to truth, particularly if we are indeed pursuing knowledge to benefit others and the societies in which we live. I have been conditioned to think in terms of interdisciplinary research—many of my colleagues in sociology, women's studies, philosophy, political science, and English think this way, too. Perhaps this is the new wave; one that allows for the possibility of a feminist political economy that has a unique epistemology. Yet we must embrace interdisciplinary research with caution, for abandoning the old for the new without self-reflexivity is very dangerous. Feminist political-economic research is self-reflexive at the core. It is critical and materialist, challenging a patriarchal institution of capitalism in its various manifestations.

Notes

1. Feminism seeks to understand and theorize power as it pertains not only to women, but also to other groups marginalized on the basis of their race, class, sexuality, religious background, ethnicity, age, dis/ability, etc. Throughout this essay I will be referring specifically to women; however, a feminist political economy, as I envision it, seeks to understand these interconnections and how different groups of people are politically, economically, and socially disenfranchised.

2. Even though many women are household wage earners, women do not always see the political nature of this because it is something that must be done for survival. This is another way in which the logic of capitalism becomes naturalized and accepted.

3. See bell hooks, *Cultural Criticism and Transformation* or *Outlaw Culture: Resisting Representation,* for a discussion of the interlocking forms of oppression of race, gender, and economics. She refers to this as "White Supremacist Capitalist Patriarchy."

4. In her presentation at the May 1999 ICA conference, Jessica Davis stressed the importance of this for black women.

5. Classical political economy, most associated with the work of Adam Smith, has roots in Enlightenment thinking and stresses both rationality and empiricism. Smith's notion of a "free market" economy stresses freedom and individuality. His concept of the "invisible hand" suggests that the market is a "free" (not subject to state or other external intervention) and "equal" (each participant has equal bargaining power) place for exchange of commodities.

Classical political economy successfully identifies forces of capitalism; however, since it is not critical, it tends to naturalize those forces.

6. Historical materialism is the Marxist doctrine explaining that the production and reproduction of social life can be understood through an examination of concrete material conditions placed in a historical context.

7. For a more elaborate discussion of feminism in communications, refer to Liesbet van Zoonen's *Feminist Media Studies*; H. Leslie Steeves's "Feminist Theories and Media Studies," in *Critical Studies in Mass Communication*, June 1987; and E. Ann Kaplan's "Feminist Criticism and Television," in *Channels of Discourse*.

8. See Joan Acker's essay "Rewriting Class, Race and Gender: Problems in Feminist Rethinking" for a further elaboration of how feminists in sociology proceeded after their critique of Marxism as male biased. Also see Lisa McLaughlin's essay "Something Old, Something New: Lingering Moments in the Unhappy Marriage of Marxism and Feminism," chapter 3 in this book.

9. See Sandra Harding's essay "Is There a Feminist Method?" in *Feminism and Methodology* and her book *Whose Science? Whose Knowledge?: Thinking from Women's Lives* for further elaboration on feminist standpoint and epistemology.

10. Even though many feminists argue that everyone looks at life through a gendered lens, we acknowledge that research does not have to call specific attention to its gendered nature in order for it to be valuable and informed.

11. Moreover, I cannot deny the indirect economic advantages of having been on a campus whose library renovation was funded by Phil Knight, CEO of Nike, or being in a school of journalism and communication that has a Nike-endowed chair (as well as other corporate sponsorships that fund faculty lines, research assistants, and several computer labs).

12. My discussion of postmodernism does not justly represent this area of inquiry or the theoretical contributions of postmodern scholars. In order to appreciate fully the significance and the theoretical underpinnings of postmodernism, one must place it in the context of a response to modernism and Enlightenment thinking—a discussion not falling within the scope of this essay. Postmodern research in communications, which tends to focus on discourse analysis as a way to theorize power, gender, race, sexuality, etc., rarely explicates the theoretical underpinnings furthered by philosophers writing in response to modernism. Often this research remains at a surface level, examining images, rather than fully explicating relations of power. For an introduction to some of the basic issues arising from postmodern research, see the introduction in Lawrence Cahoone's *From Modernism to Postmodernism: An Anthology*. Postcolonial writings, which also fall under the rubric of postmodernism and look toward theorizing subjectivity, often are critical and self-reflexive.

13. While I do not believe it is possible to separate out pleasure from capi-

talism, distinguishing and classifying social phenomena is useful to scholars provided we do not reify the categories.

14. I distinguish between these two points, truth and knowledge, to suggest how the telos of scholarly pursuit can be one of knowledge production, which is dynamic and complex, rather than being wedded to Enlightenment thinking, which stresses working toward and achieving one knowable truth.

2. Feminist Theory and Political Economy: Toward a Friendly Alliance

H. Leslie Steeves and Janet Wasko

Casual observation suggests that political economists and feminists have much in common. Both groups promote theory and activism addressing distributions of power and patterns of inequality and oppression in society. Political economists focus on these issues in the context of capitalism. Feminists are interested in all contexts, but certainly must consider the role of capitalism, which has spread globally. Statistics clearly show that women wield less power than men in capitalist political-economic systems and reap fewer material rewards as well.

For instance, all over the world female wages are lower than male wages, and unemployment is higher among women than men. Also, women constitute the vast majority of the unpaid family workers. Women have fewer opportunities than men to improve their economic status, because of greater overall illiteracy, poverty, and health constraints. Additionally, women who do obtain an education and employment may face increased risks of sexual harassment and violence as a result. In some instances the violence is extreme and escape is impossible, as in the Thai sex industry, where young girls are literally sold by their families into slavery. As few women participate at the highest levels of state and corporate decision making globally, there is usually little effort or incentive to create or enforce laws and policies that improve women's situation.[1]

From the above, it is evident that political-economic and feminist analyses could benefit from a closer collaboration, academically and politically. Yet the seemingly obvious commonalties mask sharp differences in conceptual focus and methodological approach. Though each field of study has become more complex in the past two decades in response to criticisms, it appears that the increased complexity has not produced a clear basis for merger. Rather, the two fields have taken different evolutionary paths, resulting in a more substantial paradigm shift in feminist scholarship compared to political economy. As we will show, the changes in feminist scholarship not only widen the gap between feminism and political economy, but also between theorists and activists within feminism. Therefore, despite the increased breadth and complexity of the two fields of study and activism, conflicts do exist and may be harder than ever to reconcile.

This essay examines and compares some differences and areas of overlap between feminist scholars and political economists. We begin with a general overview of each field and its recent history, including internal debates and divisions. It becomes evident that traditional political economy and Marxist and socialist forms of feminism are fairly easily reconciled. The common Marxist base provides a materialist analysis of class divisions under capitalism; and feminism demands attention to class-linked gender oppression in political-economic analysis. Our essay would end there if Marxist and socialist feminism were theoretically persuasive and dominated feminist scholarship. In fact, Marxist forms of feminism have declined because of serious weaknesses, including conceptual gaps and contradictions, their neglect of social divisions aside from class and gender, and their focus on material forms of oppression with less attention to ideology.

In the past two decades or so, feminist scholars and activists have increasingly acknowledged the heterogeneous reality of women's lives, which argues against essentialist explanations (and remedies) for patriarchy. As this has occurred, feminism has become increasingly diverse, whereas political economy has remained more unified in its basic assumptions and mission. Additionally, the overall feminist emphasis has shifted from social structures to discourses and symbols of marginality in texts, often with little attention to underlying material inequities. This change in feminist thought works against an alliance with political economy, which is fundamentally concerned with the distribution of material resources within capitalist societies.

We note that while the feminist "mainstream" has shifted from the social sciences to the humanities, there remain many feminisms, with widely varying assumptions about theory and method. The aims and methods of socialist feminism are most compatible with political economy. Further, we acknowledge the importance of studying representations and believe that political economy has much to learn from advances in feminist discourse analysis and from cultural studies in general. At the same time, and despite its present popularity, we reject a narrow focus on discourse, without considering moral, political, and economic questions. In fact, we disagree with feminist or political-economic scholarship that focuses exclusively on *any* particular facet of society or human experience without a more complex, holistic perspective. Socialist feminists' observations of links between gender and class disadvantage under capitalism remain valid and should be considered in political-economic analyses. Yet questions about the compatibility of socialism and feminism are as yet unresolved, as are questions about political economy and cultural studies. We argue that even if conceptual problems remain, a friendly alliance is politically desirable. Meantime, conceptual theorists should continue seeking the assumptive basis for quite obvious common ground.

Political Economy

The study of political economy in communications may be traced to general political economy and its roots in eighteenth-century Scottish Enlightenment thinking. Adam Smith defined political economy as the study of "wealth" (material goods and resources) and was concerned with "how mankind arranges to allocate scarce resources with a view toward satisfying certain needs and not others" (Smith 1776, 161). Smith and others, such as David Ricardo, were primarily interested in capitalism as a system for the production, distribution, exchange, and consumption of wealth. Hence, political economy evolved as capitalism evolved.

In the nineteenth century the works of Karl Marx and Friedrich Engels added class analysis to political economy, which led to a radical critique of capitalism. They took a moral stance against the unjust and inequitable characteristics of the evolving capitalist system. Hence, the study of political economy began to shift from description and relatively neutral analysis to a critique of capitalism.

Also in the nineteenth century, the mainstream focus of economic study shifted from macro- to microanalysis, with the primary emphasis on individual versus societal issues. The emphasis on the individual led to the increased use of social-scientific methodologies. As these changes occurred, the name of the discipline changed from *political economy* to *economics*. According to William Jevons, who initiated the name change, economics is the study of "the mechanics of utility and self interest . . . to satisfy our wants to the utmost with the least effort . . . to maximize pleasure is the problem of economics" (Jevons 1970, 7–8). Today, *neoclassical economics,* which evolved from Jevons's work, is considered the prevailing trend in the field.

Nonetheless, Marxist or critical political economy has survived outside the mainstream and has been applied in several fields, including communication studies. The British political economists Graham Murdock and Peter Golding have been influential in defining the parameters of the field. In contrast to mainstream economics, they describe political economy as holistic, historical, and concerned with the balance between capitalist enterprise and public intervention. Political economy "goes beyond technical issues of efficiency to engage with basic moral questions of justice, equity, and the public good" (Golding and Murdock 1991, 18).

In essence, political economy is concerned with issues of survival and control, and understanding how capitalist societies are organized to produce and maintain the necessities for survival. A primary concern is with the allocation of resources (material concerns) within capitalist societies. Through studies of ownership and control, political economists document and analyze relations of power, class systems, and other structural inequalities. Political economists analyze contradictions and suggest strategies for resistance and intervention. The approach includes both economic *and* political analysis, with methods drawn from history, economics, sociology, and political science (e.g., Mosco 1996).

Applied to communication studies, political economists are interested in studying varied questions related to the structures and policies of communications industries and their interrelations with other economic sectors, the modes of cultural production and consumption under capitalism, and communications and media as commodities produced by capitalism (e.g., Smythe 1960; Garnham 1979; Wasko 2000). Analyses have included capitalist expansionism in global communications (e.g., Schiller 1971, 1976) and media concentration (e.g., Herman and Chomsky 1988; Bagdikian 1997).

In recent years political economy has been challenged by cultural studies scholars for its neglect of ideology and the ways in which discourses shape meaning and allow for resistance.[2] In response, political economists increasingly have gone beyond studies of ownership and control to consider relationships between political economy and cultural studies and therefore to include questions about texts, audiences, and consumption (e.g., Grossberg 1995; Meehan et al. 1994; Meehan 1999; Murdock 1995; Pendakur 1993). Consequently, the tradition is more complex and diverse than some critics claim. However, economic and political analyses are still considered primary and necessary grounding for ideological readings and cultural analyses.

Feminist Scholarship

As indicated above, for political economists, economic class has been the primary social division of concern. For feminists, gender historically has been the primary social division addressed. Feminists are concerned with women's and girls' *oppression* in society, meaning all the systematically related "forces and barriers" that function to restrict options, immobilize, mold, and reduce (Frye 1983, 4, 7). *Patriarchy* may be assumed responsible for oppression, understood differently within different frameworks. Additionally, analyses of oppression or patriarchy alone are insufficient. The insights gained must contribute to social change.

Hence most feminists share the two broad assumptions that (1) women are oppressed and (2) change is necessary. With regard to the former assumption, while feminists agree that gender oppression exists, they vary enormously in how—and even whether—to analyze it (e.g., Barrett 1999). The latter assumption adds a political component to feminist scholarship, distinguishing it from "sex differences" or "gender differences" within the social sciences and from works about or by women in the humanities (e.g., Rakow 1986; Steeves 1987, 1988). However, just as feminists disagree on how or whether to explain gender oppression, or patriarchy, they also have diverse views on which interventions are desirable.

The disciplinary origins of feminist frameworks are complex and will be summarized only briefly here. Until the 1980s, most feminist scholars were concerned with issues of causality in analyses of women's oppression. Theoretical perspectives varied depending on whether the explanation for women's oppression was assumed to be fundamentally biologistic, individualistic, social psychological, or sociocultural and political economic, or a combination (e.g., Elshtain 1981; Jaggar 1983). These explanatory assumptions suggested logical interventions involving biological manipulations and separatism (radical feminism), individual actions to change laws and policies (liberal feminism), social-psychological analyses (psychoanalytically influenced feminist theories), and/or revolutionary events to alter macro-level arrangements (Marxist and socialist feminism).

Each of the above perspectives has different historical origins, which have been documented in detail by feminist theorists and historians. For instance, radical forms of feminism may be traced to Simone de Beauvoir's (1952) assumption that fundamental biological differences contributed to patriarchy, understood to mean the myriad ways in which men innately dominate women. Liberal feminism applies the principles of liberal political philosophy (of Locke, Kant, Mill, Rawls, and others), which shaped the history of American politics and capitalism and capitalist interests in the protection of individuals. Hence, from the nineteenth century to the present, feminists have confirmed gender inequity within the system (in areas such as suffrage, property ownership, employment opportunity, and salary) and have sought legal and political means to effect change. Marxist and socialist feminisms are obviously grounded in Marxist theory and argue that gender oppression is linked with class oppression under capitalism. Change requires macrolevel, if not revolutionary, political, and economic, change. Some feminists have turned to Jacques Lacan's reformulations of psychoanalytic theory to seek explanations for gender oppression. Lacan assumed that the human subject is constructed developmentally through language, such that at certain psychological crisis points, patriarchal symbols are embedded in the structure of language. The logical solution is to expose masculine and feminine symbolism in texts and also to deliberately create cultural products with alternative linguistic structures. As we will discuss later, other poststructuralist theorists besides Lacan have influenced an increased feminist focus on the symbols of culture.

Obviously the above synopsis omits much nuanced detail. It is hardly exhaustive and leaves out key strands of theory, such as Chodorow's (1978) psychoanalytic argument tracing gender oppression to the traditional division of labor in parenting. Nor are the theories mutually exclusive, and many feminist scholars draw on multiple perspectives in their work. Additionally, each perspective makes different assumptions about the role of communications processes and structures in society, their contribution to women's oppression, and how the problems should be studied. For instance, scholars who assume more individualistic explanations have tended to draw on social-scientific methods, whereas those who assume political-economic explanations have drawn on methods from history, economics, and organizational analysis. Hence, feminist scholarship in communications looks very different when published by, for instance, a liberal feminist versus a socialist feminist versus a psychoanalytic poststructuralist feminist (e.g., Steeves 1987).

Socialist Feminism and Political Economy

As socialist feminism's Marxist origins make it most compatible with political economy theory, we turn our attention briefly to this area of theory. To what extent does socialist feminism merge feminism and Marxism? This question, it may appear, is key to a collaborative relationship between feminist scholars and activists and political economists.

Feminisms grounded in Marxism reject both radical and liberal feminist perspectives. Marx opposed the notion of an essential biological human nature, which is the premise of most forms of radical feminism, and some other feminisms as well. He also rejected the liberal belief that individuals can develop their potential in a class-based society where wealth and power are held by just a few. Rather he assumed that human nature is a dialectical product of biological, social, economic, and political factors and constraints.

Explicit Marxist feminist arguments were first outlined by Friedrich Engels in *The Origin of the Family, Private Property and the State* (1985, first published 1884). Engels used anthropological data to show that men's subjugation of women did not occur before the spread of capitalism, which altered traditional kinship networks and encouraged monogamous family forms. Engels argued that capitalism moved production away from the home and created elite classes who controlled the means of production. Men left the home to become either capitalists or workers. At the same time, men of both classes gained control over the capital for their nuclear families. As men gained control over capital, they needed known heirs, hence the importance of monogamous marriage for women, though a double standard could remain in place for men. Engels's work has since been criticized for anthropological errors, for failing to recognize that women are oppressed in most families—not just monogamous ones—and for overlooking gender oppression experienced by working-class (proletarian) women (Barrett 1985). Nonetheless Engels's work was important in providing a materialist explanation for women's oppression in the context of nuclear families in capitalist societies.

Feminists influenced by Marx and Engels agree that a historical understanding of the capitalist mode of production and the accompanying class structure helps explain women's oppression and suggests a solution as well. They especially examine men's control over women's labor in most societies, evident for instance in women's concentration in lower-paying nonmanagerial positions, in inadequate maternity or child-care policies, and in the notion of "family wage," which has reinforced women's domestic role and depressed their wages. However, few feminists focus *exclusively* on capitalism as the source of women's oppression, recognizing that women were oppressed before capitalism and have been oppressed in noncapitalist societies, including in socialist states. Hence, socialist feminists have sought to reconcile theories of patriarchy with Marxist feminist arguments about capitalism, that is, to develop a coherent and persuasive theory of *capitalist patriarchy* (e.g., Barrett 1985; Eisenstein 1979; Walby 1986).

There have been problems with this theoretical work, problems that have not been adequately addressed. Most significantly, a theory of capitalist patriarchy requires an agreed-upon conceptualization of patriarchy. Yet understandings of patriarchy vary widely. There remains a wide gap between explanations in terms of men's economic and political domination over women (from Marxism), ideological explanations that focus on patriarchal systems of representation as perpetuated through communications (e.g., from Louis Althusser, Stuart Hall, and Antonio Gramsci), and psychoanalytic explanations that look to the psychic and symbolic context of Oedipal socialization (e.g., from Jacques Lacan and feminist reformulations of Lacan). The first type of explanation reflects Marxist feminist assumptions. As noted earlier, these assumptions have been criticized for their failure to recognize variations within social classes as well as complications posed by race, ethnicity, nation, and culture. The latter two types of explanations point to nonmaterial processes, to discourses, and to human agency and subjectivity. Yet Marxism has always had difficulty accepting an ideological (or other nonmaterial) explanation for oppression, especially if it fails to emphasize an ultimate economic foundation (e.g., Hall 1985; Barrett 1999). It appears that reconciling capitalism and patriarchy means theorizing a material basis for all major components of patriarchy, including ideology, and individual agency and subjectivity. This conundrum remains to be resolved (e.g., Barrett 1999).

Socialist feminism has much work to do before feminism and socialism, and patriarchy and capitalism, can be effectively linked. Identifying the material basis for and the material power of ideology, as well as of other nonmaterial aspects of human experience and human nature, remains an ongoing obstacle. As political economy assumes the material character of oppression, these problems in theorizing socialist feminism may impede collaborative work.

Feminism and Cultural Studies

Problems in theorizing capitalism and patriarchy, and their interrelations, are not the only barrier to a collaboration between feminism and political economy. Additionally, socialist feminism, which never dominated feminist scholarship, has declined even further. In general, feminist theory and scholarship have changed immensely in the past two decades. Michèle Barrett has summarized the change as a move from an emphasis on *things* (such as low pay, gender violence, and female illiteracy) to *words,* including both verbal and visual symbols in texts (Barrett 1992). Obviously this shift, which Barrett also describes as feminism's "turn to culture," is particularly significant for communications studies, as well as for literary and film studies. Poststructuralist theorists, such as Foucault, Derrida, Saussure, and Lacan, have been influential in challenging the assumptions of previously dominant feminist frameworks.

Barrett (1992) describes three major ways in which poststructuralism has influenced feminism. First, poststructuralism has changed traditional views of language. Language does not merely convey meaning. Saussure and Derrida, in particular, have argued that language actively constructs meaning. Second, Foucault and others have challenged the materialist basis of theories on which many feminisms have been grounded, including liberal political theory and Marxism. Foucault argued that material objects in and of themselves—including social structures—are meaningless, but that they are given meaning by signs and discourses. Finally, poststructuralism challenges assumptions about causality. Most feminist theories have made assumptions about the causes of women's oppression, noted earlier. Notions of causality also have been fundamental in the larger theories and philosophies on which these frameworks are based. Yet poststructuralists argue that it is far more valuable to identify meaning in ongoing representations than to search for an explanatory origin. In other words, there are no determining social structures. Rather, the meanings of these structures are constructed by words and symbols.

Poststructuralist arguments have been supported by postmodernism, which has accompanied postindustrial capitalism and the globalization of communications and information systems. Postmodernism is difficult to define, as it means different things from different disciplinary perspectives. Like poststructuralism, however, it tends to reject the grand conceptual projects of Enlightenment thought and to focus attention on a plurality of meanings, on "pastiche and parody," and on surface meanings rather than depth (Barrett 1992, 206).[3]

Alongside poststructuralist and postmodernist influences have been critiques of traditional feminist frameworks by minority and international feminists, especially Third World feminists. These feminists have rightly noted that the assumptions and political agendas of traditional frameworks reflect the experiences of their creators, and do not include all women. Black U.S. feminists have challenged the white, middle-class basis of liberal and radical feminisms (e.g., hooks 1984). Minority and immigrant British feminists have challenged the white basis of Marxist and socialist feminism (Barrett 1999, 146). Third World feminists have effectively critiqued the ethnocentrism evident in perspectives originating in the West (Mohanty 1991a, 1991b). Many of these feminists have argued against gender—or gender and class—as the primary social division(s) in feminist thought, agreeing with Foucault's view that there are no totalizing explanations, whether gender, class, race, or nation. Rather, the nature of gender oppression shifts by historical and cultural context and cannot be generalized. However, while these feminists agree with postmodernists and poststructuralists on many points and disagree with traditional frameworks, noted above, their work retains a material political agenda. As Barrett notes, "the voices now most effectively addressing questions of class, inequality, poverty and exploitation to a wider public are those of black women, not white socialist feminists" (1999, 149). Like poststructuralists and postmodernists, minority and international feminists may not wish to theorize links among—or origins of—specific social inequalities, but the material relevance of these links is evident in their work.

In general, an outcome of all of the trends discussed above—poststructuralism, postmodernism, global feminisms—has been a turn away from the social sciences and toward the arts and humanities, both conceptually and methodologically. Questions of concern less frequently relate to issues of social structure, including capitalism and patriarchy, and more with issues of culture, sexuality, identity, and political agency. The focus of interest has moved toward processes of symbolization and representation, as well as of consumption and reception, in order to understand issues of subjectivity, psyche, and self (Barrett 1992, 204–05). Accordingly, methodologies have favored discourse analysis, with decreased uses of the methods of history and social science.

Another more troubling outcome, especially of poststructuralist influences, has been decreased academic feminist interest in activism and a widening of the gap between feminist scholars and activists. Activists seek to reveal and reform oppressive structures and practices in society. Analyses of discourses and practices of consumption and reception may be considered activist if they are contextualized within or clearly contribute to an activist political agenda. Yet, as Grossberg (1995) acknowledges, feminist cultural studies scholars vary in the extent to which they situate their work in the larger context of social structures of power. For instance, some who study consumption equate pleasure with resistance; others recognize that pleasure may be empowering, yet do "not deny the exploitive, manipulative, and dominating aspects of the market" (73). The meaning and basis of resistance and of political activism remain points of difference between feminists, as well as between many feminists and political economists.

Finding Common Ground

Marxist and socialist forms of feminism, which share some fundamental concerns with political economy, have lost popularity for a number of reasons, including their neglect of the role of ideology in women's oppression, and also their failure to seriously consider social divisions aside from gender and class. In contrast, much current feminist scholarship emphasizes discourses of gender, with little or no attention to structures of inequality, which both shape and are shaped by discourses.

First, we reemphasize that predominant trends in feminist scholarship do not represent all feminist scholars and cannot address all questions. Despite its present decline and conceptual flaws, key observations and premises of socialist feminism remain valid, observations that have been largely ignored by political economy. These include analyses of the family and the workplace as key sites of oppression in society. While the movement to the humanities in feminism is welcome in raising questions previously neglected, much is lost by going too far in rejecting theories and methods from political science, sociology, economics, and history, as Michèle Barrett has argued. Yes, words, symbols, and discourses are important in shaping structures of inequality. Yet words and symbols are the products of individuals who have histories and spend their lives in specific contexts, which include families, workplaces, nations, communities, schools, and religions—and more. These histories and structures are far more complex than words and symbols alone.[4]

Feminists, political economists, and cultural studies scholars must continue seeking ways to theorize connections between and among material and ideological factors contributing to social inequalities, as well as to progressive social change. Additionally, other nonmaterial contributions must be considered, such as personal agency. What is the material basis for ideology? How does ideology acquire material power? What is the role of individual agency and identity in social change? Until these and other questions have been addressed more broadly and effectively than they have been so far, most political economists and feminists will continue to study different kinds of problems, problems consistent with their own conceptual and methodological histories.

Yet studying one type of question does not necessarily mean rejecting other questions, as Grossberg (1995) points out. Most feminist and cultural studies scholars reject extreme views that dismiss the importance of structural relations of power and historical context. Most political economists recognize the significance of representations and of consumer and audience experiences. This suggests the logic of mutual respect and friendly alliance, an alliance that may catalyze collaborative activism and conceptual progress.

This is happening to some extent with research projects that embrace feminism and political economy, such as Eileen Meehan and Jackie Byars's study of the Lifetime channel (2000), Ellen Balka's work on women's use of computers (1991), and Michéle Martin's study of gender and telephone systems (1991). Much more of this kind of research is needed to develop the theoretical and methodological relationships between these approaches.

Additionally, we believe that the political imperative is more compelling than theoretical gaps and contradictions. Readily observable problems, listed at the beginning of this essay, demand political action. Barrett suggests that the critical theory of Jürgen Habermas may provide one avenue "to rescue feminism from the irrationalism and political limitations of postmodern perspectives" (1999, 33). Maybe so. Feminist revisions of Habermas along these lines already are under way.[5] But should we need a persuasive conceptual rationale for collaborative action? History shows that we do not, as activism seldom is grounded in a coherent and persuasive theory. Rather, political agency arises from a messy combination of observed and experienced problems, timing, access to material resources, and personal values.

Conclusion

Much has changed since the 1970s. Political economy and feminism have become more complex, to consider both material and nonmaterial analyses of power. The nonmaterial focus is on words and discourse, with less attention to structures of inequality and their histories. At the one extreme, that complexity may seem to suggest a merger. If both may include anything, depending on the history and context of the situation examined, then they should be able to reconcile differences.

The reality is that the meaning of political economy and the meaning of feminism depend on the values and assumptions of the scholars using them.

To the extent that political economists are unwilling to consider the gendered relations of power, as well as class relations, feminism will be neglected. Feminisms that recognize the need to consider multiple social divisions, depending on context, will be dissatisfied with an exclusive class/gender focus. To the extent that feminists are unwilling to consider a material analysis of power, the insights of political economy will be neglected.

We assume that gender is one of several key social divisions (which also include class, race, ethnicity, sexual orientation, age, disability, and more) that must be included in political economic analyses. The social divisions foregrounded, as well as the feminist theory used, depend on the historical context of the situation analyzed in each instance. Additionally, we assume the importance of ideological as well as political economic analysis. The material nature of ideology remains inadequately theorized, though it has been assumed in political economic studies. At present, a merger between feminism and political economy is difficult to theorize. Yet urgent global problems of injustice and inequality necessitate both kinds of analyses. At the least feminists and political economists can be friends, with much to gain from one another conceptually and strategically.

Notes

1. For data and examples, see, e.g., Nelson and Chowdhury (1994); Seager (1997); UNDP (1997, 1998); United Nations (1995); World Bank (1999). For a powerful discussion of the Thai sex industry, and other examples of economy slavery globally, see Bales (1999).

2. See especially a "Colloquy" on the debate between cultural studies and political economy in *Critical Studies in Mass Communication* 12 (1995): 60–100, with an introduction by Oscar Gandy Jr. and articles by Nicholas Garnham, Lawrence Grossberg, James Carey, and Graham Murdock.

3. See other essays in *Destabilizing Theory,* ed. Michèle Barrett and Anne Phillips, for discussions and definitions of postmodernism and poststructuralism and their impact on feminist theory.

4. We note that the original Sapir-Whorf hypothesis, that language determines thought and culture, was revised to recognize the dialectical influence of language, culture, and other aspects of environment, as well as the capacity of

humans to learn new languages and to borrow or assimilate elements of myriad other cultures.

5. For a good overview of the value of Habermas for feminism, alongside feminist critiques, see Johanna Meehan's (1995) introduction to her edited collection, *Feminists Read Habermas*. In general, Habermas may assist feminists who argue conceptually for a social and relational view of self-identity (e.g., Weir 1995), and who consequently seek "programs, policies, and solutions to our controversies that embody differentiation without cutting off the possibilities for change" (Warnke 1995, 258).

3. Something Old, Something New: Lingering Moments in the Unhappy Marriage of Marxism and Feminism
Lisa McLaughlin

For a number of years now, the battlelines have been drawn between cultural studies and critical political economy. By the time that the debaters have finished hurling epithets and the spectators have chosen sides, it is easy to forget that, since the inception of British cultural studies, a number of scholars have recognized the importance of a steady stream of systematic dialogue between the approaches (Meehan 1986; Mosco 1996). An interesting development in recent years is that allusions to feminist sites of conflict appear to have become a vehicle for disagreement, as cultural studies and political economy are described as separate spheres, each requiring "its own methodologies and theoretical frameworks" (Fiske 1994b, 469). In one memorably caustic exchange, Nicholas Garnham and Lawrence Grossberg address the disharmony between the two approaches within a framework reminiscent of "The Unhappy Marriage of Marxism and Feminism" (Hartmann 1981), in various configurations involving marriage, divorce, and reconciliation.[1]

I wish to argue that references to "the unhappy marriage" and "separate spheres" indicate more than that scholars have borrowed a convenient framework for expressing their differences. In fact, these allusions point to a gendering of the cultural studies/political economy debate, a formation of "separate spheres" in which the greater number of Western feminists have occupied the sphere associated with cultural studies. As cultural studies and political economy have broken down into two sides of an "academic apartheid" (Murdock 1995, 90), this division also reflects and reinforces something of a "gender apartheid."

Mosco (1996, 231) notes that although some leading political economists have begun to recognize that the incorporation of gender relations within the political-economy perspective is long overdue, "one observes remarkably little effort to theorize gender within a political economy approach to communication." There is not a substantial body of research in North American or European political economy on the relationship of gender to cultural industries (111). A large number of feminists recognize the importance of political economy to the analysis of communication and culture. Yet, among First World feminists, only a very few have pursued a research agenda that involves a sustained consideration of both feminist and political-economic concerns; among those who do are Gallagher (1980, 1985, 1992), Martin (1991), Spigel (1989), Roach (1993), and Meehan (1994).

Historically, cultural studies has provided a more amicable environment for considerations of gender and patriarchy than has political economy, but to note this is to return to where we began, with the substantial feminist presence within cultural studies, for feminists were instrumental in creating—not simply inheriting or borrowing—the field.[2] In cultural studies, as elsewhere, the feminist interrogation of difference was effective, if not transformative, in ameliorating the orthodox Marxist tendency to think in terms of a single structure of domination, exposing the gendered assumptions of Marxism, and rendering women visible within the Marxist analysis of class dynamics. Although British cultural studies was never populated by devout disciples of orthodox Marxism, much of its early work focused on working-class culture and tended toward silence on questions of the ways in which "popular racism" and "popular sexism" were expressed through the cultural practices of the working class (Tester 1994). Feminists helped to break this silence by challenging male-oriented models and assumptions and gender-biased practices, particularly within ethnographic studies. McRobbie's (1978a, 1978b, 1980, 1982, 1984) studies of working-class "girl culture," through which she challenges the primacy of class considerations, have had an enormous impact on cultural studies, and for feminists in particular, as one of the first of many responses to the masculinist bias of British cultural studies. In providing a concerted challenge to many of its gender-biased practices, particularly within ethnographic studies, feminists became integral to the trend in which British cultural studies turned away from class as a key structural determination in relations of domination and began to take up questions regarding the articulations of multiple social dimensions that included gender, race, class, and youth culture.

There are distinct ties that bind the cultural studies/political economy dispute to the "Unhappy Marriage" debate, notably through questions of whether class is the central structure of domination, with differences in gender, race, and sexuality following from the mode of production, or whether these differences constitute alternative structures of domination undetermined by class. Any attempt to explain the gathering of feminists on the side of cultural studies must begin with feminists' struggle for recognition within and against Marxist politics, and here there is no better place to start than with the debate initiated in the early 1970s, when the Marxist "woman question" became an embattled political and theoretical site of contention between the often divergent goals of feminism and Marxism. In the collection *Women and Revolution* (Sargent 1981) and elsewhere, many feminists objected to "the woman question" as a misguided, patriarchal attempt to align the interests of men and women within the context of relations of production. Hartmann (1981), in her influential essay, "The Unhappy Marriage of Marxism and Feminism," argued that "the woman question" has never been "the feminist question," which is, instead, directed toward understanding men's dominance over women. Conceptually speaking, "the feminist question" described by Hartmann and others located patriarchy and capitalism as separate struggles with separate mechanisms ("dual systems") while "the woman question" located women's oppression within the interests of capital ("unified systems").[3]

But the separation of patriarchy from capitalism posed a number of political and conceptual problems. By severing domestic space from political-economic space, the dual systems approach seemed to reinforce the notion of separate spheres by creating a gendered division of labor between Marxism and feminism and their respective concerns with capitalism and male dominance. The dual systems approach, ironically, proposed a "marriage" in which Marxism takes care of the public world of economics and feminism takes care of the private world of family, reproduction, and sexuality, thus reinforcing the dominant ideological construction of the public/private dichotomy. As Acker (1999, 47) writes,

> Capitalism/patriarchy and other dual systems theories . . . sidestepped the problems with class analysis by creating a separate system to explain the special subordination of women, leaving intact the original class concept that had been widely criticized as implicitly based on a model of the male worker.

Since women's subordination was assigned to a separate system, "class came to be seen as less central for explaining women's subordination than for explaining men's subordination in capitalist societies" (48).

One of the more productive developments to emerge from the "Unhappy Marriage" debate was a form of materialist feminism that refused to sever feminism from Marxism. Instead, materialist feminists attempted to transform the Marxist problematic in order to account for how a sexual division of labor is produced at the intersection of patriarchy and capitalism. Moreover, by insisting on material analysis, they countered a tendency within feminist theory to idealize and essentialize "woman" (Hennessy 1993, xi). Still, as Acker (1999) suggests, even when feminists made an effort to transcend dual systems theory by positing one system of relations that unites gender and class, the central conceptualization of class remained intact, with considerations of the relations involved in women's work added on to it. The lack of success in linking theories of gender and class meant that dual systems persisted in practice (50). This separation made it easier for class to slip out of the feminist picture, except for its role as the taken-for-granted addition to "gender," "race," and other categories of social identity. With the postmodern shift in concern for questions of class and gender consciousness to questions of identity, class was largely abandoned as a central theoretical concept.

While it is not at all clear whether many feminist media scholars nominally subscribe to a dual systems or a unified systems approach, the former is followed most often in practice. Although a focus on patriarchy may be obviated by feminist politics, this is the central, and often only, antagonism described in most studies, even though considerations of race and ethnicity have made momentous appearances in recent years.[4] With a "postmodern turn" that finds a number of feminist critics as uncomfortable with a totalizing approach to patriarchy as they are with that of Marxist theory, contingent and contradictory expressions of multiple differences and identities are explored, but rarely is it acknowledged that differences flourish within the capitalist mode of production. The history of feminist communications scholarship appears to follow a pattern established through the feminism/ Marxism encounter. It is tempting to suggest that those who forget history are condemned to repeat it, but this would be to forget that the "Unhappy Marriage" and cultural studies/political economy debates *share* a history. If the "Unhappy Marriage" provides an effective framework for evaluating the "Great Divide" between cultural studies and political economy, this is because, in many respects, it is not possible to separate the two.

Feminism and the Cultural Studies/Political Economy Debate

The schism between political economy and cultural studies that is invoked by the Garnham/Grossberg debate focuses most precisely on the differences between two left approaches, critical political economy and scholarship influenced by British cultural studies, reflecting the predominant Marxist or neo-Marxist form of each approach as it has been institutionalized within the field of communication. Garnham (1995, 71) defines a critical approach to the political economy of culture as the view that the capitalist mode of production has certain core characteristics (such as waged labor and commodity exchange) and that these "constitute people's necessary and unavoidable conditions of existence." In turn, these conditions shape, in determinate ways, the terrain of cultural practices: "the physical environment, the available material and symbolic resources, the time rhythms and spatial relations . . . they set the cultural agenda." As a field, cultural studies has become almost too diffuse to define. Appadurai (1996, 51) broadly defines it as one whose subject matter concentrates on

> the relationship between the word and the world . . . so that word can encompass all forms of textualized expression and world can mean anything from the means of production and the organization of life-worlds to the globalized relations of cultural reproduction. . . .

The more specific and central site of conflict in the cultural studies/ political economy debate, however, is that scholarship evolving from British cultural studies, which originated in the 1960s and 1970s and whose inception is most closely associated with the Centre for Contemporary Cultural Studies in Birmingham, England.

Although feminists' participation in the development of British cultural studies was often oppositional, their affinity with the approach was sustained through a shared discomfort with traditional Marxism and a mutual interest in publicizing and politicizing the activities of subcultural groups or communities whose "private" activities have been culturally, socially, and historically devalued. The key insight for British cultural studies scholars was that an elitist scholarly approach decrying economistic determination and ideological manipulation is ill-served for advancing a politics of the marginalized. The scholars directed their attention toward the study of subcultures, subcultural styles, and the contradictions experienced in the everyday lives of members of subcultures. In the case of feminist cultural studies, these subcultures have often included the audiences for "feminine" cultural forms such as soap operas, romance novels, and melodramas. The analysis of popular culture's insertion into everyday life promised to open up the category of struggle, beyond "official-political" and economic struggle, to account for specific audience responses to mass culture through questions of resistance, pleasures, and plurality of meaning.

Over the years, several of those who are affiliated with critical political economy have registered an appreciation for cultural studies' approach to culture as the product of everyday life, audience members as active subjects, and the importance of recognizing differences in addition to class (Curran 1991; Meehan 1986; Meehan et al. 1994; Mosco 1996). However, many critical political economists have also criticized the New Left scholars for pushing their insights to the extreme, as cultural studies approaches began to affirm and valorize the resistant capacities of "ordinary" people while largely ignoring the structural constraints imposed by political and economic realities. A number of critics have suggested that British cultural studies lost its Marxist leanings as it became institutionalized in the United States in the 1980s (Morley 1992; Budd et al. 1990; Hardt 1992). While there is some accuracy to this assessment, I would also suggest that cultural studies' populist inclination was not created but intensified through the export of British cultural studies into an American context that lacked a Marxist tradition. While it is true that the American myth of classlessness, expressed through the ascendancy of the notion of a huge middle class, did not offer the clarity and specificity of British class relations, the history of the evolution of British cultural studies suggests that, by the time it began to take hold in the United States, the approach had on offer a set of progressive politics that could be assimilated to the American context (McLaughlin 1997).

After its early work, which focused upon class relations as primary in the organization of British society, the history of British cultural studies is marked by its increasing distance from Marxist analysis of class structures. Because British cultural studies developed out of the perceived inadequacies and evasions of Marxism, the relationship between cultural studies and Marxism was always more antagonistic than conciliatory (Hall 1992, 279). Grossberg (1995, 77) effectively summarizes the relationship: "Both cultural studies and the New Left, with which many of its leading figures were affiliated, distanced themselves from Marxism and its various models of culture, even while they operated within the space it opened." The approach to Marxist political economy was often ambivalent. On one hand, British cultural studies developed in dialogue with political economy. On the other hand, it attempted to marginalize the approach (Nightingale 1996, 54), justifying this through allegations of orthodoxy, determinism, reductionism, economism, and belief in false consciousness. The distanciation of cultural studies from political economy expanded with a growth in ethnographic criticism, which often pursued the Gramscian analysis of culture and hegemony at the expense of the analysis of structural determination. Although Hall, Morley, and other researchers at the Centre for Contemporary Cultural Studies had stressed the importance of the relationship between encoding (the textual inscription of dominant ideology) and decoding (audience activity), the development of ethnographic criticism eventually tipped the scales in favor of the latter, and in so doing, tipped the scales in favor of a neo-Gramscian culturalism and against an Althusserian structuralism.

Tester (1994) suggests that the Gramscian political agenda of British cultural studies made almost inevitable the breakdown of the synthesis between structuralism and culturalism. The Gramscian concept of hegemony maintains that "the ruling class is able to get subordinated social groups to consent to the prevailing state of affairs and it does this by offering the subordinate a stake in the status quo" (16). Because the ruling class must "construct its dominance over and over again on a day-to-day basis . . . popular culture is itself inevitably a place of conflict, struggle and resistances" (16). With the concept of hegemony in hand, neo-Gramscians-as-organic-intellectuals set out to study the lived cultural practices and realities of oppressed groups, so that, through understanding "the people," they might enable them to become politically, socially, and culturally self-aware to the point of creating new hegemonies (21). Because the neo-Gramscian orientation defines popular culture as "of the people" and cultural studies as "for the people," the cultural activities of "the people" are of overwhelming concern. And "the people" are where the media are at, especially that media previously denigrated as "low culture." Therefore, there is the risk of elision of two types of popular culture: that "of the people" and that "liked by many." Tester (1994) identitifes a key cultural studies dilemma: if its political agenda is to be "for the people" and mediated popular culture is "of the people," then it becomes difficult to take a critical stance toward the forms and practices of popular culture. If they are "of the people," they are potential sources of resistance to hegemony. The Achilles' heel of cultural studies is that the popular culture of the oppressed cannot be judged oppressive without undermining the approach, and, ultimately, the entire political agenda. The result is that cultural studies risks becoming morally and culturally flat, responding to the question of the value of popular culture with silence, ambivalence, or celebration (Tester 1994, 30).

The Achilles' heel is laid bare with the shift from subcultures' appropriation of popular culture to audiences' consumption of popular culture, where the populist political agenda of being "for the people" and "letting the people speak" has often become a political liability through, first, treating the relationship between both consumption and production and agency and structure as a dualism rather than a dialectic and, second, overinvesting in the first term of each polarity. Although British cultural studies began with a critique of Marxist political economy's overemphasis on relations of production and structural determination, in marginalizing political economy, it ultimately opened itself up to charges of celebrating audience activities around the consumption of commodities while neglecting the issue of their production.

As Corner (1991) suggests, cultural studies' advocacy of reception analysis coincides with a turn toward postmodernism within several arts and sciences disciplines. With the "postmodern turn"

> a heightened sense of ambivalence towards the artefacts and pleasures produced by the resources and market inventiveness of the Late Capitalist culture industries has been displayed at the very same time as it has become fashionable to be elaborately nervous about ideas of truth, reason and power. (269)

In arguing for the fragmentation of the concepts used in modernist social theory, postmodernists have tended to shift the focus from structure and Marx to discourse and Foucault, and, in doing so, they "conceptualize power as highly dispersed rather than concentrated in identifiable places or groups" (Walby 1992, 49). There is little sense of the specificity of power because it is treated as ambiguous, organized through discourse, and unrelated to prevailing material conditions or the activities of agents and institutions (Whitworth 1994, 22).

Despite its rhetoric of power and resistance, cultural studies finds it difficult to connect audience agency to individuals' subjective relationships to political participation and their roles in forming, reforming, and overturning practices and institutions.[5] This dilemma is carried through from early feminist cultural studies to the postmodern scholarship of recent times. Feminist research that came out of the Centre was based explicitly in a political orientation modeled on consciousness-raising, giving the private a social dimension through exposing and recovering voices and resistances; it attempted to replace masculine modes of research (which resulted in patriarchal or chauvinist analysis) with research grounded in the values and beliefs of feminist communities, and tried to extend the "community" rules of such groups (rules of loyalty and recognition which redressed the neglect of patriarchy) to a research agenda which endorsed and valued women's popular cultural forms. (Nightingale 1996, 75)

Although their work was oriented to culturalist, Marxist, and feminist ends, the attempt to recuperate women's experience and recover the subjective often involved the avoidance of Marxist and structuralist theories (Nightingale 1996, 75). This, Nightingale suggests, is evident in Hobson's (1982) highly regarded ethnographic study, *Crossroads: The Drama of a Soap Opera*. Here, Hobson rejected the sort of psychoanalytic textual analyses published in the film journal *Screen* (known as "*Screen* theory"), which described the way subjects are "inscribed" in and "constructed" by popular film texts. Instead, she attempted to understand how female audience members related the television program to their own experiences. Nightingale suggests that, by pursuing a culturalist analysis and eschewing the topic of ideology, Hobson substituted "the right to determine the fate of a character" for "the right to exercise power in a patriarchal and ageist society" and, ultimately, provided "clear documentation of just how little power is exercised by audiences" (Nightingale 1996, 72).

Similarly, Radway's (1984) study of readers of romance novels rejects *Screen* theory and argues that romance readers actively make sense of their own experience of reading; yet she concedes that romance reading left the domestic role of women in patriarchal culture virtually intact. The women did not challenge the system of social relations, but instead made incremental demands, such as the right to be alone or to spend money on romances. Radway convincingly shows that reading romance novels leads to reading more romance novels. Nevertheless, she suggests that "if oppositional impulses or feelings of discontent such as those prompting romance reading can ever be separated from the activity that manages them in favor of the social order, it might be possible to encourage them, to strengthen them, and to channel them in another way so that this very real disappointment might lead to substantial social change" (18).

The problem suggested by Radway is that reader or audience agency often acts on a different terrain than that occupied by forms of political activity that seek influence beyond one's immediate sphere. That viewer agency is politicized by cultural critics and authorities cannot be denied, but, as Radway recognizes, the "citizen" constructed as active within an interpretive community is not the same as that which produces political activity in the public arena. The notion of political agency suggests that if mass-mediated popular culture is to be truly "of the people," the people would have to engage in the creation of effective sites for the strategic distribution of public issues and interests, the mobilization of representational politics, and the struggle for alternatives to existing hegemony. For some postmodern cultural critics, however, the critic's advocacy of political agency amounts to a scholarly elitism toward the audience. Ang (1996), who adopts something of a "don't ask, don't tell" posture toward feminism, argues that Radway's entreaty that the women become more activist has the unfortunate "therapeutic" effect of restoring the authority of feminist discourse, thus invalidating "the significance of the craving for and pleasure in romantic feelings that so many women have in common and share" (107). She suggests that, in expressing her "feminist desire," Radway draws "dangerously near a form of political moralism, propelled by a desire to make 'them' more like 'us'" (104).

With "woman" deconstructed almost out of existence and both second-wave feminism and critical political economy disparaged as though their intentions are fascistic, it appears that politics must come in the form of an ethnography that "promises to offer us vocabularies that can rob television audiencehood of its static muteness" (Ang 1991, 170). The attempt to follow the threads from the old "Unhappy Marriage" debate to the "new" one has brought us to a postmodern turn and a place where both totalities and emancipatory politics would seem to have become a dead end.

Class Difference and Indifference

Jameson (1993, 45–46) suggests that cultural studies' rhetoric of power is, in fact, a repudiation of economic analysis, "an anti-Marxist move, designed to replace analysis in terms of the mode of production." The replacement of the mode of production by relations of power is accompanied by an inattention to class experience. In place of the old modernist conceptions of "class," we now have new, postmodern conceptions of "audiences," "communities," and "fans." Murdock (1995, 91) argues that although class was central to the founding moment of the field of cultural studies, it "has become a category that dare not speak its name" (91). I would suggest, however, that the replacement of the mode of production by relations of power is not necessarily accompanied by an indiscriminate rejection of and disregard for class experience. While the history of the development of feminist cultural studies of the media reveals a keen discomfort with Marxism and its emphasis on class, few feminists would suggest that a nod to class is irrelevant or damaging to this scholarship. Yet, when class does speak its name within feminist scholarship, it tends to do so modestly, from its tertiary place in the "holy trinity" of gender, race, and class or as one difference in a vast chain of differences.

Political economy and questions of class have made limited appearances in feminist cultural studies of the media, in the form of institutional analysis, textual analysis, and reception analysis. Radway's original work on romance readers was conceived as the study of a complex social process beginning with the romance novel's publication within an institutional matrix and culminating in the "actual construction of texts by real women who inhabit a particular social world" (1984, 12). Far more compelling from a political-economic perspective is her subsequent work (1989), which examines the history of the editorial structure and middle-brow discourse of the Book-of-the-Month Club. Likewise, Ang (1991; 1996) has focused on the forms of cultural authority that emanate from the construction of the audience concept within television industry and academic discourse.

As Jameson (1991, 346) suggests, however, a review of institutions does not allow one to arrive at the mode of production so much as it has come to replace it. "Institutions" are the externality of "groups," while "mode of production" and "class" seem to have become more difficult to identify, let alone analyze. Institutional analysis is no substitute for either class analysis or an expanded critique of capital. When "class" explicitly appears in feminist media studies, it is most often separated from institutional analyses. Moreover, "class" is presented as a designation of a group identity or a form of the subject's psychic identity. Even in studies in which "class" enjoys a privileged place, it tends to be categorically confined to something that can be read off the text or the audience. For some time, feminist film theorists have analyzed working-class representations in films including *Mildred Pierce, Stella Dallas, Gentlemen Prefer Blondes,* and *Silkwood* (e.g., Williams 1988; Williams 1990; Kaplan 1990). Explorations of the rare representations of the working class produce valuable insights; yet, there is often a sense that only those films that feature the working class are "about class," as though other films were not also ripe for class analysis. As

Jameson (1991, 349) has observed of "the cultural logic of late capitalism," any adequate representation of the ruling class is excluded.

In naturalistic and ethnographic forms of research, scholars set out to explore the lived experiences of respondents, but often place limits on the lived experience of class because its association with audiencehood turns class into a relation of consumption but not of production. Moreover, the criteria employed for judging the differences among social classes work more effectively in describing social status that in describing social class. For example, in one of the more sophisticated analyses of the class-specific appeal of certain 1980s Hollywood films, Traube (1992) concentrates on the professional middle class, whose status derives from education rather than capital or property. Similarly, the traditional sociological measures used by Press in her study, *Women Watching Television: Gender, Class, and Generation in the American Television Experience* (1991), would seem to indicate more about the status levels of blue-collar, pink-collar, and white-collar occupations than of class positions.

The problem is that status and class, while related, do not describe the same structural phenomenon. Status is based on social stratification, which may have its roots in class relations but is also sustained by value systems that often work to camouflage the class structure through ideological means. Unlike a status group, which is defined by the place it occupies and the function it performs in society, a class is defined by the fact that it is in structural contradiction with another class at the intersection of forces and relations of production (Saffioti 1978, 23). In a precise sense, social classes are "human groupings which occupy antagonistic structural positions in the system of goods and services, that is, groupings whose chief difference lies in the fact that one of them creates, directly or indirectly, the surplus value appropriated by the other" (Saffioti 1978, 25). The phenomenon of social class belongs more to the economic infrastructure, while the phenomenon of social status belongs more to the ideological superstructure. The infrastructure and superstructure mutually determine one another so that a relationship is sustained between class structure and social stratification.

A Marxist view of class would suggest that the distinctions drawn between social classes in reception analyses are unnecessarily divisive since all of the respondents would be defined as working-class if we were to foreground control over the mode of production and production of surplus value. Interestingly, Ang (1996, 116), coming from a staunchly postmodern position, is also troubled by the use of sociological categorizations for describing class experience, but objects to "the creeping essentialism" that risks reifying and absolutizing differences by forcing them into two distinct class and cultural formations. Although she does not deny class differences, Ang would seem to want class to emerge through audience location, rather than to come into being through struggles between organized class forces. Assuming the class position of women in advance, she argues, places a premature explanatory closure on the multiple ways that women belonging to both classes can make sense of the media (117). In wording reminiscent of Judith Butler's (1990) criticism of essentialist gender polarities, Ang suggests that, "Pushed to its logical extreme, this would lead not only to the positing of fixed differences between working-class women and middle-class women, but also to the projection of unity and coherence in the responses of the two groups" (117). Pushed to *its* logical extreme, the approach advocated by Ang would annul the possibility of ever engaging in class analysis.

In treating class as either a demographic category or as something that may or may not emerge through audience encounters, we lose a very important conception of class in the Marxist sense, where class refers to "the structure of access to the means of production and the structure of the distribution of the economic surplus" (Garnham 1995, 70). Although categorical analyses of class are important, they do not have the political potential of a relational approach that would question how inimical classes are both opposed and united through a specific antagonism at the site of property, division of labor, mode of production, and the state (Balibar 1994, 99). Given the difficulty of undertaking a full analysis of class in this sense, it is not surprising that the more easily defined status groups become the vehicle for expressing attributes of class. Jameson (1991, 346) observes that "Classes are few; they come into being by slow transformation in the mode of production; even emergent they seem perpetually at distance from themselves and have to work hard to be sure they really exist as such." Groups seem somehow more recognizable and representable, united in difference rather than in economic exploitation. But, if we are not to give up on class, we must recognize how classes become classes, how, as Marx discusses in *The Eighteenth Brumaire of Louis Bonaparte* (1963), class-in-itself becomes class-for-itself.

Today, one antagonism that is ripe for intervention is that between an expanding, merging, and increasingly powerful for-profit media and those who are unable to access this media except as consumers. One feminist case in point is the effort toward mobilizing a transnational women's movement within the context of a transnational economy dominated by media conglomerates and characterized by disparate access to resources. A political-economic approach to this specific antagonism might foreground the relationship of global citizenship to global resources for communication, thereby addressing structural dimensions of media access that are often disregarded in feminist and cultural studies.

Several scholars have attempted to conceptualize such a movement in a manner reflective of the heterogeneity of the world's women, one that does not only represent the concerns of white Western feminists (Mohanty 1991a, 1991b; Grewal and Kaplan 1994; Hegde 1998). But the promotion of dialogue that is capable of accounting for differences in individual and collective experiences should be accompanied by an awareness that emancipatory movements must engage in struggle with levels of economic, political, and ideological power that can constrain or sabotage dialogue among women (Steeves 1993, 226). As this should suggest, the disharmony in orientation between cultural studies and political economy becomes an irreconcilable difference for feminism whenever political economy's analysis of class relations excludes other differences and cultural studies' analysis of multiple differences fails to acknowledge that these thrive within the capitalist mode of production so long as they do not pose a threat to capital.

For feminists, the problem posed by the cultural studies/political economy schism is that we are too often summoned to choose sides: class or difference? As I have suggested, the trend in cultural studies has been to marginalize one difference: class. Nancy Folbre (1994), one of the pioneers of materialist feminism, has proposed a unisystemic approach that avoids forcing a choice because it attempts to recognize the differences within capitalism. Her notion takes into account structures of constraint based on gender, class, nation, race, age, and sexual preference, among other factors (38), all of which coexist with and coinfluence one another and are aligned and realigned in ways that form differing bases for collective identity, interest, and action around issues of political and economic justice (60). Folbre's conception of collective structures of constraint advances an effective framework for a "feminist question" that is capable of exploring the limitations on choices made by human agents within the context of social structures, the expression and suppression of identities and interests through forms of collective action, and the formation of alliances among individuals by virtue of their location in respect to interlocking structures of constraint.

With this political-economic recognition of "sectional identities," what becomes of the Marxist emphasis on class, the belief that the development of capitalism would erode gender and other differences and that the undoing of capitalism and the transition to socialism would be the work of a unified, class-conscious proletariat? Does "class" no longer make a difference, by itself, in itself, and for itself? One response to this question might be to revive Negt and Kluge's (1993, xiv) defense of the use of the term "proletarian" in the expression "proletarian public sphere": "it is wrong to allow words to become obsolete before there is a change in the objects they denote." But the development of global capitalism *has* engendered a change in the "object" denoted by the word "proletarian." With the expansion of the world's markets, women have emerged as a new kind of proletariat, located at the center of developments as global trade and interactions intensify and international trade affects the survival of local economies (Moghadam 1999; Jaggar 1998).[6] What this would suggest is that class continues to make a difference; it may be "something old," but it is not an antiquated concept. Yet when we see that unequal relations of gender, race, ethnicity, and nation also help to sustain global capitalist expansion, it becomes evident that we need "something new" in the way of an alliance between feminism and political economy, one whose strength is in moving beyond the limits of analyzing class *by itself* in order to confront the configurations and complexities of structured inequalities within capitalism.

Notes

A significant portion of this chapter is a synthesis of material from two of the author's previously published articles: "Class Difference and Indifference in Feminist Media Studies," in *The Public* 4 (3): 27–40, and "Beyond 'Separate Spheres': Feminism and the Cultural Studies/Political Economy Debate," in *Journal of Communication Inquiry* 23 (4): 327–54.

1. Here I refer to a somewhat infamous 1995 colloquy, published in *Critical Studies in Mass Communication*. In the end, Grossberg spurns Garnham's half-hearted attempt at reconciliation, asserting that cultural studies and political economy "don't need a divorce because we were never married" and lamenting that the two approaches have not found a way to live in the same

(left) neighborhood, even as feuding neighbors. Meanwhile, another participant in the debate, Graham Murdock, refrains from the marriage metaphor in order to advocate that scholars might behave something like comrades working to build a bridge over "the Great Divide" (94).

2. One reason for the amassing of feminists on one side of the cultural studies/political economy divide may be "the prevailing academic division of labor" (Murdock 1995) and women's location within it. Cultural studies has tended to make its institutional home in the humanities, while political economy is often pursued through the social sciences (90). Women, who have been traditionally represented and recognized in larger numbers in the humanities, are often theoretically and methodologically separated from political economy as it is conducted across the boundaries of politics, economics, and sociology. Although the field of communication studies is a hybrid of both humanities and social science disciplines, a gendered division of labor prevails here as well. More women are represented in the humanities-oriented study of popular culture, while more men are represented in the social science-oriented areas of political communication, new technologies, and public policy (van Zoonen 1994, 124). However, this can only be a partial explanation, since neither feminist studies nor cultural studies is otherwise averse to border-crossing.

3. The political separation between many feminists and Marxists was not only conceptual but also organizational. In one respect, the separation of "the woman question" from "the feminist question" was in reaction to women's experiences in left organizations, which many feminists charged with a masculine bias. With the separation of women from the left, socialist-feminists became a minority, as those who wanted to participate in left and feminist causes were often asked to choose between causes (Echols 1989, 136).

4. The predominant conception of patriarchy is most often, exclusively and transhistorically, located in the family system, as private patriarchy, despite patriarchy's increasingly public management by the state in the interest of the economy (Brown 1981; Fraser 1989; Mann 1994).

5. In many respects, cultural studies' avoidance of political economy reflects the pervasive problem of felt powerlessness throughout the populace at large. Young (1990, 56) argues that the primary division of labor in advanced capitalism is between professionals and nonprofessionals, and, among the latter, exploitation and oppression takes the form of powerlessness. The powerless are those who lack authority, status, and sense of self; they exercise no power but have power exercised over them, take orders but make no decisions. The hierarchical structure of policy-making and implementation, in particular, prevents the powerless from direct participation in public-policy decisions. In the face of this, and given the overdetermination of powerlessness in respect to gender, race, and class, the retreat from a political-economic critique appears as self-imposed exile. But this may be more a matter of historical conjuncture than of a conscious attempt to avoid political economy. As scholars including

Murdock (1995) have noted, the growth of cultural studies is nearly concurrent with the dominance of neoliberal economic social policy and the left's exclusion from political and economic decision making.

6. As Jaggar (1998, 7) writes, women "constitute a large and increasing part of the labor force in many newly industrializing as well as industrialized countries; they (with their children) constitute 80 percent of the world's refugees; they are trafficked in a world wide prostitution trade; and their bodies are the site of technological interventions designed to promote and control fertility."

II

In the Public Sphere: Work, Technology, Law

4. An Unsuitable Technology for a Woman? Communication as Circulation
Michèle Martin

"Women's use of men's technology would come to no good end," said telephone developers and so-called experts in the early expansion of telephony (Marvin 1988, 23). For them, the telephone was too serious a technology to be used as women would for what men called frivolous matters. Many feminist studies on new information technologies adopt a position close to that of early telephone developers and claim that technologies such as the Internet embody male culture and hence are hostile to women. Are communication technologies gendered? My previous research shows that who can have access to and who can determine the uses of systems of communication depends on a complex relationship among the social, political, and economic conditions under which such systems developed. From my position, a central element in the development of systems of communication is their role in the process of circulation and accumulation of capital. It is this role that I wish particularly to examine in this chapter. The importance of capitalist accumulation in the development of modern systems of communication is largely absent from the feminist studies that I have reviewed.

Given the rapidly changing conditions of the field, I limited the corpus of my analysis to feminist studies on women and new technologies of communication published from 1993 to 1999 in feminist or other types of journals or in books. Though my analysis is not exhaustive, I believe it to be representative of the kind of feminist research done on such issues. The stress put by feminists on empirical studies, though important and useful, raises questions as to the shortcomings of conceptual approaches: Can we sustain, theoretically, that communication technologies are gendered? Could there be other ways of conceptualizing what seems to be an a priori gender-bound conceptualization? I do not pretend to give a satisfactory answer to these questions, but I think they deserve to be raised. The aim of my discussion is to suggest some paths of research that might be useful to consider in feminist analysis of modern systems of communication. To do so, I begin by reviewing some of the most recent works on women, the globalization process, and communication technologies, thereby uncovering some leading recurrent themes and questions. Then, using Marx's approach to communication technologies, I discuss the link between communication and the circulation and accumulation of capital. Finally, I examine how modern systems of communication are mutually related to different spheres of society: the economy, the state, social relations, and how and why this relationship may affect women's relation to modern systems of communication.

Some Themes in Feminist Research

Various themes are explored in the works reviewed for this discussion. The theme of women's labor related to diverse situations in the global economic structures seems to be of particular concern for some scholars: women's exploitation by big conglomerates, especially in less-developed countries (e.g., Marchand 1996; Giri 1995; Spivak 1996, 1999); the impact of information technology on household female workers in subaltern occupations (e.g., Menzies 1996); the appropriate training given to women to integrate successfully in the globalization of capital (e.g., Peterson 1996; Hurgenberg et al. 1994); and the impact of the development of information technology on women scholars (e.g., Morritt 1996, 1997; Taylor et al. 1993). The role of the state in relation to issues raised in this area of study has emerged frequently, particularly the state's weak or lacking intervention in regulating gender discrimination on the net or in media production (e.g., Knupfer 1996a, 1996b; Shade 1996, 1998); in developing policies eliminating the unequal accessibility of new technology for women (e.g., Taylor et al. 1993) or in erasing hate speech, pornography, sexual harassment on the net (e.g., Shade 1996); in supporting the construction of gendered identity within the process of globalization of communication (e.g., Peterson 1996).

The use of the Internet has particularly attracted the attention of feminist research on new technologies. As stated earlier, there seems to be some consensus among feminists that technology is embedding a strong male culture that may prevent women from using it. Many studies are concerned with the ways such a culture could be overcome, or circumvented—through legal interventions (e.g., Kramarae and Kramer 1995); teaching women a critical approach to systems of communication (e.g., Luthra 1996); increasing the number of women using the net (e.g., Senjen and Guthrey 1996; Shade 1996, 1998); creating a world of exchange on specifically feminine networks (e.g., Lucek 1995; Star 1996); and training women in ways to use the Internet (e.g., Senjen

and Guthrey 1996; Hurgenberg et al. 1994) or other types of information technologies in a transnational world.[1]

Various pragmatic questions, ranging from the most general to the
most particular, were put forward in these studies: What is the situation of women in the global economy? How has the development of information technology allowing the globalization of economy and culture affected women's power locally and globally? In what way would
women be affected? How can we preserve and universalize less familiar
strategies, particularly used by women, on social reproduction and
representation in face of globalization? How can women circumvent
male-organized networks on the net? These are important questions,
and answering them helps to identify some barriers to gender equality
related to systems of communication. Still, the reviewed works mostly
look at *how* gender discrimination is experienced, so that the reasons
why it happens are rarely discussed. I suggest that to understand fully
the relationship between women and systems of communication developed, or taken over by capitalist interests as in the case of the Internet,
one has to consider that communication must be seen primarily as a
means of circulation of capital reproducing power relations based on
class and gender. Looking at this issue from a political-economic and
sociological point of view should help us to understand why women's
contribution to these systems takes particular forms.

Communication as a Means of Circulation of Capital

The capitalist process of circulation is at the origin of the development
of modern systems of communication. It is impossible to understand
the place and role of women in relation to these systems without looking at the characteristics given them by capital. Modern sophisticated
systems of communication tremendously increase the velocity of the
circulation process of both money and the ever-increasing mass of information, a reality that has its importance, since money spent in that
process belongs to the cost of production. The more time it takes to
transform the commodity into exchange value, the higher the cost of
production. At this point, space is fixed into time. The moment of fixation of space into time is part of the circulation process and is fundamental in the development of systems of communication. The more
rapid and reliable the systems, the more they are worth to industrial
capitalism, not in the production of surplus value, which is exclusively
produced by labor, but in saving it. Within the process of globalization

of the economy, it becomes crucial to find ways of decreasing circulation time as much as possible.

In 1867, when systems of communication were still in their infancy, Marx asserted that there was no capital realization/accumulation without circulation/communication. Not only did communication technologies such as the telegraph reproduce capitalist relations of production, but more and more rapid systems of communication were the basis for the acceleration of the process of circulation and, then, for the accumulation of capital. What he could not foresee, though, is the significance of that process for the circulation of information as a commodity and, consequently, the importance of the systems allowing that circulation.[2]

Systems of communication allowing interactive exchange of information are becoming increasingly sophisticated with the development of computers and satellites and have become an essential element for capitalist production in the global restructuring of the economy not only in relation to the labor process, but also in the marketplace, allowing international coordination of mass production and circulation of capital at a level of abstraction never reached before, and of a mass of information growing exponentially. The expansion of these systems is of consequence since their monopolization by one class leads to the control of the kind of information being sent and of the structure of its transmission. Still, the dialectical relationship between the processes of production and communication goes beyond issues of structures and equally involves social agents.

Modern Systems of Communication and Society

At the base of the communication processes involved in the globalization of the economy lie different types of interests. For instance, the capitalists' private interests in increasing their profits must adjust to the general social interests, namely those of the majority, related to the monetary relations implied within the global market. On the other hand, the workers' individual interest in finding jobs in a competitive market must adjust to the compulsory socialization of the relations of production in the workplace that is submitted to an ever-increasing geoeconomic expansion. This reciprocal dependence owes partly to the fact that private interests are themselves socially developed within the conditions laid down by society and with the means produced by society (Marx 1976). Thus, in modern society, private interests are mediated by general interests, and both take different forms and expressions that are class- and gender-specific. This state of affairs leads to contradictions between the processes of production, labor, and consumption and creates situations in which different types of interest take on different meanings. These contradictions are necessarily reproduced in forms of communication emerging from specific systems of communication and must be taken into consideration in an attempt to understand the production of new forms of communication suitable or not for women.

Individuals are perpetually facing a contradiction between private and general interests, a contradiction within which the general has to be always prevalent, dominant, for the private to be realized, a contradiction within which general interest dictates private interests, but within which private interests are often disguised as general interest. For instance, telecommunication industries cannot increase their subscription fees without justifying the increase in the name of the general interest (usually presenting it as necessary to give people better service), while in fact the specific intention is to increase the industries' rate of returns.[3] Marx asserts that this paradoxical relationship between these two types of interests exists because monetary relations involve an interdependence of production and consumption as well as a large gap between the consumers and producers. This alienation between objects and subjects may produce economic crises, however: surplus production in some areas, and underproduction in others.[4] As this alienation developed, some attempts were made historically to overcome it in expanding systems of communication that allow the diffusion of information among producers of all the world market activities and to adjust their own accordingly.[5] The interconnections among these activities were successively made through interactive means of communication—such as the mail, the telegraph, the telephone, and, later, the information technologies—that grew at the same time as the exchange market. Nowadays, global systems of communication are meant to create a connection between the different groups of producers and consumers.[6]

It follows that systems of communication become the real instrument of capitalism as transnational tools for the production and reproduction of capital, in the hands of those who control and have access to them. In the form of socially determined types of communication, systems of communication are commercially produced[7] and used for the multiplication of capitalist private interests, and are offered for consumption as general interest. Such is the Internet, which is becoming more and more of a marketplace but is still presented as a social process emerging from people's conscious will. Thus, people's forms of communication are based on an alien social power standing above them, though it is often presented as "natural," as was the development of the telephone in the nineteenth century. Yet modern systems of communication created by capitalist power are not entirely controlled by it but are constituted of elements of social and political nature as well. As such we may say that they create hegemonic forms of communication.

The development of systems of communication involves the political institutions. Marx and Engels (1968) argue that the antithesis between private and general interests takes form in the state as an independent form divorced from the real interests of society and thus as an illusory representation of the general interest. In fact, looking at the conditions offered in some developing countries by authoritarian governments for capitalist interests to build telecommunications infrastructures linked to information technologies, one would tend to agree with Marx and Engels. However, the nature of political interventions is more complex than suggested by these authors and may be affected by internal conditions or by external pressures.[8]

In general, however, forms of communication developed by capital and sustaining the existing social relations of class and gender are approved by state interventions and/or maintained by their absence. Further, more often than not, the state provides attractive conditions (guarantee of a certain rate of return, tax rebates for a number of years, etc.)[9] that favor the involvement of capitalist interests in the expansion of new systems of communication. States, in either developed or developing countries, see the expansion of such systems as a necessary asset for the stabilization of their economy, or for the reinforcement of the national identity, as was the case in Canada in the early expansion of the telephone. Still, some governments create state agencies whose task is to provide universal access to the modern systems of communication being developed in their countries. This occurred in France, with the expansion of the Minitel in the early 1980s.[10] However, unless pressured to the point of action, neoliberal states, and even social democratic states nowadays, wholly support the so-called market economy, at the expense of social issues related to class and gender. Yet systems of communication are bound to reproduce the social relations that they entail either in the labor process or in the social and/or domestic sphere.

Modern systems of communication contribute to the increase of already existing forms of exploitation of labor and to the creation of new ones. A critical level of taylorization of the labor process through mechanization and computerization fixes time into space. In these highly computerized labor processes, "time is everything, man [or woman] is nothing, he [she] is only the body of time," to use Marx's words. Time is fixed into a quantitative measure filled with commodities: into a space. At this stage, the labor process acquires characteristics antithetical to circulation process in terms of time and space. In the production process, *time becomes space* for the workers and space must be extended in order to increase the intensity of labor time. The exploitation of labor power by capital, then, follows the same rules as the acceleration of the process of circulation in relation to the reproduction of capital, albeit applied reversely. Indeed, in order to decrease the time necessary for a measurable quantity of work, the object of labor is scientifically decomposed into small parcels, each corresponding to a specific time. Accordingly, the subjects must also be rationally decomposed. This is the case, for instance, of an occupation such as word processing, in which women predominate. Their work is to produce the greatest number of bytes in the shortest amount of time.

In the circulation of information, *space becomes time,* and the velocity of communication must be such as to shorten as much as possible the time of exchange and thus to lessen the cost of circulation.[11] Modern systems of communication have reached such a degree of velocity and performance as to make geographical space disappear. This creates new sociological and cultural concerns. At the sociological level, instantaneous control at a distance allows capitalist producers facing union organizations, strikes, and wage increases in one country to move their labor process to a more accommodating country where the labor force, often constituted of women, has few means of resistance. From the cultural point of view, these systems of communication may appear as a threat when cultural products coming from industrial countries into more vulnerable communities interfere with their own cultural practices and products, the more so that they carry with them the gender, cultural, and race stereotypes still part of Westernized societies.

At the domestic level, private and general interests have different meanings. The forms of communication developed in modern society and allowing privacy correspond to the "general" interest, namely the private interests of individuals coming from all classes. As such, it gives the developers a "moral" passport for imposing forms of communication fit to the conditions necessary for accumulation of capital, as well as to the "ideal" conditions for the reproduction of the labor force.[12]

Nonetheless, this "moralization" of a form of communication obscures one side of the relationship between private and general interests: *the compulsion of a hegemonic form of communication over particular groups*. This, however, by no means excludes the fact that access to such a form of communication may be liberating for some groups of individuals, including women, in different ways. This was the case with the early development of the telephone in Canada.[13] In such cases, private and general interests in the economic and social spheres seem to coincide.

The imposition of systems of information technologies in the workplace has been particularly strategic in the latest development of the cottage industry based on computerized domestic labor processes. Here, capitalists' interests are disguised as social interests as they take the appearance of personal freedom and individual equality for everyone, while in reality that personal freedom has a different meaning according to class and gender. For instance, women working in the computerized cottage industry are in mainly low-waged, highly controlled jobs, are cut off from peer support, and are usually responsible for the domestic chores as well (Menzies 1996). Thus the "moral" definition of the notions of private interests and general interest, applied in an undifferentiated and general manner in the development of these systems, hides important differences based on class and gender, but also on race, ethnicity, or other group differentiation. These differences, inherent to modern society, are not taken into account in the development of modern systems of communication in which private and general interests are defined in a way that makes disempowered groups disappear.

Yet communication infrastructures created by the industry and more or less controlled by state policies, national or international, are molded by the gendered structures of power already existing in society. Because of their position in such structures developed by the private industry, not only have men greater access than women to systems of communication, but their access is from a better location in the structures, and as Mosco (1998) would put it, places matter. So a truly democratic development of systems of communication should be concerned with local practices and needs, including those of women. A critical approach to these systems of communication should take into account, in addition to the process of globalization involved in the expansion of the economy, the internationalization of a political model in which women's struggles for recognition and women's right to communicate within a transnational system based on complex forms of power relations would be integrated. Still, this does not mean that communication technologies are gendered and thus not fit for female use. In fact, some work has shown that young girls are as skillful as, and sometimes more skillful than, young boys in using information technology, skills that seem to decrease when they get older and more conscious about their gendered role! This suggests that the discrimination encountered in women's use of these systems of communication is a reproduction of that experienced in society and based on structural as well as social elements.

Conclusion

Much feminist study of new technologies pays little attention to the structural relationships sustaining systems of communication. Its microlevel concern with specific issues related to women is mostly apolitical and ahistorical and rarely is related to wider political, economic, or technological elements. On the other hand, political economy's macrolevel concern with critical issues related to communication processes, flows, and structures in relation to so-called globalization mostly ignores the significance of these phenomena for women. Rather, this approach concentrates on the globalization of the economy by the mobilization and transfer of capital by large transnational corporations and their political and economic impact at the national level. In consequence, "women's issues . . . come to be separated off from the 'mainstream' of scholarly and political debate," to be ghettoized. Yet women participate in the processes of transnationalization both as consumers and as workers (Gallagher 1985a, 4) and as such they are concerned with and involved in the transformation of the economy. So women's interests are left to the discretion of transnational corporations, which consider communication as circulation of capital and integrate women into their communication strategies as consumers or as cheap labor. Could state intervention counter the market-oriented development and use of these technologies based on gender and class differentiation? There is no guarantee that a neoliberal government would develop legislation to force equal opportunities of access and use for women and low-income classes on those in control of systems of communication, even less so with an authoritarian state.[14]

It follows that there is a general understanding in the critical feminist perspective that all forms of feminism need to be counterhegemonic in developing approaches to new technologies of communication that will prevent the use of inequitable elements of conceptualizing some aspects of the field that may subvert the aims of feminist politics. Looking at systems of communication as entailing essential characteristics such as patriarchy is unhelpful because it means focusing on a nonexistent feature of the technology. It is no surprise, then, that no conceptual approach was developed to understand that object of analysis.

A more useful task, it seems to me, is to demystify the way private capitalist interests have been constructed as the general interest, thereby annihilating the representation of disempowered groups. Perhaps the first stage of this deconstruction would be to answer some questions about power. Where is power located in the infrastructures and processes of systems of communication? Who has control within the social agencies related to these structures and what are their interests? Are any shifts in power and control possible? If so, which ones? In short, in which ways should we conceptualize power relations within the field of research on new technologies of communication to unmask and eradicate capitalist private interests at the sources of inequality related not only to gender, but also to other disempowered social groups and even countries?

Notes

1. For more information on these and similar works, see Martin (1998).

2. For more information on this particular issue, see Gandy (1995).

3. One could also give as an example the exploitation of female workers in developing countries. The big conglomerates present the situation as in the general interest of these workers, who would not otherwise be employed, but the aim is actually to fulfill the industries' private interests in expending lower wages for higher levels of productivity and profits.

4. The economic crisis of the late 1990s in Asia was partly the result of this alienation, despite the tremendous development of information technology systems.

5. For example, the list of current prices, rates of exchange, etc. For more information on this and related issues, see Martin (1988).

6. For example, this is the case with any conglomerate such as one that would have its headquarters in Toronto, its factories in Malaysia, and its consumers in different Western countries.

7. I am not discussing systems developed and used by the military here.

8. For more information, see Petrazzini (1995).

9. This has been recently the case in Canada, when the federal and provin-

cial governments provided a group of conglomerates with very attractive conditions to develop a multimedia complex in Montreal. For more information, see Martin (1999).

10. Minitel is a telecommunications system based on the same characteristics as the Internet, but whose diffusion and distribution is limited to France. For more information, see Atten (1994), Vedel (1991), and the journal *Réseaux* no. 37, 1992. In Canada, the federal government has made some recommendations concerning gender disparity related to information technologies and has provided funding to study the issue of universal and equitable access; see Shade (1996).

11. In effect, commodities are often exchanged on the market even *before* they are produced.

12. This issue is discussed at length in Martin (1988).

13. For more information on this issue, see Martin (1991), chapters 5 and 6.

14. We have an example of extreme oppression of women in Afghanistan, where, were it available, there could not be any access for women to information technologies.

5. The Invisibility of the Everyday: New Technology and Women's Work

Ellen Balka

In the small community of Heart's Content, Newfoundland, a museum chronicles the glory days of telecommunications in Newfoundland. It marks the site where the transatlantic cable first reached land in North America, which led to prosperous jobs. Although women represented at least half of the telegraph operators in Newfoundland telegraph stations between 1893 and 1896 (Bradbrook 1980), historic accounts of Newfoundland's telecommunications industry made little mention of the sex of workers when it came to the economics of the industry. This pattern reflects larger patterns of the omission of sex as a variable of analysis in the political economy of women's work in telecommunications.[1]

Although only a fraction of the workers in the telecommunications sector today, women warrant consideration because their labor has played an important role in the delivery of communications services. The mechanisms through which women's labor has been leveraged to service the needs of the market, and the costs borne by women in the process, have long gone unaddressed. Here I argue that the sex of workers in Atlantic Canada's[2] telecommunications sector is intimately tied to how technology is used to increase telecommunications sector profits in Atlantic Canada, where as the industry has grown, huge profits have been realized at the expense of women's jobs. New telecommunications technology has played a central role in this process, as it has facilitated the movement of jobs between communities, provinces, and countries and contributed to job loss and deterioration of working conditions in many remaining jobs held predominately by women.

Although traditional analytic tools used in political economy might allow one to discover how political economic changes translate into changes in the everyday lives of women, their use does not ensure that the significant links between sex and money will become apparent. These only become evident when sex is a variable of analysis, and analytic tools aimed at uncovering women's everyday experiences are employed. Below, after briefly outlining the theoretical perspective on which this work is based, I describe the Atlantic Canadian telecommunications industry. Next, I tell a sex-blind story of changes in the Atlantic telecommunications industry to demonstrate how sex can be overlooked in traditional political-economic approaches. I then outline some of the changes that have occurred in women's work in the Atlantic Canadian telecommunications industry, as a way of drawing attention to the value of focusing on women's everyday experiences in our efforts to understand the political economy of women's work in telecommunications. Such a focus also renders technology visible as a factor in the political economy of women's telecommunications work.

Theoretical Framework

Mosco (1996) identifies three points of entry into the study of political economy of communications: commodification, spatialization, and structuration. Commodification refers to the process of transforming use value to exchange value, and the ways the processes of commodification are extended into the social field of communications products, audiences, and labor. Spatialization refers to the transformation of space and time, or the process of institutional extension. Structuration refers to "the process of constituting structures with social agency" (Mosco 1996, 138). Structuration results in social and power processes organized around class and gender and race that may correspond to or oppose one another.

Mosco (1996, 231) suggests that one goal for political economy is "to determine how best to theorize gender within a political economic analysis" and to find terms of engagement between political economic frameworks and those that more adequately address gender. Here I suggest that although commodification, spatialization, and structuration are extremely useful in explaining the macrodynamics of women's work in the telecommunications sector in Atlantic Canada, they fall short as conceptual tools when it comes to explaining the micro- or day-to-day experiences of women workers in the telecommunications sector—a frequent shortcoming of political economy that has been noted by others (e.g., Connelly and Armstrong 1992; Pendakur 1993).

Political economy has been criticized for its failure to uncover "the ideological dimensions of economics that present a male-controlled system of work as characteristic and natural" (Mosco 1996, 61). Women's day-to-day experiences become invisible in many accounts of political economy (Smith 1987), which suggests that we need a political economy that analyzes how women's lives are caught up in historic, political, and economic processes. One of my tasks here is to stress the need for a political economy that draws on the everyday experiences of women. In the absence of an analysis of everyday labor (paid and unpaid), it is easy to "miss" the significance of sex in political economy. Random people don't fill random jobs in the provision of telecommunications services—those jobs are filled by workers of a particular sex. Spatialization does not have random impacts on social groups, but rather, in Atlantic Canada's telecommunications industry, spatialization works as an invisible stick with telephone and call center operators, most of whom are women. When one does make sex a focal point of political economic analyses, it is quickly evident that women fill specific roles in the political economy of the telecommunications industry. Partly because of the predictability of roles women fill—within a sex-segregated paid labor force and as lower wage earners than men, for example—it is possible to introduce new technology into the telecommunications industry and end up with social and power processes organized around gender.

The Atlantic Canadian Telecommunications Industry

In recent history, each of Atlantic Canada's four provinces had its own telephone company[3] and operated independently, under federal regulation. In 1992 significant regulatory changes occurred in the telecommunications industry, opening it up to competition, which included deregulation of long distance calling.

I have argued elsewhere (Balka 1998) that the Atlantic Canadian telecommunications industry has gone through four distinct phases in the last decade. In the first phase, provincial reorganization allowed provincial telecommunications providers to test new technologies that would be deployed to transfer jobs throughout the region. In the second phase, faced with deregulation, the "old" telecommunications providers (former Bell affiliates) formed the Atlantic Provinces Telecommunications Council (APTC). The APTC allowed the provincial telephone companies to form strategic alliances and reposition themselves by coordinating subcontracting opportunities among themselves, in hopes of warding off recent entrants to the telecommunications arena. In the third phase, these strategic alliances have led not only to regional specialization (which has dire consequences for the availability of work for women in each of the Atlantic provinces), but also to a remonopolization of the industry. In the fourth and most recent phase, remonopolization of the industry is being strengthened through increasing exportation of Atlantic Canadian telecommunications technology to the Third World and through efforts to exploit new markets in Canada, which are emerging as the convergence of communications technologies occurs. Mosco's (1996) points of entry to the study of political economy provide insights into the functioning of the Atlantic Canadian telecommunications industry in recent years.

Structuration, Spacialization, and Commodification in Atlantic Canadian Telecommunications[4]

Mosco's (1996) mapping of political economy encourages a focus on structuration, spatialization, and commodification. These three interrelated sets of processes can be used to describe changes in the Atlantic Canadian telecommunications industry. Here, I deliberately use them to tell a sex-blind story of Atlantic Canadian telecommunications as a way of highlighting the significance of women's everyday experiences in the political economy of women's work. I am certain this is not how Mosco, quite sympathetic to feminist concerns, meant for this framework to be used. My point here is that unless one either specifically considers sex as a variable for study, or utilizes methods that ensure the discovery of sex as a variable, women's experiences and the significance of sex are likely to remain invisible.

Structuration: The State, Employment, and the Telephone Companies in Atlantic Canada

We can view the APTC as a structure, or institution, with social agency. The APTC engages in activities (e.g., allocating tasks, such as the development of a new customer service computer system and the development, maintenance, and operation of directory assistance databases between its members) that lead to changes in the distribution of work between provinces and the content of jobs. However, the APTC is only part of the story. The activities the APTC engages in are supported directly and indirectly by provincial governments in Atlantic Canada. For the state, support of the telephone companies combines the good politics of supporting major private-sector employers with sowing the seeds for what on the surface looks like growth industries. Regional telecommunications practices and policies may well be deepening class, gender, and regional divisions, as the telephone companies, APTC, and provincial governments engage in the development and delivery of telecommunications services that ultimately will ease the movement of service jobs out of Canada's eastern provinces.

In Atlantic Canada, the telephone companies play a significant role as private-sector employers. In Nova Scotia, Maritime Telegraph and Telephone Company (MT&T) was the province's second largest private-sector employer in 1997. That same year it paid $16.5 million in income tax, which represented 15 percent of all corporate tax paid for 1997 in Nova Scotia (KPMG 1997, 3). In 1998, NewTel was Newfoundland's largest private-sector employer (NewTel 1998). With unemployment rates as high as 25 percent in many areas of Atlantic Canada, the state has a vested interest in supporting the telephone companies. In some cases the government may purchase services directly from the telephone companies. As has been the case in Newfoundland, the state may, through a variety of means, create favorable conditions for conducting business related to the telecommunications industry.

In 1994 the province of Newfoundland and Labrador disposed of Newfoundland and Labrador Computer Services Limited (NLCS). It was purchased by Newfoundland Telephone (and its name was changed to NewTel Information Solutions Limited, or NISL) as part of NewTel's strategy to remain competitive in the face of telecommunications convergence. The provincial government subsequently signed an agreement with NISL that made NISL the primary information technology supplier to government for seven years. When combined with the transfer of some Newfoundland Telephone employees to NISL, NISL became Atlantic Canada's largest information technology company (NewTel 1995). Many other examples of state support of provincial telecommunications companies abound (Balka 1998), including the formation of a company by a provincial government and public university, developed to market expertise and develop new products and markets through telecommunications in distance medicine and education (NewTel 1995); and a joint venture between NewTel and the Newfoundland government called Network Newfoundland and Labrador, designed to "strengthen the position of the province as a location for call centre and related businesses" (NewTel 1996, 3–4).

State support for the telecommunications industry has taken a similar form elsewhere in Atlantic Canada. For example, in Nova Scotia as well as in New Brunswick, state funds have been used to create educational programs catered to the needs of the telecommunications industry. In Nova Scotia, along with its research and development partner Telecom Applications Research Alliance (TARA), MT&T has contributed to the development of a master's degree program in software engineering at Dalhousie University (MT&T 1998). NBTel was a partner in developing Canada's first undergraduate program in computer telephony integration, which was offered through the University of New Brunswick in September 1998 (NBTel 1998). The province of New Brunswick has also directly supported the call center industry[5] through a variety of tax incentives and financial contributions to businesses.[6]

A former British Columbia employment minister noted that the New Brunswick government promised the United Parcel Service $6 million to aid the company in relocating, in order to lure 850 jobs to New Brunswick (Cernetig 1995). In another instance, New Brunswick contributed $200,000 ($4,000 per job) to Imperial Kool-Ray to help cover relocation and start-up costs (*The Globe and Mail* 1995). The former British Columbia employmnet minister also noted that a New Brunswick promotional document titled *New Brunswick: The Call Center Capital of North America* advertised changes to the workers' compensation laws in New Brunswick that reduced employee costs borne by employers (Cernetig 1995). New Brunswick's corporate taxes and workers' compensation premiums are among the lowest in Canada (Cooper 1995).

Although the APTC fills a significant role in the reorganization of telecommunications work in Atlantic Canada, clearly it is a result of the combined efforts of APTC members, their industrial partners and allies, and the state that jobs have disappeared in Atlantic Canada (and those jobs that remain offer women working in the telecommunications industry very limited opportunities). With the collaboration of the state, Atlantic Canadian companies have been engaging in numerous practices that in the short term leave workers competing with others in the region (or nation) for jobs, and in the long term will leave Atlantic Canadians competing with workers elsewhere in the world for jobs.

Spatialization: Time-Space Compression and Institutional Reach

Competition for jobs of an increasingly narrow scope in the telecommunications industry reflects spatialization processes that in recent years have increasingly separated workers from both the tools and materials they require to perform their jobs (e.g., directory assistance databases for all four Atlantic Canadian provinces are now located in New Brunswick) and the location of those people who consume the products and services their labor produces (e.g., people all over Canada now call customer service representatives who are located in New Brunswick). New switching technologies have increasingly allowed companies to locate workers at a distance from the markets they serve. The technology, tested initially in Newfoundland and Labrador, where telephone operators' jobs were moved from smaller communities to the province's largest city, where the main phone company offices were located, is now being used increasingly to separate jobs and workers spatially from the markets and customers they serve.

Commodification

Commodification of communication services has been central to APTC members' strategies to maintain and increase profit as deregulation has allowed new entrants into the local and long distance telephone service markets. For example, Newfoundland Telephone reported a 4.7 percent increase in revenues in local service in 1993 (NewTel 1994, 6), which it attributed partly to the success of enhanced services such as "Custom Calling" and call management services (such as voice mail). Many of the new services have been marketed through telemarketing services, handled in house by telephone operators who now perform an enlarged array of tasks.

In their 1993 annual report, NewTel Enterprises indicated that in the previous 18 months, Newfoundland Telephone had introduced a record number of new products and services. In their 1995 annual report, NewTel Enterprises declared that intensive marketing of value-added services took on greater importance as a source of revenue generation during 1994. During that year marketing of data products and high bandwidth uses (e.g., video conferencing) also increased. In 1994 Newfoundland Telephone entered into an agreement to spend $172 million over ten years to build a broadband network that can deliver interactive multimedia services throughout the province (which has a high out-migration rate and a population of just over half a million people). This initiative was expected to produce 270 jobs. In 1995 Newfoundland Telephone introduced an unprecedented 32 new products and services.

Consistent with its efforts to have New Brunswick identified as the call center capital of North America, the main offerings for sale of Bruncor, the holding company for NBTel, are customized interactive voice response (IVR) services. NBTel interActive provided 170 different IVR applications to a range of business and government customers in 1997. Topics and issues addressed by the IVR applications included entries in a draw for moose-hunting licenses, recorded messages for Celine Dion (a Canadian pop star), and queries to the "Name that Number" service that allows callers to locate the names associated with phone numbers. Through the Bruncor subsidiary NBTel interActive,

Bruncor has also become a leader in processing prepaid long distance phone cards (NBTel 1998). Like MT&T (MT&T 1997), New Brunswick Telephone (NBTel) hopes to expand its market by entering the cable market and combining telephone, cable television, and Internet technologies in new combinations for customers.

The Intersection of Sex and Money: Women's Work in Atlantic Canadian Telecommunications

The Invisibility of Sex in Macroprocesses

The interrelated processes of structuration, spatialization, and commodification have dramatically altered the content of women's jobs in telecommunications in Atlantic Canada as the region has sought to establish itself as a telecommunications giant of international proportion. Although these concepts are extremely helpful in guiding investigations of macroprocesses that together constitute the political economy of the telecommunications industry, and such investigations yield valuable insights about the structure of that industry, there is nothing inherent to political economy in general or these analytic categories in particular that necessitates an analysis of the relationship between sex, money, and the use of technology. Indeed, as my use of these analytic tools above suggests, the sex of the workers can remain unknown, their daily working conditions hidden, and the interconnectedness of sex, technology, and profits undocumented. In order for these connections to be rendered visible, methods that focus on both the sex of the workers and their everyday experiences at work are required.

Feldberg and Glenn (1983, 60) argued that "an accurate assessment of the effects of technology requires identifying the social divisions within the labor force, describing the impacts for each group, and analyzing the connections and differences between what happens to one group and what happens to another group." They advocate an investigation of technological change that addresses the effects of technology on three levels: the occupational structure, the organizational structure, and the work process. Occupational-level changes are reflected in changes in the content and/or scope of activities that constitute a job. Such changes are reflected in changes in the number and types of jobs, the ratio of one job category to another, and elimination of some occupations through labor savings. Changes at the organizational level refer to changes in the ratio of workers in different job categories within a workplace or organization. Changes in the work process refer to changes in the content and organization of jobs. Such changes are reflected in changes in job content, including the amount and type of skill associated with a job and changes in the extent to which jobs are specialized, varied, or routine (Feldberg and Glenn 1983).

Sex Matters: Making Women's Work in Telecommunications Visible

The use of such analytic categories draws our attention toward sex as an important variable in the political economy in telecommunications. Although changes in the occupational structure can be difficult to track because of the long time intervals between censuses, evidence of such changes can also be gleaned from changes in employment advertisements, where, for example, one might begin seeing advertisements for "call center customer service representatives" (reflecting the growth of the call center industry, made possible through processes of spatialization), or "telemarketers" (reflecting the increasing commodification of telecommunication services). A further investigation, focusing on the sex of workers holding these new jobs, allows us to see where women's labor fits in the new telecommunications economy. Although at this time little data detailing the sex of workers in these new occupations exists, anecdotal reports from call center operators suggest that in the New Brunswick call center industry, as much as 80 percent of the labor force is composed of women.

An analysis of organizational level changes and work process in the Atlantic Canadian telecommunications industry directs our attention much more toward the interconnectedness of sex, technology, and money. An investigation of changes in the organizational structure at Newfoundland Telephone between 1987 and 1995 shows that in all three groups of unionized workers (the all-male "craft" workers, who do line work; the all-female clerical group; and the predominantly female telephone operators), levels of employment increased between 1987 and 1989, and all three groups of workers experienced a slight decline in 1990. The numbers of craft and clerical workers increased slightly in 1991. After reaching their highest level of employment in 1989, the number of telephone operators declined steadily through 1995, and the volume of calls handled by the company nearly doubled. Craft workers also declined in numbers from 1992 to 1995, while the number of clerical workers employed remained relatively constant throughout the period, as they handled the data entry needs associated with nearly constant change of the phone company's administrative computer system. Tracing technological changes and identifying how they are related to changes in work processes of telecommunications industry workers sheds further light on why sex is an important variable in political economic analyses, and why an understanding of women's everyday lives contributes to political economic analyses. I address this by looking at changes to the work processes of telephone operators in Newfoundland, linking these to organizational and occupational changes that occurred during the same period.

Prior to 1991, when the number of telephone operators employed declined dramatically, a division of labor existed among telephone operators. One group of operators handled directory assistance inquiries, another group handled long distance calls, and a third group handled special services, which included ship-to-shore communications, radio calls from remote areas, and TTY calls (for hearing- and vocally impaired persons). Telephone company offices all over the province performed a mix of operator services. In 1991 the office in Goose Bay (Labrador) was closed down, and long distance and special service and directory assistance calls were rerouted. Women workers in the Goose Bay office (a majority of whom had partners employed in Goose Bay) were given "an opportunity" to move to St. John's. For most of the women workers in the Goose Bay office, the economics of having a male partner with a more lucrative job in Goose Bay prevented a move to St. John's.

Around the same time, automated directory assistance service was introduced, and multipurpose positions (computers that, unlike previously used technology, made it possible for a single telephone operator to handle directory assistance or long distance calls) were introduced in the St. John's office. With the automated directory assistance system, directory assistance work went from a completely manual system (where operators looked up phone numbers and then recorded the caller's number on slips of paper for a computer-based billing system) to a fully automated system. The automated billing portion of the directory assistance system automatically traced the caller's number, which eliminated a component of the directory assistance job (asking for and recording the caller's number).

With the "multipurpose" workstations, operators came in to work and logged onto a computer as either a directory, long distance, or multipurpose operator (handling both types of calls). "Cross-training" (teaching directory assistance operators how to handle toll calls and teaching toll operators how to handle directory assistance calls) has virtually eliminated the distinction between directory assistance and long distance operators. The combination of digital communications switching equipment and computers made it easy to reroute telephone traffic between locations. As a result, the phone company was able to shut down offices by rerouting calls to St. John's, as well as to change the mix of services handled in other locations. Directory assistance jobs were eliminated in all areas of the province except St. John's, and the combination of new technology and cross-training resulted in an elimination of the division of labor among telephone operators. Part of what allowed the strategy to succeed was the gendered economics of work: women who are attached to male wage earners are unlikely to move for a job, because it means giving up what is usually a significantly higher male wage.

With automation, the phone company was able to reduce the number of offices handling Special Operator Services Traffic (SOST) from four to one (located in St. John's). In 1993, SOST was a separate group of operators that also provided after-hours telemarketing. The displacement of the SOST operators-turned-telemarketers was slowed somewhat by the increasing commodification of telephone services, made possible through the very same switching equipment that was used to move jobs throughout the province initially, and subsequently elsewhere in the region.

In July 1993 an automated billing system was introduced for toll calls. It eliminated the live operator interface and allowed customers to make collect and third-party calls with no operator intervention, which led to a further reduction in the number of telephone operators. One operator viewed this as a threat to jobs and also noted that many customers (especially seniors) found the new automated billing system difficult to use. A phone company supervisor countered this by suggesting that customers could choose to bypass portions of the automated billing system when placing long distance calls. An advertisement placed in a local St. John's newspaper (*Express*, 20 October 1993) by Local 410 of the Communication, Electrical, and Paper Workers representing the telephone operators provided instructions toward this end. The advertisement, which began with the heading "YOU HAVE A CHOICE!," included the following text: "When placing third party, collect and credit card calls, dialing '0' when the recording begins, will get you an operator. Insist on an operator. It's your right. It's your choice!"

A spokesperson for another telephone company, speaking about a similar computerized automated billing system, commented, "neither we nor the phone companies view this system as a replacement for operators . . . rather than replace them, it displaces them to do other things for telephone users," such as act as service agents, set up conference calls, handle emergencies, and so on (*Vancouver Sun* 1991, B11). Not surprisingly, extensive use of new technology at Newfoundland Telephone has led to massive service increases in areas in which women are employed, which have been accompanied by declines in staffing levels.

For those operators who have kept their jobs, new technology has resulted in poorer working conditions. For example, the new multipurpose positions used by both directory assistance and toll operators in St. John's diminish operators' ability to pace work (calls are fed into the operators' consoles as soon as they have disconnected from a call). At the same time, the new positions allow supervisors to monitor how long operators spend on each call. The new multipurpose positions also allow supervisors to determine how long operators have been unplugged from their consoles (for example, to go to the bathroom). The new system also tracks call volume, which has made it possible to schedule operators' shifts more accurately to coincide with high call volumes. Where in the past an operator's shift might have included some busy and some slow times, "traffic monitoring" has enhanced the company's ability to schedule operators to handle higher call volumes throughout their shifts. Thus, the technical capability of monitoring call volume has facilitated an increased workload handled by operators, while the same technology has facilitated electronic performance monitoring.

Finally, labor savings related to the automated directory assistance and toll systems have resulted in layoffs and significant scheduling changes for those operators who remain. Both labor savings and the redistribution of work (e.g., moving all night shifts to St. John's, made possible through a feature of the company's computer system that allows entire services to be moved from one location to another through a computer console) have necessitated that operators with extensive seniority return to night and weekend shifts in order to retain their jobs.

In 1993 the APTC made decisions about rationalizing work (e.g., by moving all directory services to New Brunswick, where the database is maintained, moving all billing to another Atlantic location, and so on) and eliminated some tasks in some provinces. Ironically, the threat of lost work is, for telephone operators, made possible as a result of the telecommunications services that they are helping to provide. The same technology that made it possible to close down telephone company offices employing telephone operators outside of St. John's made it possible to set up a huge call center industry in the province of New Brunswick, where women labor under poor working conditions providing services for businesses and companies located elsewhere in Canada. The relative poverty of New Brunswick has ensured that wages paid to the call center workers remain low, as workers in New Brunswick work in jobs that could be removed from their community literally with the flick of a switch.

In the period prior to 1993, Newfoundland Telephone introduced several new technologies that made it possible for workers who provide telecommunications services to be located in any geographic location served by Newfoundland Telephone's switching equipment. During the early 1990s, Newfoundland Telephone was able to install and implement new technologies that would become the basis for their long-term business strategy, as they entered into strategic alliances with the other Atlantic province telephone companies. Newfoundland in effect became a test bed for new technology that made it possible to locate telecommunications workers who provide telecommunications services at a distance from the markets they serve. The same technologies tested by Newfoundland Telephone and adapted widely elsewhere in Atlantic Canada are now serving a bustling call center industry in New Brunswick. As emphasis on the transfer of technology to less developed regions of the world is undertaken by the phone companies, call center workers in New Brunswick may well find themselves in competition with women workers elsewhere in the world, just as they have recently found themselves competing with call centers elsewhere in Canada for scarce jobs.

Conclusion

In Atlantic Canada, new technology has been introduced into a labor force that is highly sex segregated. The new technology has been at the heart of processes of spatialization (the compression of space and time in moving jobs around a province and then a region). It has played an important role in the commodification of telecommunication services (e.g., voice mail, three-way calling, etc.). Evidence of structuration can be found in both the existence of agencies such as the APTC and the intersection of jobs and gender. Women in different parts of Newfoundland were initially competitors for the same jobs, no longer linked to the communities in which women lived. As the technology matured, women in one province competed with women in another province for the same scarce jobs. In the final stage, women in Atlantic Canada will begin competing with women elsewhere in the world for jobs. The new technology with which women work has become an invisible stick for women workers in telecommunications, the ever-present awareness that jobs can move at the flick of a switch ensuring compliant behavior.

Although the concepts of structuration, spatialization, and commodification do not demand a focus on women, when combined with Feldberg and Glenn's (1983) focus on understanding the role of technology in the gendered nature of occupations, the relations between groups of workers within organizations, and the content of women's jobs, it is possible to uncover not only how the telecommunications industry in Atlantic Canada works from a political economic perspective, but also how women workers fit into and experience that industry. Mosco's (1996) mapping of political economy gives us a macroperspective of the industry. It is tremendously useful in terms of developing a sense of broad industry patterns. But its use can (precisely because it focuses on macroprocesses) obfuscate the special role played by women in relation to technology, in the Atlantic Canadian telecommunications industry. Feldberg and Glenn's framework, however, can be used to focus attention on both sex as a variable for analysis and on women's everyday lived experiences, upon which many telecommunications services are built. Such a microperspective is essential in developing an understanding of the role sex plays in the political economy of women's work.

Despite claims in each of the Atlantic provinces about how corporate strategy has been designed to keep provincial telephone industries competitive, there has been a decline in the numbers of jobs in both the telecommunications industry in Atlantic Canada and in other sectors (service and clerical) that have traditionally been dominated by women. Areas of employment traditionally dominated by women (e.g., service areas such as banking) have been particularly vulnerable to job losses related to the introduction of new telecommunications technologies (such as home banking and banking by phone). Although some of these jobs have been transferred to other locations (e.g., bank call centers), many other jobs have been eliminated through the advent of technologies such as interactive voice response systems, which in many cases eliminate workers (mostly women workers) from the process of providing information to customers.

Notes

1. There are, of course, exceptions. See p. 231 of Mosco (1996) for a discussion.

2. Atlantic Canada includes the four provinces of Newfoundland, New Brunswick, Nova Scotia, and Prince Edward Island.

3. A fourth telephone company, Terra Nova Telephone, operated in Newfoundland until 1988, when it was acquired by Newfoundland Telephone.

4. Arguments made in this section are based on a considerably more detailed account of events, documented in Balka (1998).

5. Call centers bring a range of telecommunications technologies together, which makes it possible for call center workers in one location to provide a range of services to callers (or target clients) in other locations. Call centers handle inbound calls (where orders are processed, information is provided, or problems are solved), and outbound calls (where calls are initiated by the call center, usually for the purposes of selling something, such as extended warranties).

6. McFarland and Buchanan (1997) have begun the task of documenting New Brunswick's call center industry, which has also received substantial coverage in Canadian newspapers amid calls of unfair interprovincial trade practices.

6. The Political Economy of Women's Employment in the Information Sector

Stana Martin

Prior to Machlup's publication of *Production and Distribution* in 1962, economists traditionally divided the economy into three parts: primary/extractive, secondary/industrial, and tertiary/services. Machlup was the first to conceptually carve out a fourth sector: the knowledge/information sector. The Industrial Revolution largely shifted the U.S. economy from a primary/extractive economy to a secondary/industrial economy. The industrial economy was characterized by two factors: (1) the majority of the nation's wealth was produced in manufacturing, and (2) the majority of the civilian labor force was employed in industrial jobs. Today, however, much of the U.S. national wealth derives from the production, distribution, and manipulation of information.[1] Similarly, the majority of the civilian labor force work in information jobs, or jobs whose primary output is the production, distribution, and manipulation of information.[2] This economy is now known as an information economy, and the largest sector of employment is known as the information sector. This paper analyzes the relationships among gender, information technology, and work in the information sector.

There is no consensus in the literature about how women will fare in an information-centered economy. Bell (1973) argued that, since women are heavily employed in services and since demand for services would grow in an information-centered economy, women workers would be more in demand. Webster's and Robins's (1986) argument is somewhat less rosy. They assert that women will be particularly vulnerable because they usually hold positions in the workforce that are the least skilled and least likely to be unionized. Hartmann et al. (1986) predict neither job loss nor growth for women but merely shifting in occupational structure as some jobs disappear while others appear. Then primary objective of this paper is to scrutinize the patterns of women's employment in the information sector and, in the process, explain how these patterns have evolved and what trajectory may lie ahead. The section below looks at the patterns by gender in information employment and gives some theoretical explanations for sex-segregation in information work. The next section looks at the role that information technology plays in reshaping women's occupational structure in the information sector. The last section briefly addresses two oft-cited predictions for employment growth in the next century and relates these to the analysis presented here. Before we arrive there, however, we must first turn to patterns of employment in the information sector by gender.

Gender Patterns in the Information Sector

Table 1 details employment by gender in the four sectors of the economy from 1970 to 1995.[3] First and foremost, both agriculture and industry continue to decline in share of all employment for both genders. Employment in these sectors as a proportion of all employment is waning even as services and information grow. Secondly, the gendered nature of occupational structure is clearly evident. Men have historically dominated in industry while women have dominated in information. Looking at the total numbers of men and women in the information sector, it is clear that women outnumber men for all years. In 1970, 1.06 women worked in information work for each man. By 1990 the ratio of women to men had grown to 1.43 to 1. Clearly, women have been the "preferred" worker in information employment.

While the information sector has been dominated by women workers, it has also dominated women's employment. Unlike men's employment, the information sector has long been the bastion of women's work. From 1970 to 1995, the majority of women's employment was in information. In 1970, 57.96 percent of all women's work was in information. By 1995 that percentage had risen to 63.84. The largest employing sector for men, on the other hand, was industry in 1970 at 46.27 percent. From 1970 to 1995 employment in industry progressively declined for men (down to 39.58 percent) and employment in information increased (up to 41.18 percent by 1995). It is important to note that this shift occurred in the last five years of the data. Even as late as 1990, men were about equally divided between information work and industrial work. Thus, though men's employment in information rose dramatically, women have been characteristically the dominant workforce for the information sector, and the information sector has dominated women's employment.

Underlying these trends, however, are more subtle microtrends. From 1990 to 1995 women's employment experiences negative growth. Women's employment drops from its 1990 high of 64 percent to 1995's 63.8 percent. In the same time span, men's employment gains

Table 1. Employment by Gender in Four Sectors as a Percentage of
All Employment

			Women			
Sector	1970	1975	1980	1985	1990	1995
Agriculture	0.83	1.40	1.21	0.99	0.81	1.04
Industry	16.43	13.16	12.74	10.58	9.85	9.01
Service	24.78	26.72	25.30	25.42	25.18	26.11
Information	57.96	58.72	60.75	63.01	64.16	63.84
Total	100%	100	100	100	100	100

			Men			
Sector	1970	1975	1980	1985	1990	1995
Agriculture	5.21	5.32	4.48	4.07	3.41	3.39
Industry	46.27	42.50	42.60	41.57	40.71	39.58
Service	13.06	13.94	14.02	15.14	15.53	15.85
Information	35.46	38.24	38.90	39.22	40.35	41.18
Total	100%	100	100	100	100	100

Source: Martin (1997b)

nearly a full percentage point (.83). Until 1990 women's employment
in the information sector exhibited regular and steady growth. I will
argue that this shift to negative growth for women is not an aberra-
tion, but rather the beginning of far-reaching changes that result from
the interrelationships of (1) patriarchal occupational structures, and
(2) technology-led changes in the occupational structure of work. To
make this argument, we must first discern the occupational patterns of
information work for both men and women.

Routine Information Employment and the "Helping" Professions

Conceptually, information occupations can be divided into several different types. Machlup (1962) identified six different types of information work:

1. A *transporter* will deliver exactly what he *[sic]* has received, without changing it in the least. . . .

2. A *transformer* changes the form of the message received, but is not supposed to change its contents. . . .

3. A *processor* changes both form and contents of what he has received, but only by routine procedures which subject different pieces of knowledge received to certain operations, such as combinations, computations, or other kinds of rearrangements, leading to definite results, independent of the processor's tastes, moods, or intuition, dependent solely on conventions concerning such processing rules. . . .

4. An *interpreter* changes form and contents of the messages received, but has to use imagination to create in the new form effects equivalent to those he feels were intended by the original message; for example, the translator of subtle speech or sensitive poetry in a foreign language.

5. An *analyzer* uses so much of his own judgment and intuition in addition to accepted procedures, that the message which he communicates bears little or no resemblance to the message received.

6. An *original creator,* although drawing on a rich store of information received in messages of all sorts, adds so much of his own inventive genius and creative imagination, that only relatively weak and indirect connections can be found between what he has received from others and what he communicates. (33)

Implicit in this scheme lies a continuum of information-handling tasks. Occupations that are transporters, transformers, and processors are typified by formalized rules for handling information. Occupations that fall into the categories of analyzers, interpreters, and creators, however, are the least likely to have codified rules.

The more the information handling tasks can be codified into sets of rules, the more likely the job is to involve routines. Thus, we can categorize information occupations according to the extent of routinization of their information-handling tasks. Occupations that create, analyze, or interpret information are nonroutine information occupations, while occupations that process, transform, or transport information are routine information-handling occupations.

Figure 1 below charts information employment by routine and nonroutine work from 1970 to 1995. Two patterns clearly emerge. First, the information sector has been and is still dominated by routine information handling. Equally clearly, however, the trend over time is less routine information handling and more nonroutine information han-

Figure 1. Information work by type.

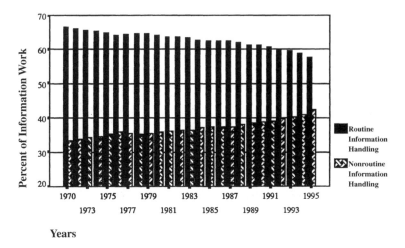

Years

Source: Martin (1997b)

dling. In short, the information sector appears to be headed for significant occupational restructuring as routine information handling increasingly gives way to nonroutine information handling.

If we look at this same data and control for gender, we can see that women's employment in the information sector has been typified by routine information jobs. Figure 2 graphs employment in routine and nonroutine information-handling occupations by gender as a percent of all information work for that gender. Over the period of this study, women accounted for the majority of the routine information workforce. In 1970 women were 59.46 percent of all routine information workers and by 1995 they were 60.44 percent. Interestingly, routine information work is also the majority of all women's employment. In 1970 nearly 80 percent of all women's employment in information work was routine information handling. By 1995 this number dropped to just over 63 percent but still dominated women's employment in the information sector. Conversely, men's employment in routine information handling has been consistently less than women's and has very nearly equalized with nonroutine information handling as of 1995. Clearly, women are heavily segregated into routine information handling.

Looked at over time, the data seem to indicate that, though women have been historically segregated into routine information handling, they are now making gains in employment in the information sector

**Figure 2. Routine and nonroutine information work as percentage of all
information work, by gender.**

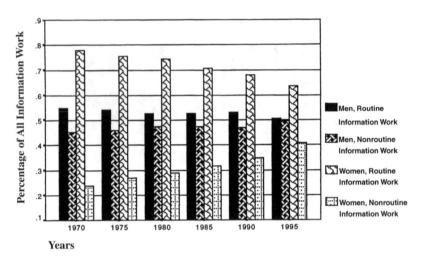

Source: Martin (1997b)

largely in nonroutine information handling. At this microlevel, we
might conclude that the Information Age is eradicating (albeit slowly)
gender inequities. Such a conclusion, however, is facile as it fails to account for underlying patterns that contribute to the macrostructural
changes. When we look closely at the patterns in nonroutine information work by gender, we can see that women's gains are not in "gold-
collar" (i.e., highly paid, in-demand, technologically oriented information occupations) work, but rather in the "helping" professions.[4]

Space limitations do not allow us to look at employment by gender
by detailed occupation. However, a few exemplary cases will solidify
the pattern. Table 2 below lists the eleven occupations that were the
"top performers" in terms of producing growth for men and women in
nonroutine information occupations. Of these occupations that represent the highest share of growth, the majority of them for women (72
percent) fall into the "helping" professions. Conversely, less than a
third (27 percent) of men's do. Furthermore, men's gains are far more
likely than women's to be in the "gold-collar," highly paid, highly
trained technical jobs. Of the occupations listed below for men, 45.5
percent are "gold collar," while only .9 percent of the occupations are
for women.

Table 2. Occupations with Highest Percentage of Growth in
Nonroutine Information Handling, by Gender

Occupation	Women	Men
Computer programmers		3.6
Educational administration	4.0	
Engineers		7.6
Entertainers		16.3
Financial managers	3.3	13.8
Health administration	6.0	12.1
Lawyers and judges		5.7
Math and computer specialists	4.0	9.3
Managers, public relations and advertising		3.4
Management analysts		2.6
Other financial officers	3.9	
Public administration	3.2	
Sales managers	18.0	
Scientists		2.7
Social workers	2.8	
Teacher aides	6.0	
Teachers, college	3.0	
Teachers, not college	17.0	4.4

Source: Martin (1997b)

Thus, even where women are making gains in nonroutine information handling, they are still far more likely than men to make gains in
"helping" professions. Men, conversely, are more likely to be making
gains in technical "gold-collar" occupations. In combination, the preponderance of women in routine information handling and their tendency to make gains in "helping," nonroutine information professions
lets us conclude that sex segregation is alive and well in the information sector.

It would be tidy at this point for the data to support one or the
other of the theories discussed earlier about how women will fare in
an information-based economy. However, this is not so. Bell (1973)
predicted strong employment for women based on the existing preponderance of women in clerical work. As it happens, employment
for women is on the rise in the information sector, but not particularly
in the types of occupations Bell identified. Webster and Robins (1986)
are also correct in pointing out that women are vulnerable in the

information sector labor force. Women, primarily hired in routine information handling, will suffer heavy redundancies in an information-based economy. Hartmann et al. (1986) may come closest to this data by predicting neither significant gain nor loss, but simply shifting occupational structure. The question left unanswered by their argument, however, is why these particular patterns emerge in the data over other possible ones and what this might mean for women's employment as the patterns are extrapolated into the future. The next section briefly reviews the literature on sex segregation in the labor force while the following section analyzes the implications for women workers in the next century.

Sex Segregation in the Labor Force

Feminists have long criticized the sex-segregated nature of employment. Two of the earliest theories came from neoclassical economics: human choice theory and human capital theory. Human choice theory, a supply-side explanation, argues that the supply of men and women for any given job will be gender biased, as all workers will make occupational choices that allow them to maximize their earning potential over their lifetime. From the demand side, human capital theory contends that employers will opt to hire workers who have the maximum human capital attached to them (meaning education, years of work experience, etc.). In both neoclassical theories, human actors, whether workers or employers, are making rational choices based on maximizing earnings and profit margins. The theories ignore, however, the role of gender power in creating segmented markets. Neoclassical economists "ignore patriarchy, a social system with a material base" (Hartmann 1986, 140).

Marxist feminists, on the other hand, explain sex segregation as a function of dual operating systems: patriarchy and capitalism. Patriarchy has proven rather slippery to pin down as either a definition or as a system of subjugation (see Bradley [1979] and A. Pollert [1996]). Originally patriarchy meant the rule of the father over the son. However, in feminist thinking it is generally used as the rule of men over women. Hartmann (1986) defines patriarchy as

> . . . a set of social relations which has a material base and in which there are hierarchical relations between men, and solidarity among them, which enable them to control women. Patriarchy is thus the system of male oppression of women. (138)

Hartmann argues that job segregation by sex is both an *outcome* and a *source* of men's power over women:

> Job segregation by sex . . . is the primary mechanism in capitalist society that maintains the superiority of men over women. . . . Low wages keep women dependent on men because they encourage women to marry. Married women must perform domestic chores for their husbands. Men benefit, then, from both higher wages and the domestic division of labor. This domestic division of labor, in turn, acts to weaken women's position in the labor market. Thus, the hierarchical domestic division of labor is perpetuated by the labor market, and vice versa. This process is the present outcome of the continuing interaction of two interlocking systems, capitalism and patriarchy. (139)

This combination of men's power over women in both the home and in the labor force provides a powerful theory for sex segregation at work.

Men benefit from women's unpaid labor in that they are freed of the major responsibilities of hearth and home. They can sustain full-time, uninterrupted employment as they are unhampered by the demands of young children. Because men can give greater dedication to full-time employment, they are able to take on the debt load of higher education and training as they can be assured of eventual return over a lifetime of work. Thus, it is to men's economic benefit to hold women responsible for "nurturing" and domestic labor. Women, faced with the responsibilities of young children and household care, often forgo extensive training, thus taking lower-paid and lower-social-prestige positions. Women's continued responsibilities for children and household care mean that women are more likely to seek part-time work or work that will accommodate absences from the labor force. If a woman does opt for a career, she is more likely to have to take time off from work and thus jeopardize her promotion potential. Thus, women's starting positions are often lower than men's and they rise slower, if at all. Men as workers benefit both because they can compete better with other men in the labor force as long as a woman performs the unpaid domestic labor, and they have less competition from women as women are not very successful competitors for the higher-paid, higher-prestige jobs.

Marxist feminists' combination of patriarchy and capitalism serves to explain both the supply and demand factors as well as the role of gender power in the creation of sex segregation in the labor force. Furthermore, the explanation matches closely the trends evident in employment in the information sector. Routine information handling requires much less training than does nonroutine information handling. This means that workers can be fairly interchangeable, wages are low, and temporary or long-term absence from the workforce has minimal adverse effects on employability.

Contrasted to nonroutine information handling, patriarchal relations "channel" the sexes into various types of information handling. Nonroutine information work pertains largely to professional occupations. These occupations usually require a great deal of education, commitment to ongoing full-time employment, and frequently the ability/willingness to work more than 40 hours per week and/or sublimate all personal concerns to meeting project deadlines. As long as women are held ideologically and physically responsible for family care, it is far more difficult for a woman to render herself a competitive professional in the nonroutine information workforce. Earning the requisite credentials (school and on-the-job-learning), fielding the requisite job history, and having peer and supervisory evaluations that indicate professional commitment are much harder for a woman than for a man. Women are thus segregated into routine information handling occupations, and routine information occupations typify women's employment because of the practical problems inherent to women's employment. For those few women who are making inroads into nonroutine information handling (as there are some), they will make inroads primarily in "helping" professions, or professions where the mental and physical well-being of the client is a primary aspect of the job.

If the tracking of women into routine information handling and into "helping" professions occurs because of the intertwined ideological and economic apparatus in the United States, we can have every expectation that these patterns will continue until the ideological and economic underpinnings change. As there is little indication in either data or recent thinking that significant change is imminent, we can anticipate that (1) routine information-handling jobs will continue to disappear and that (2) women will primarily be the type of worker most likely to "lose" in the employment market. We can also anticipate that (1) where women "win" in the information job market, they will do so primarily in "helping" professions and not in the "gold-collar" section of the information sector.

Implications for the Turn of the Century

What then are the implications of these patterns? If the jobs that have historically been the bastion of women's employment are progressively suffering from redundancy, where will these women find re-employ-ment? One scenario is that health care will see significant growth into the first part of the new century.[5] A portion of health care occupations are information occupations. Furthermore, the majority of health pro-fessions are also "helping" professions. Thus, should health care con-tinue to grow, we may very well see growth in women's employment in health care because the synergy of the ideological and economic struc-tures will progressively track women into this field.

Problematically, the health industry can be divided into two "camps" of workers between which there is very little crossover. Some health occupations require a great deal of education and handle infor-mation in complex ways (i.e., physicians, physical therapists, registered nurses, etc.), while others require very little education and handle in-formation in routine ways (i.e., records technicians, receptionists, etc.).

The first "camp" of workers (professionals) will undoubtedly con-tinue to grow. As the population ages, as medical techniques become more sophisticated, and as long-term health care and rehab needs grow, so will the need for workers to render services. Furthermore, these types of occupations, because they require person-to-person exchange of information, will be relatively protected from the effects of techno-logical redundancy.

One of the more difficult problems faced by computer programmers is "meaning making." As Hofstadter (1979) points out, though a com-puter can be programmed to write a grammatically correct sentence, the machine cannot evaluate whether or not the sentence is meaningful. A machine may write "The dog picked a purple pickle," but the ma-chine will not be able to identify it as a nonsense sentence—something even young children can do. Taking this one step further, computers are not able to read body language, tone of voice, or many of the other symbol systems that human communication relies upon for accuracy. Thus the professions that require person-to-person exchange of infor-mation will be sheltered from technological redundancy simply because we have yet to program the complexity of information handling re-quired in human communication.

The same cannot be said, however, of the second "camp" of work-ers (nonprofessional information technicians). The bulk of these jobs handle information in highly codifiable, routine ways. Thus, though the need for record keeping will hardly diminish, the need for employees to perform the record keeping will as technology increasingly over-takes the tasks once performed by human laborers.

The upshot of this is that growth in health occupations will most likely happen for women along class lines. For health occupations that are predicted to grow (i.e., the professional occupations that require higher education and person-to-person exchange of information), most of the women who find employment will be from middle socioeconomic backgrounds. These women are more likely to be able to invest in the education credentialing process necessary to be competitive in these jobs. Furthermore, the person-to-person requirements will further benefit women from middle- to upper-middle-class backgrounds. Well-educated, middle- (or higher) class women will be better prepared to communicate effectively with people from a wide range of cultural, economic, and age backgrounds.

For the other "camp" of workers where the training requirements are low, where workers are easily interchangeable, and where the work is often part-time with no benefits, employees will primarily be women from lower socioeconomic backgrounds. Confoundingly, the need for workers to staff these positions will continue to decline with the advent of information technology. We can conclude, then, that under the first scenario—growth in health care—it will primarily be women from middle- to upper-middle-class backgrounds who will benefit.

The second scenario is that there will be growth in the personal service sector. This sector, comprising jobs whose primary output is not information but person-to-person services (such as janitorial, hair-stylists, food service, etc.), is also predicted to absorb many of the workers displaced from information work. Interestingly, this sector has also long been associated primarily with women's employment. Characteristically, however, this sector is notorious for jobs that are part-time, low-pay, low-prestige, and without benefits. Because of the low education requirements in this sector, however, it is very likely to be the sector that absorbs the bulk of women from lower socioeconomic situations. The majority of women displaced from the information sector will be women from the routine information handling jobs. As these jobs are primarily filled with women from lower socioeconomic standing in the first place, their shift into personal-service sector work is entirely predictable. The largest drawback with this transition is that women are exchanging full-time (often with benefits) white-collar work for increasingly part-time, no benefits, service-sector work.

Conclusion

Women are tracked via political and economic constraints into (1) jobs that are dissapearing and (2) the helping professions. For women displaced from white-collar work (routine information handling), employment options are most likely to be in either health occupations or in the closely allied personal service sector. For women from higher socioeconomic categories, this will mean full-time jobs in a growing health care industry. For women from lower socioeconomic categories, this will mean employment in lower-paid, lower-status, less-secure work than they had in an economy dominated by information employment. In either case, women are and will be missing from the new "gold-collar" (i.e., well-paid, technologically oriented white-collar work) technology jobs. Thus, though the information age may be upon us, it clearly bears the gender stamp of the industrial and agricultural ages before.

Notes

1. There are several studies that document this shift. One of the most comprehensive was done by Marc Uri Porat (1977).

2. Though the figures and measuring schemes vary, most studies document majority employment in the United States in information. Machlup, writing in 1962, found that 31.6 percent of the labor force was engaged in "knowledge production." Porat (1977) documents just over 40 percent of all employment in the information sector by 1970. Martin (1998) documents roughly 52 percent of the workforce as information workers by 1995.

3. The economy can be aggregated in different ways. The method used here generally follows that of Machlup (1963), Porat (1977), and Rubin (1986), where jobs are categorized as belonging primarily to agriculture (examples: farming, ranching, and fishing), industry (mining, manufacturing, transportation), services (food service, janitorial, hostels, child care), and information (managerial, sales, clerical).

4. The helping professions are largely "other centered," and the primary output is in communicating with and caring for others—teaching, social work, clergy, counseling, and health professions, as a short list. These can be contrasted with professions such as lawyer, judge, underwriter, etc., jobs that involve a great deal of communication but not necessarily caring, and with jobs like computer specialist, drafting specialist, systems analyst, and researcher, jobs that primarily involve analytic tasks rather than communicating or caring tasks.

5. Health care is expected to grow in the United States because (1) our population is aging, especially as the baby-boom generation begins to retire; (2) new medical techniques keep people alive longer as well as preserve accident victims who would have otherwise perished; and (3) the number of chronic illnesses such as AIDS and cancer is rising.

7. Sexual Harassment as an Economic Concern: Swedish and American Coverage of Astra
Nancy Hauserman

This chapter uses allegations of sexual harassment against Astra USA to link two important topics: sexual harassment and the power of the media as a cultural influence. It considers how the media contribute both to the condemnation and prevention of sexual harassment and to its persistence in an attempt to further our understanding of the underlying problem of sexual harassment and the cultural descriptions and manifestations of sexual harassment.

Relying primarily on two U.S. newspapers, two Swedish newspapers, and an international business newspaper published in Britain, the chapter focuses on various conversations about sexual harassment in the print media and in U.S. and Swedish society. For U.S. coverage, a national business paper, the *Wall Street Journal,* and a national daily paper, the *New York Times,* were used. For Swedish coverage, a comparable business daily paper, *Dagens Industri,* and the only daily paper that is regularly read around the country, *Dagens Nyheter,* were used. One international paper, the *Financial Times,* was used to get a sense of how an international business paper, published outside the countries most directly involved, covered the case.

As well as national papers, several local papers were considered: the *Boston Globe,* the *Worcester Telegram and Gazette, Svenska Dagbladet* (widely read in Stockholm), and the more tabloidlike Swedish *Expressen.* Although the primary focus of the research was to analyze national coverage of the case, the local papers occasionally provided additional details.

In addition to consideration of the print media, dozens of interviews were conducted primarily in Stockholm, Sweden. The interviews focused on sexual harassment in Sweden and the Swedes' perceptions of sexual harassment in the United States.

This chapter considers some of the similarities and differences in coverage, with emphasis on the ways in which the media portray sexual harassment as an issue and the prioritization of economic concerns over human concerns. The chapter also contains observations about cultural differences that affect—and are affected by—this coverage.

The Public Beginning: *Business Week* Exposes Astra USA

On 13 May 1996 the cover story of *Business Week*, an American business periodical with a circulation of more than a million paid subscribers, was titled "Abuse of Power: The Astonishing Tale of Sexual Harassment at Astra" (Maremont 1996). Written by then–*Business Week* reporter Mark Maremont, the story chronicled years of alleged sexual harassment at Astra USA, the American subsidiary of the Swedish pharmaceutical Astra AB. Located in Westborough, Massachusetts, Astra USA is a wholly owned subsidiary of Astra AB, a Swedish pharmaceutical company with subsidiaries around the world, that markets hospital and outpatient products in the United States. It has $2.8 billion in gross sales and approximately 13,000 employees worldwide.

According to Maremont, who spent six months working on the story, Lars Bildman, CEO of Astra USA (Astra) for the past fifteen years, and several of his top executives fostered an environment in which relatively young saleswomen were badgered to engage in sex or to endure the sexual innuendoes, gropes, and grabs of senior management. According to the story, and later court documents, "Within one year of Bildman's arrival at Astra, the company began to replace female secretaries and assistants who were over age 40 or married with children with females between the ages of twenty and thirty. By 1990, Bildman was requiring every new sales representative, typically 'an attractive young woman just out of college,' to attend nightclubs or bars with him and other top executives as part of the Astra 'training program.' Trainees were required to attend the 'Astra' bar every night of the nine-week program. At the bar, female trainees were 'picked up . . . fondled, rubbed . . . and propositioned for sexual intercourse' by Astra's top executives" (Maremont 1996). Those who resisted their advances worried about their jobs, and those who complied, called "The Chosen," advanced rapidly. Between 1992 and 1994, up to fifteen middle managers were fired under the pretext of poor performance for objecting to the harassment of women at Astra. Women who did not "go along" were fired and men who complained were let go. A follow-up piece in *Business Week* contained allegations of lavish parties held on yachts at which prostitutes were provided to visiting businessmen.

It was not as if the employees at Astra had not complained about the alleged behaviors. In the past decade, Astra had been the subject of several lawsuits and had entered into at least eleven settlement agreements. In these agreements, parties complaining of sexual harassment accepted a sum of money in return for leaving the company and signing confidentiality agreements in which they agreed not to talk to anyone about what they claimed had happened to them at Astra. They also agreed not to file suit against Astra or help anyone else who might file suit.

Just before the *Business Week* story broke, Astra AB received an advance copy by fax and quickly suspended Bildman.

The Coverage: Some Similarities

In many respects, the coverage of the Astra case was similar in the two countries. Both countries' business newspapers, *WSJ* and *DI*, offered about the same number of stories. Between 30 April and 1 August 1997, *WSJ* ran seventeen stories specific to Astra. *DI* ran twenty-five stories in the same time period. There was more difference in the number of stories offered by the national dailies: between 30 April 1996 and 29 May 1997 *NYT* ran nine articles, including one that focused on one of Sweden's wealthy families, the Wallenbergs, whereas in Sweden *DN* ran thirty-six stories. In the same time period, the *FT* ran nine stories.

In addition to the amount of actual coverage given to the Astra story, there were similarities in the substance of the stories. First, they suggest that the occurrence of sexual harassment is to be expected, and its eradication is apparently not a goal, or, alternately, that sexual harassment is not a problem and therefore needs no solution. Second, the coverage prioritizes economic concerns over the protection of employees from sexual harassment. Third, sexual harassment is viewed as isolated and individual aberrant behavior rather than the responsibility of the business community or society as a whole. The similarities suggest views of sexual harassment that I believe are at best problematic and at worst erroneous. In order to understand the significance of this coverage, it is important to consider separately these common concepts of sexual harassment as presented in the news stories.

The first commonality, the expectation that sexual harassment will necessarily exist, is evidenced, in part, by stories that position the incidents at Astra relative to similar incidents in the world of business. All of the newspapers pick up and repeat Astra's assertion that, although it has settled approximately eleven other sexual harassment cases in the United States, this number is relatively low. The implications are that Astra is no different, and certainly no worse, than other U.S. companies, and this situation is "par for the course," to be expected as a part of doing business in America. Notably, this implied conclusion is offered only in the abstract, since the newspapers do not mention the number of suits filed against comparable companies or the number of settlements comparable companies have actually reached.

What is the newspaper reader encouraged to think about these prior settlement agreements? Are we to congratulate Astra for having only eleven serious cases of sexual harassment in ten years? At least one article does, in fact, congratulate Astra for its handling of *this* case without mentioning the prior eleven cases following which Astra appears to have done little to change the corporate culture. There is a paucity of stories and editorials questioning whether eleven prior cases is really a small number, although in fact many lawyers and affirmative-action officers who handle sexual harassment complaints for their U.S. companies consider eleven settlement agreements significant, especially in a white-collar industry.

The newspapers offer very little explanation about these settlement agreements between Astra and its former employees and raise few questions concerning the implications of this history. The press might have raised questions about or sought to discover what actions the company took after the earlier settlements, whether anyone was fired, or whether any training was instituted. Indeed, they raise few questions about why Bildman continued as Astra's CEO when he apparently was not successful in stopping the sexual harassment in the company and may indeed have perpetuated it. What if the complaints had involved allegations of fraud? If Bildman had not immediately put a stop to such behavior, would not serious questions about his leadership ability have been raised? Even in the unlikely event that Bildman was not the subject of prior sexual harassment complaints, he was responsible for the culture of the company.

The second similarity in coverage involved the prioritization of certain economic concerns over the fair treatment of employees. Virtually every story contains some sort of economic information about Astra, and many articles focus on economic issues such as Astra's total sales volume, its entrance onto the New York Stock Exchange (NYSE) in May 1996, Bildman's economic misdeeds, and Astra's economic loss from Bildman's fraud. In part, this focus reflects the safety of talking about economics rather than gender issues. In part, it suggests the myopic focus on economic issues.

The press coverage mirrors Astra's version of its actions. When Astra fired Bildman, he was fired for economic reasons, and, almost as an afterthought, "inappropriate behavior" ("Astra USA," A3; Gilpin 1996; Johannes 1996). Astra refers to the sexual harassment as "inappropriate" behavior, like bad manners. It is never referred to as behavior that is harmful. None of the five major newspapers that were the focus of this research printed comments about why sexual harassment is a problem for society.

Astra's spokespeople appear to reframe the issue successfully from a focus on sexual harassment to economic fraud. By June 1996, when Bildman was fired, the focus had been redirected from Bildman's sexual harassment and his and Astra's failure of responsibility to their employees to Bildman's economic transgressions against Astra. Astra emphasizes that Bildman was fired without compensation so that even in his termination the focus is on economics rather than the substance of his wrongdoing.

The Swedish press immediately comments on market issues and the potential effect of this case on the market. This focus implies that the firing of Bildman is sufficient to redress the wrongs he and others at Astra committed. It is impossible to know whether he would have been fired but for the apparent economic fraud or the fact that this story appeared as the cover story on *Business Week* at the same time Astra AB was getting set to list on the NYSE. In fact, the allegations of sexual harassment did not affect either the listing of Astra on the stock exchange or its prices. This may reflect the fact that stockholders do not really care about such events; that such occurrences are to be expected as a price of doing business; or as Lars Ramquist, a member of Astra AB's board, suggested, perhaps this was simply "good press" for Astra.

In all of the economic information provided, including the mention of past settlement agreements, there is no emphasis on the financial effects of sexual harassment. No article contained a description of the various costs associated with sexual harassment. Other than generally noting that the settlements ranged from $20,000 to $100,000, little is made of the fact that these agreements cost Astra and its stockholders a fair amount of money. Real costs include the actual dollar amounts of the agreements and, especially, the implicit costs of sexual harassment. These implicit costs include sick days, time off work, psychological injury, and lowered morale and productivity generally. Why is this kind of economic information not a priority? Perhaps because to make it so would be tantamount to admitting that sexual harassment is bad business!

The third similarity in coverage, implied by the focus on certain economic issues, is the lack of discussion of responsibility for the sexually harassing behavior. In spite of Astra's potential for legal liability, the U.S. and the Swedish press gave little attention to Astra's moral or ethical responsibility to provide employees with a harassment-free environment. Indeed, there were relatively few articles that actually criticized Astra or Astra AB or seriously suggested that Astra AB may have resisted firing Bildman years earlier because he was "successful" in bottom-line results!

The financial focus mitigates, and may avoid altogether, certain issues of business ethics. It avoids discussion of the culture of business while accepting business's quest for profit. Moreover, by focusing on the act of an individual, Lars Bildman, neither business nor society is held accountable for sexual harassment.

Astra's public stance presents a view of the corporation as an innocent. Astra maintains and the newspapers repeat that Bildman duped them. Astra's refrain is "we didn't know and when we found out we were swift. We, too, were the victims of Bildman. He duped us for money and injured our reputation and the reputation of our country." Astra claims it is the victim of everybody: the press, Bildman, even the concurrent Mitsubishi case. Staffan Ternby, Astra AB's public relations director, said that one person, Lars Bildman, caused the scandal. Meanwhile, in the United States, Bildman is also claiming victim status, describing himself as the victim of plaintifs and Astra AB. "Although everyone is a victim in this tragedy, no one, it seems, is a villain"(Lipari 1994).

The media stories are narrowly focused on Bildman, his deeds, and his responsibility. The focus was individual wrongdoing rather than corporate and societal responsibility for sexual harassment. The reader's conclusion is likely to be that Bildman may be despicable, but Astra is not.

The Coverage: Some Differences

There are, of course, differences in the coverage of the five primary newspapers. Here I discuss two of those differences: the explicit use of Bildman's name as the alleged harasser and the provision of educational material about sexual harassment. A major difference in the coverage between the two countries involves the identification of the players. While all of the U.S. newspapers name Bildman and the other defendants, in Sweden, only one, *DI,* identifies Bildman by name. This is important not only because of issues surrounding the naming of defendants generally, especially criminal defendants, but because *all* of the newspapers name the plaintiffs in the cases. This difference reflects a long-standing print media tradition in Sweden in which the identity of defendants, usually in criminal cases, is not made known until they are found guilty and sentenced. The underlying rationale for such nondisclosure appears to be both that the person is not guilty when simply charged and that after he or she is tried the legal system will take care of the punishment. Publishing the defendant's name, the argument continues, would subject him or her to further punishment and would make rehabilitation difficult since the public would forever remember the person's misdeed.

In the United States, adult defendants' names are usually printed when a person is charged with a crime or when a civil suit is brought. The resolution of the case is usually published. If the person is acquitted, the same is publicly noted.

Admittedly, I have an American bias in favor of disclosure of a defendant's name. I believe that disclosure makes the case real for people. In the Astra case, it is also important to note that the sexual harassment cases covered were not criminal cases. The fraud charges later filed against Bildman were criminal in nature, but the sexual harassment cases were civil cases in which the remedy focuses on redressing injury to individuals. The decision by most of the Swedish press not to print Bildman's name is not clearly grounded in any attempt to avoid conflict with the goals of the criminal justice system.

Although the Swedish newspapers do not print the name(s) of the alleged harassers, they do print the name(s) of the women who complained about the behavior. To name the victims but not name the defendants puts an added burden on people who are likely to be already stigmatized by the events—the victims. The victims will be known to the public, subjected to public scrutiny and surmise while the defendant remains cloaked in and protected by anonymity. The choice of whom to name and the effect of naming the victim but not the perpetrator suggests the responsibility for the sexual harassment lies with or on the victims. The focus is placed on the victims and away from the perpetrators and the inappropriate and illegal behavior.

The second difference in coverage appeared in the various definitions of sexual harassment. Although neither U.S. nor Swedish newspapers tended to define the term "sexual harassment," the *WSJ* and *NYT* printed a few educational articles that included more detail. In the Swedish stories, only one newspaper included a thorough definition of sexual harassment from the United States. Most Swedish stories implicitly trivialized sexual harassment by offering relatively minor examples of what constitutes sexual harassment in the United States. There is no definition of sexual harassment under Swedish or European Union (EU) laws, although one article does criticize Sweden for having a less stringent law than the EU, of which Sweden is a member.

By failing to provide good definitions, the U.S. and Swedish newspapers ignore an opportunity to educate the public about sexual harassment. If the definition given is particularly brief or noninformative, the reading public may not "get" sexual harassment and may think it is unimportant. Definitions that trivialize sexual harassment trivialize the whole concept of sexual harassment, inaccurately portray most cases, and cast the complaining victims, usually women, in the role of overly sensitive females. For example, one Swedish newspaper provided only examples of sexual harassment that many people would consider silly or minimal infractions, such as a single off-color joke. If sexual harassment is considered trivial, people may become cynical about or uninterested in it and quit paying attention to the issues.

Cultural Issues

Of course, news stories do not exist in a vacuum. They reflect, extend, and sometimes create values. As Sally Merry writes, "The ideas can be better understood as parts of a conversation in which expectations about audience, context, and history affect the way statements are framed and understood" (1996, 90). Further, according to Merry, "The pervasiveness of any frame depends on the extent to which it reflects a convergence of views based on shared cultural themes, mass media depictions, personal experiences, and differential experiences based on race and class locations"(91). Even the same texts can mean different things or be understood differently in various contexts. What does a story mean when read through the lens of cultural differences? How do the stories reflect cultural differences?

For instance, I noted initially that the press in both countries failed to raise many questions about Astra AB's responsibility for these actions, especially in light of the existence of prior complaints of sexual harassment. In the United States, this failure of inquiry might be attributed to a high tolerance of sexual harassment by certain segments of society, especially businesses, or a failure or unwillingness to educate themselves about sexual harassment. The U.S. news articles contain repeated references to the increasing number of sexual harassment cases and complaints received by the Equal Employment Opportunity Commission (EEOC). The increasing number of sexual harassment cases may lead society to expect such cases and not be especially surprised when they occur. Instead of being critical of companies that tolerate the behavior, if only by not stopping it, society may assume that sexual harassment is part of doing business. While there may be an interest in reading stories about sexual harassment, the behavior merely confirms various expectations of business, government, or women as employees.

In Sweden the failure of the newspapers to raise questions about the continuance of, and responsibility for, the sexually harassing behavior may reflect the society's dismissal or avoidance of sexual harassment as a relevant and consequential issue. Repeatedly, Swedes whom I interviewed in both the United States and Sweden told me that Swedes are more "natural" about sex and that relations between genders are more natural. Conversely, they say, in the United States, relations between the sexes are more "complicated." This may, in part, account for why some Swedish women told me that Swedes see sexual harassment as "ridiculous" and for comments in articles that seem to trivialize sexual harassment. Swedes express, and may hold, a different attitude toward sexuality than the attitudes of many Americans. But sexual harassment is about the abuse of power and not about sex, so this argument about "natural relations" between the sexes seems somehow misguided or even irrelevant to questions of sexual harassment.

Importantly, the existence of cultural explanations for the failure to address certain issues in the print media does not necessarily justify the absence of critical coverage. Sexual harassment is really abuse of power, and questions about why it continues to be tolerated in both the United States and Sweden need to be raised in the media and in society generally.

A second cultural issue raised by the coverage concerns notions of privacy. Both U.S. and Swedish newspaper stories reflect the interest of each country in the privacy of its citizens and businesses. In the United States, privacy interests are paramount in the use of settlement agreements. These agreements generally contain confidentiality clauses that seek to prohibit the signatories not only from instigating future lawsuits but also from talking about the issues. The signatories to these agreements in the Astra case were prohibited from later filing claims against the company or even from talking to the EEOC unless subpoenaed to do so. The rationale was that it is in the public interest to promote private settlement of disputes. But what is really being protected, or given priority, in this case appears to be the company's autonomy and its right to settle problems and keep them quiet. The privacy interest that is really protected, then, is the company's.

Furthermore, settlement agreements often protect "the alleged harasser and the organization from answering discomforting questions. Confidential settlements also treat the actual details of harassment as unspeakable, thus perpetuating the stigma many victims feel"(Weaver 1992, 25). As long as each complainant assumes that he or she is the only victim, the culture looks less poisoned and the details of the particular settlement are considered in isolation. The victim can be isolated, "cut from the herd," and implicitly charged with being disgruntled, vindictive with no effective recourse.

Privacy is also a strong part of Swedish culture, and the press coverage of the Astra case both reflects and enforces this priority. The ethical code for Swedish press says that the press is to protect privacy. For example, the press is enjoined from identifying defendants by name unless the public interest outweighs such a need for privacy. But Swedish journalists tell me that convincing an editor that printing a name of a defendant is in the public interest is extremely difficult. So names of defendants in cases are most often not printed: the secret is protected. Arguably such secrecy has the same effect as the settlement agreements in the United States: questions remain unanswered, the truth is not discovered, and the victims are isolated.

Both manifestations of privacy protect people other than the complainants or victims of sexual harassment. Settlement agreements protect the company from lawsuits and from negative publicity while nonpublication of a defendant's name in the Swedish press protects the individual defendant from negative publicity. Both the company and the individual defendants continue to have credibility. In a settlement agreement, the complainants usually get some of what they want (for example, money) faster than they might have through the court system. So for the immediate victim, the settlement agreement might be a positive gain, but for future victims and company culture, the value may be far less positive since the information is not public and companies may not feel compelled to eliminate the behavior. I am not sure what a sexual harassment victim gains from not having a defendant's name published in the newspaper, especially if her own name is made public. Arguably, there is some greater social good that is achieved by the nonpublication, and the particular victim can share in the good. Whatever the greater good, the cost to the victim is high as the focus turns to his or her character, history, and intentions in filing a complaint.

Conclusion

The need to educate ourselves about sexual harassment is critical to its eradication and the empowerment of its victims. "We need to create a community of discussion about the issue of sexual harassment"(Hill 1997, 268). If we are serious about and committed to equality in the workplace, knowledge is the key towards greater equality in working life. "Language is power. Writing and talking about sexual harassment in terms of legal philosophy, morality, social relations, psychology, power, ethics, or politics"(Lipari 1994, 307) is different from writing about sexual harassment simply as something that affects the price of a company's stock, as a soap opera, or as an abridged factual accounting. The impact of sexual harassment on individuals and companies is great. If the media are going to focus on the costs of sexual harassment, they should accurately reflect all the costs incurred by the victims, including the loss of work time and emotional distress, and all the costs incurred by the companies, including loss of productivity and lowered morale.

The media have a responsibility to hold corporations and governments responsible and accountable for actions that are damaging to people. It is in the best interests of the public and it is the public's right to know about occurrences of sexual harassment. The media could facilitate change through the dissemination of accurate information regarding complaints filed, persons and businesses involved, and the outcomes of sexual harassment cases. In this instance, there were few questions raised about why Astra, or any company, tolerates this kind of behavior at all much less after the first settlement agreement.

As to the parties in the Astra case, we do not know what has happened to the various plaintiffs. Some have received a settlement, but we do not know, from the print media anyway, where they are working, if they are working, or how they are faring psychologically. Bildman entered into a plea bargain agreement in January 1998 and is serving time in prison for tax evasion. Astra USA has a new CEO and a human resources department. Astra AB is doing more educational programming for all its managers and has developed an international human resources policy. Astra AB spends more time talking to managers about issues of diversity; they are more "careful" about what they think sexual harassment is. Apparently, one executive at Astra said that when he attended the fiftieth anniversary celebration of Astra USA at the end of the summer of 1997, he did not dance with any U.S. women because he did not want to risk any behavior that might be considered sexual harassment.

In February 1998 Astra settled the case with the EEOC for $9.9 million to be apportioned among the eligible claimants. They issued a public apology for the actions of their management. They filed a suit against Bildman for $15 million in damages. Written prior to the settlement, their annual report for 1996 mentioned the EEOC investigation and private actions for sexual harassment against Astra USA, but did not mention Bildman or detail the accusations. The closing line reads, "While it is not possible to predict or determine the ultimate outcome of these negotiations and legal proceedings, the Company believes that the outcome will not have a materially adverse effect on the financial position, liquidity or results of operations of the Company" (Astra Annual Report 1996).

8. Single Moms, Quota Queens, and the Model Majority: Putting "Women" to Work in the California Civil Rights Initiative
Roopali Mukherjee

No longer would people like Janice Camarena, a white, widowed mother of three, be thrown out of outreach classes because her color or racial background does not fit the racial template of the institution.

—Ward Connerly

Women are mothers, wives, daughters and sisters. No one is better placed than a woman to see the double-edged nature of racial and gender preferences. It is clear to a mother that an institutional preference for her daughter is institutional discrimination against her son.

—Sally Pipes and Michael Lynch 1996

I begin this chapter with the foregoing quotes to draw attention to the ways in which the category of "women" and representational claims on their behalf have performed subtle yet significant discursive work in recent public debates over affirmative action policies in the United States. In particular, I am interested in the ways in which these statements illuminate the operation of the public policy process as a powerful site for the ideological construction of race and gender. While scholarship in media studies has amply demonstrated that preferred constructions of race and gender identities are fixed in specific ways in popular culture and mass media texts (Dent 1992; Fiske 1994; Hall 1986; hooks 1992; Mercer 1994), this chapter argues that the public policy process, not unlike the mass media, plays a critical role in circulating dominant knowledges of race and gender. Emerging out of economic, political, and discursive pressures, such knowledges do not necessarily reflect the "truth" about race and gender, but they do legitimize a limited but powerful knowledge of them.

Specifically, this chapter attends to constructions of women, "that phantasmatic construction which has its purposes, but which denies the internal complexity and indeterminacy of the term" (Butler 1990, 142), visible within ongoing and perhaps irreversible shifts in the career of race and gender-based affirmative action policies. Voters in California passed the California Civil Rights Initiative (CCRI), also referred to as

Proposition 209, in general elections in 1996, eliminating "preferences" in public education, employment, and contracting in the state of California. The CCRI has been followed by copycat measures like Initiative 200, which was approved by public referendum in Washington in 1998, and there are reports of similar proposals in as many as twenty-one states and at the federal level in the United States (Freedberg 1997, A1; Honan 1996, 14).

In the wake of changes in welfare, public education, and immigration policies, these attacks on affirmative action may be located within a larger albeit fragmented assault, what Brenkman refers to as a "turn toward the excision of social justice from public discourse and its demise within public policy" (1995). Such a turn is likely to impact women's participation in the political economy in significant ways. It is likely to slow the pace with which women have entered the workforce over the last thirty years, and to frustrate their ambitions for promotion and higher education. This, as the chapter will elaborate, is particularly critical with respect to nonwhite and poor women who have reaped at best modest rewards from affirmative action programs thus far. Mirroring larger concerns over the "proletarianization of women of color" urged on by the global restructuring of capitalism (Davis 1998/1977a, 308), early reports on the impact of the passage of the CCRI in California point to declines in opportunities for Latinas and black women, and the resegregation of workplaces and classrooms (Katz 1997; Parker 1998).

These assaults on gender- and race-based affirmative action policies offer insights into the ways in which gender and race considerations are not irrelevant to but related in complex ways to political-economic structures and practices (Davis, 1998/1977b; Folbre and Hartmann 1989; Shultz 1992). Affirmative action programs seek to redefine established parameters for entry into political-economic institutions. These programs were designed to limit an employer's power to shut out female and nonwhite applicants. They forced accountability for sexist and racist impulses in hiring and admissions decisions. Thus, affirmative action policies by their very existence suggest that political-economic practices are not necessarily rational nor always merit-based but rather are deeply intertwined with cultural imaginaries about women and blacks, and their value as workers.

Current assaults on affirmative action, like the creation of these programs, then are ultimately about women's and blacks' entry into economic life, and their access to political-economic power. Representations of women within these attacks offer useful keys to the imbrications of gender, race, and class in the structures of contemporary economic life. Attention to gendered narratives and deployments of particular images of women as they circulate within the assault on affirmative action illuminates the ways in which public policies are culturally articulated, and how they "tacitly structure the ways in which identities are formed, recognized, legitimated, and delegitimated" (Butler 1996, 75). Toward these ends, the present analysis seeks to uncover the kinds of representations of women we find narrativized in the current assault on gender-based policies. It asks how racialized representations of gender work within ongoing appeals for the elimination of gender-based social justice, and seeks to understand how the category of women may have become, as Christian asks, a hidden, though powerful, construct in the anti–affirmative action arsenal (1996, 120).

Affirmative action programs were designed in part to ensure equal opportunities and fair representation for American women in public education, employment, and contracting. In 1967, Executive order 11375 amended Title VII of the Civil Rights Act of 1964 to provide the legal basis for affirmative action for women in employment in the United States. It was believed at the time that women, like black Americans, were among those who were "historically disadvantaged." Thus, employers and admissions committees were asked to take affirmative action to remedy economic disadvantages historically inherited by women. Title VII prohibits discrimination by any employer or labor union on the basis of race, color, religion, sex, or national origin.

Similarly, the Educational Amendment of 1972 provided the basis for affirmative action for women in education, which the Civil Rights Restoration Act of 1988 restored after Supreme Court decisions to the contrary. These provisions require educational institutions receiving federal funds to take "specific steps designed to encourage individuals of the previously excluded sex to apply for admission."

Despite generally low levels of Title VII enforcement, affirmative action programs have witnessed the entry of large numbers of women into the workforce. The percentage of women in executive, administrative, and managerial positions rose from 17.6 in 1972 to 43.8 in 1996 (Equal Rights Advocates 1999). Although black women have not shared in these gains to the same extent, particularly in the most desirable occupations, white women's share of management jobs increased by about one-third—from 27.1 percent in the 1980s to 35.3

percent in the 1990s (Hartmann 1996, 78–81). Blacks, men and women both, show the greatest increases in blue-collar jobs in which fewer white women work (Hartmann 1996, 92).

Changes visible since the implementation of affirmative action policies also indicate the continued impact of the glass ceiling faced by women and nonwhites. White males account for almost 97 percent of senior managers of Fortune 500 corporations. In contrast, women occupy approximately 3 percent, blacks 0.6 percent, Asians 0.3 percent, and Latinos 0.4 percent of these positions (Equal Employment Opportunity Commission 1995; Glass Ceiling Commission 1995). Stagnating corporate careers may be among the reasons why growing numbers of women have launched their own businesses since the beginning of affirmative action programs—from around 400,000 in 1972 to almost 8 million in 1996 (Equal Rights Advocates 1999).

Other concerns such as sex segregation and income inequities remain significant. In 1994, women were more likely to be schoolteachers, nurses, and social workers while men were more likely to be doctors, architects, and engineers (Hartmann 1996, 81). Further, the wage gap between men and women stands at approximately 85 percent after adjusting for differences in education, experience, and other factors. This gap is wider still between white men and men and women of color. Latino men, for instance, earn 81 percent and Latinas less than 65 percent of the wages earned by white men at the same educational level (Blau and Ferber 1992; Stith 1996). While affirmative action programs enjoy a mixed record of effectiveness, the representation of women in economic life is unlikely to be strengthened by the elimination of policies geared to their inclusion. And yet the current assault on affirmative action does not propose to overhaul existing policies. It seeks to end them.

The nation's first voter- and court-approved ban on affirmative action, the CCRI amends the constitution of California as follows:

> The state shall not discriminate against or grant preferential treatment to any individual or group on the basis of race, sex, color, ethnicity, or national origin in the operation of public employment, public education, or public contracting (California Constitution, Article I, § 31(a)).

The CCRI contains three exceptions. It does not affect the practices of private corporations and nongovernmental groups. It does not apply to state affirmative action programs that are needed to maintain eligibility for federal aid. Also excluded are positions where "bona fide qualifications based on sex are reasonably necessary for normal operation." This last exception would allow, for instance, the hiring of female prison guards in women's correctional facilities.

As Volokh clarifies, the CCRI specifically outlaws affirmative action programs that confer "preference" (1997). However, the measure does not define "preferential treatment." Moreover, the CCRI has in recent months been interpreted by California courts as disallowing even "soft affirmative action" such as focus outreach or contract recruitment programs that make specific efforts to hire subcontractors who are women and members of nonwhite groups (Chiang 1999). Thus, the CCRI limits inclusion mechanisms to the presumption of good faith to hire members of historically disadvantaged groups, arrangements that, as Steinberg points out, were ineffective until the implementation of "goals and timetables" in the 1970s (1995, 164).

The remainder of this chapter presents an analysis of the year-long CCRI public campaign that helped secure the popular vote in California to end affirmative action in 1996. The analysis examines public speeches by spokespersons, brochures, bulletins, and television advertisements prepared as part of the "Yes to 209" campaign, as well as literature made available on official CCRI web sites.

Attending to the ways in which gender concerns were both given voice and silenced, the analysis makes visible the operation of a "model majority" of economically successful women—a gendered but race- and class-effacing category that performs critical disciplinary work. Next, the analysis locates appropriations of familiar gendered narratives of the single mom and the quota queen—women who fail as a result of or despite race- and gender-based programs. These narratives are seen working to encode affirmative action issues in racial terms that erase their reference to race even as they reinscribe it. Finally, the analysis examines how the eclipse of gender by racialized appeals against preferences in the CCRI campaign may have made the category of "women" available as a subtle but powerful construct within the anti–affirmative action arsenal.

The Model Majority

Among the official spokespersons for the CCRI campaign were Pete Wilson, then governor of California, and campaign cochairs—Ward Connerly, one of the regents of the University of California, a black Republican and businessman; and Pamela Lewis, a white female attorney and a Clinton Democrat.

Far from accidental, Connerly's and Lewis's presence on the front-lines of the assault on affirmative action in California reveals a particular performance of authenticity that worked well for the campaign. Echoing familiar, all-American mythologies of individuals who pull themselves up by their bootstraps, Connerly often told the story of his life as a black man growing up in a racially segregated South and rising out of poverty on his own merits. Lewis was similarly seen extolling the virtues of color- and gender-blindness as she narrated her experiences as the successful attorney who represented Jack Bras, a white male architect in a "reverse discrimination" law suit. Together, Connerly and Lewis embodied the distance that blacks and women have traveled since the 1960s, their careers evidence of the potential of an idealized color- and gender-blind meritocracy.

The CCRI campaign made full use of these visibly en-raced and gendered spokespersons. Connerly and Lewis appeared in television advertisements often, and typically as themselves expressing frustration and fatigue over race- and gender-based programs. In one such testimonial, they state, "we're tired of people dividing us by race and gender" (Skelton 1996). They declare that despite their diverse backgrounds and their political differences, they agree that affirmative action policies have become "buzzwords for preferences and quotas" (Skelton 1996). Their opposition to affirmative action programs is race-blind and gender-blind, erasing its reference to race and gender even as it secures much of its discursive force from visible displays of en-raced and gendered authenticity.

Presenting a glossy "we *can* all get along" image of the future, Connerly and Lewis served the CCRI campaign as no white male spokesperson could. Individuals like Connerly provide what Williams Crenshaw refers to as a "racially correct voice-over to narrate the story of black pathology and dependence" (1997, 281). Such representatives work to provide the salve to soothe lingering doubts about sexism and racism in America, while they nudge widespread consent to public policy shifts with serious consequences for women and persons of color.

Lewis's presence among the spokespersons for the CCRI is almost a cliché in the context of stories of breakthroughs in gender equity that dot the landscape of contemporary public knowledge. Major news stories of women ascending to powerful cabinet offices and legislative seats, high executive ranks in business, and command positions in the nation's space program make for a comforting view of the distance women have covered since the 1970s. Like other homegrown G.I. Janes, fiercely individualistic and scornful of gender-based policies, Lewis played a critical but familiar role in the CCRI campaign. Her opinions fit comfortably within a discursive context that reiterates the nightmare of gender preferences using a variety of narratives of "reverse discrimination," "token hires," and "diversity candidates."

These narratives that reiterate the myth that women and nonwhites are typically token hires and therefore often unqualified for their jobs find themselves reproduced in everyday, casual conversations at the office and at home. My own conversations with white male acquaintances who speak of not making it to short lists for job interviews because "the department was looking for a black woman to *colorize* its offices" are a case in point. Some of these reactionary tales are found dramatized in election-year campaign advertisements that tell horror stories about white males who are victimized by race- and gender-based programs. One such antiquota advertisement was used by congressional and assembly candidates in Northern California during the 1996 elections and depicts a young white husband walking into the kitchen and telling his wife he didn't get the job because of quotas. The advertisement ends with the focus on the wife who "stands by her man" exclaiming, "It's just not right" (Skelton 1996).

Such avowals serve to legitimize knowledge of declining gender bias and the impropriety of continued affirmative action programs. Archetypal hegemonized subjects, these wives and career women alike are effectively disciplined into the dominant practices and institutions of the male-centered workplace. As Lewis demonstrates, these are model women who play by the rules, for whom gender is irrelevant, and who deny their debts to social justice programs. They perform significant work by their very presence and serve as representatives of women as a group, a "model majority" that denies the internal complexities and indeterminacy of the category of "women."

As the myth of the model minority works as a site of discipline for Asians and non-Asian minorities (Takaki 1993, 414–17), here I argue that the CCRI campaign constructed an imagined "model majority" that served to discipline successful women as effectively as it did those who "fail." These are the "mothers, wives, daughters, and sisters," each of whom can be relied on to see clearly that an "institutional preference for her daughter is institutional discrimination against her son" (Pipes and Lynch 1996). To wit, 48 percent of women voters in California elected to end affirmation action in the 1996 referendum ("Women Helped Push" 1996). Furthermore, since all nonwhites, men and women both, made up only 26 percent of the Californian electorate, a sizable proportion of the 48 percent pro vote from women reflects the opinions of white women (*Los Angeles Times Exit Poll* 1996). It is notable that white women, whether wives, homemakers, or career women, are seen giving voice to these laments most often. As the myth of the model majority generalizes the experiences of white women to women as a group, it simultaneously evokes and erases its reference to race and class, thus performing crucial disciplinary work that is race- and class-blind. The deployment of the model-majority myth minimizes the circumstances of class and color among women with critical effect, constructing exceptions to gender bias as the rule, and fictionalizing the experiences of poorer and nonwhite women. The accomplishments of some white women are generalized to women as a group, while the experiences of working-class black women or poor single mothers are delegitimated.

Single Moms and Quota Queens

If Lewis performed critical disciplinary work by her presence as an economically successful woman, Janice Camerena's experiences served the CCRI campaign in quite a different way. While arguments for individualism and merit and stories of "reverse discrimination" highlight the follies of affirmative action as they impact the meritocracy and the lives of white men, Janice Camarena's story brought the dangers of preferences home for white and working-class women.

Camarena comes as close to being a poster girl for the CCRI campaign as can be found. Connerly told her story often.

> After her husband, an American of Mexican descent, died and left her with three children to support, Janice decided to go back to school. She enrolled in a remedial English course at San Bernardino Valley College. On the first day of the term, the instructor said, "There are two people who will have to leave." She singled out Janice and the only other white student, saying, "This class is reserved for African Americans." There was laughter as they were escorted out of the room.
>
> It seems the course was part of a special out-reach program financed by the University of California, and admission was based on race. Janice could not graduate unless she passed remedial English. So, she signed up for another course. But it was restricted to Latinos. She was thrown out again. (Connerly 1996)

Janice Camarena's experiences tell a story of "reverse discrimination" that is left out in stories of such practices as they victimize white men. But quite like the harried white husband who is excluded from opportunities, Camarena is excluded because of her race. Her example was an important one for the CCRI campaign, for it simultaneously drew white men and women together while it widened the distance between white women and women of color.

Well within the parameters of legitimate reproductive moralities and established gender roles, Camarena is among the "truly needy" and precisely the type of woman who deserves assistance but who is tragically left out. Her story is, however, as instructive in its articulations as in its silences. She is a widow. Her children were born within the institution of marriage. Her sexual practices were morally condoned. She sought ways to provide for her children. She sought to complete her education toward a better job and better pay. She made several attempts to enroll in local training programs. She was excluded by the very policies that were intended to assist her.

Camarena's story subtly confirms that the beneficiaries of affirmative action are not the working-class and perhaps white women who truly need help, but rather other less deserving and perhaps nonwhite women. Within a discursive context rich with narratives of irresponsible, promiscuous, and unfit black and Latina single mothers, the tragic but conscientious Camarena emerges in stark contrast. Dark and delinquent quota queens who have access to outreach programs that are racially exclusive are thus recalled in the silences in Camarena's story. Existing affirmative action programs fail to provide assistance to the most deserving of women at least in part because they enable preferences for unfit, nonwhite others.

Race Eclipses Gender

While previous sections of this chapter have highlighted the ways in which the category of "women" was put to work in the service of anti–affirmative action appeals, on the whole gender was frequently on the sidelines of campaign strategy. From public speeches by spokespersons to brochures and bulletins available at CCRI web sites, there is little evidence of serious and sustained discussion of the benefits that women have reaped from affirmative action programs, or of the impact that eliminating such programs may have for them. Thus, even while the CCRI campaign addressed itself to women voters, questions of gender were frequently silenced and on the sidelines of campaign strategy.

If the majority of beneficiaries of affirmative action over the past thirty years have been white women, the CCRI campaign could have been expected to raise gender issues more centrally and more frequently. White women may have been identified as being most directly responsible for "reverse discrimination" against white men, and therefore as the villains in the affirmative action equation. Instead, as we have seen, women and particularly white women are located among the unfortunate victims of affirmative action programs.

Campaign strategy to diffuse gender issues may reveal "the delicate but pragmatic recognition that the politics of gender are less volatile than the politics of race" (Boxall 1996, A1). Elsewhere I have documented the ways in which Connerly and his overwhelmingly racial message enjoyed so large a presence in the CCRI campaign that gender considerations remained eclipsed by race (Mukherjee 2000). CCRI proponents' deliberate effacing of gender considerations may have enabled a strong indictment of affirmative action programs on grounds that they primarily benefit unqualified racial others. Placing a prominently racial face upon affirmative action issues, the eclipse of gender worked to facilitate what Christian refers to as the "trigger effect" of racial appeals (1996, 122).

Further, since women made up 52 percent of the Californian electorate, the CCRI needed a strong vote from women. Thus, the CCRI campaign may have relied upon devices like Camarena's story to persuade women that continued affirmative action was contrary to their interests. Toward these ends, the CCRI campaign is seen engaging in a strategic politics of division, one that separated women along color and class lines.

As the foregoing section suggested, Janice Camarena, the emissary of working-class women in the CCRI campaign, served primarily to raise anxieties over preferences for racial others. Camarena's example also offered support for the "class not race" emphasis found repeated over the course of the CCRI campaign. But while attention to class concerns may have enabled CCRI organizers to propose color-blind solutions to the problem at hand, as Roediger has argued, the assurance of color-blind affirmative action could be relied upon to elicit overwhelmingly racialized reactions (1997, 60).

If cochair Pamela Lewis epitomized successful, middle-class women who no longer needed affirmative action, Camarena's story confirmed that affirmative action had degenerated into racially exclusive preferences for unqualified racial others. Together, Lewis and Camarena served the CCRI campaign to affirm the folly of color-based programs, and in so doing they contributed effectively to undoing women-focused and gender-based affirmative action programs in California.

This chapter set out to examine the ways in which the discursive category of "women" has operated as a potent signifier within current anti–affirmative action efforts. It sought to uncover the ways in which appropriations and manipulations within the category of women served anti–affirmative action voices. The analysis focused upon strategic appropriations of gendered narratives, constructions of women's successes and failures, and the eclipse of gender as color and class took center stage in the CCRI's attack on affirmative action. It examined the ways in which the CCRI campaign constructed "poster women," some who by their accomplishments herald a gender-blind and color-blind meritocracy, and others who forcefully demonstrate the folly of race- and gender-conscious regimes.

This examination of the CCRI campaign reveals that women are playing crucial roles in the ongoing anti–affirmative action assault. Economically successful white women are held up as model women and are seen parading on the CCRI podium, representatives of an imagined majority that no longer needs preferential treatment. Transparent in its whiteness, this model majority is inscribed in racial and class terms even as its discipline is race- and class-blind. Other carefully selected poster women serve the CCRI effort by highlighting the ways in which existing gender- and race-based programs are so poorly designed that they fail to serve even their own constituents. Together these narratives of "women," some successful and others less so, served the CCRI campaign well, constructing affirmative action as either unnecessary or racist or both.

The public policy process is revealed in this analysis as a powerful site for the production and legitimation of particularized gender and racial identities. Dominant representations of women in the CCRI campaign include successful career women, coded white, and working-class women who are urged to find allies in white men and women rather than in working-class persons of color. The affirmative action debates examined here offer a glimpse into the ways in which voices in the public policy process lift circulating narratives and images from available cultural contexts, legitimating some to the stature of "truth." Existing stereotypes of the single mom and quota queen are reiterated, as the experiences of working-class women of color are silenced and delegitimated. Voices within the public policy process are seen engaging in a manipulative politics of division that capitalizes on the economic realities of working-class women like Janice Camarena, while the solution to the problem as defined remains the vilification and exclusion of women themselves. Complex intersections between race, gender, and class are thus made visible with public policy debates over affirmative action, categories that are neither collapsible nor separable.

Arguments in the CCRI campaign reveal a context marked by racialized economic anxieties over the influx of nonwhite immigrants to California, and transformations in employment opportunities for Californian workers given the incentives of multinational corporate employers for whom foreign labor has proved immensely profitable. Within such a context, the events of the CCRI confirm that markers such as race and gender hold a critical valence in economic life. Foundational constructions of capitalist economies such as the meritocracy, the free market, and fair competition are imbued with meaning and salience as strategic deployments of race and gender identities "make sense" of tightening economic realities. As racial and gendered others are held responsible for economic hardships and uncertainties, and social justice policies designed for their inclusion are redefined as un-American and unfair, the ongoing assault on affirmative action programs illuminates how race and gender are imbricated with the disciplinary mechanisms of contemporary capitalist economies.

9. Selling Women (Down the River): Gendered Relations and the Political Economy of Broadcast News
Karen Ross

> The relation between gender and communication is primarily—
> although not only—a cultural one, concerning a negotiation of
> meanings and values that informs whole ways of life and which is
> vice versa informed by existing ways of life, with configurations of
> power and economic inequities being a key element within them.
> —Liesbet van Zoonen, *Feminist Media Studies*

This chapter is concerned with the relationship between sex (gender), politics (agenda), and the economy (money) and uses the particular nexus of women and broadcast news as a way to explore the ways in which news media's "treatment" of women in news domains—where women are objects of news interest (selling sex) or else rendered invisible (ignoring women news consumers)—and the experience of women working in news media organizations themselves (gendered economic relations) are each the products of a world system of patriarchal capitalism whose globalizing tentacles (see, for example, Herman and McChesney 1997) currently threaten the small gains achieved by a hundred years of feminist campaigning. It begins by considering the role of the media generally in the democratic process before moving on to explore women's location in and experiences of media industries, and it closes with a discussion of the ways in which women and our political concerns are covered in broadcast news media, using the British general election campaign of 1997 as a case study. The central argument is that women continue to function as commodified bodies, that their/our sex is always the primary signifier no matter how else we are producing or making news, and that therefore the political economy of news production relies on reducing women to cheap(er) labor as workers in the industry and on sexualizing them/us in the social world more generally (when they are not erasing us altogether from social, political, economic, and cultural life) as yet another way of selling sex.

Media and Power Relations: Issues of Definition and Control

The mass media are often described, especially by their own members, as constituting a "fourth estate," an independent and impartial public sphere through which the polity gain insight and information about local, national, and international affairs and where, through the diligent ministrations of the corps of journalists, the government of the day (and any other appropriate target) is held to account. Clearly, such scrupulous accountability requires complete independence from the "targets" of the media's interest, especially from government, as John Thadeus Delane argued, but the media's rhetoric in this regard has been seen increasingly as more aspirational than real.

> To perform its duties with entire independence and consequently with the utmost public advantage, the press can enter into no close or binding allegiance with the statesmen of the day, nor can it surrender its permanent interests to the convenience or ephemeral power of any government. (John Thadeus Delane, editor of *The Times* 1841–1877, quoted in Baistow 1985: i)

That the independence of much of the media has been questioned for quite some time now (see, e.g., Tunstall 1977; Baistow 1985; Jones 1996; Franklin 1997; Negrine 1998) will not be considered here, but it is important to acknowledge that, despite the famously independent nature of the media that the industry claims for itself, few people really believe the homily. On the contrary, I would argue that the relationship between politics and the media is a mutually dependent one, both politically and economically, each tied to the umbilicus of the other to keep its lifeblood of credibility/visibility (politicians) and stories/sales (news industries) pumping. But news media do not merely report the important events of the day, they decide what are the important events of the day—they construct the agenda, if not telling us what to think, then at least telling us what to think about. This circulation of meaning is not ideologically neutral but rather carries with it certain assumptions and certain perspectives that frame (in every sense of the word) the news agenda in particular ways, ways that, I argue, privilege the dominant socioeconomic paradigm of capitalist patriarchy that functions to ensure a male-ordered and global system of social and economic control. It thus becomes merely a commonplace to argue that broadcast media (especially, but other media too) regularly and routinely perform an important affirmatory function in reinforcing dominant norms and values to "the public" and confirming the cherished and comfortable beliefs of most of their consumers. Existing and unequal social, economic, political, and cultural relationships are routinely (and unproblematically) promoted through both fictional and factual programming strands; and the ways in which women particularly (but also other disadvantaged groups) are represented on and in broadcast media transmit important messages to the viewing public about women's place, women's role, and women's lives (see, e.g., Tuchman et al. 1978; Root 1986; Soothill and Walby 1991; Creedon 1993; Ross 1995a; Carter 1998; Wykes 1998). Much contemporary research effort on broadcast media has focused on analyzing the ideological effects of television, that is, how the dominant ideology is mobilized by the media, and especially television, to produce an apparently shared, uncontroversial, and unproblematic understanding of the world (see, e.g., Dines and Humez 1995; Eldridge 1995; Fiske 1994a; Ross 1996). But within this more general project of identifying how ideologies work as conveyors of meaning, how they constitute specific belief systems, who believes them, and what circumstances continue to support them are particular questions of gender. How are women framed in news agendas? How do women viewers read news media? Do my concerns, as a woman, coincide with those of media producers? Do we see the issues that affect our lives reflected in the media's agenda?

The media, and in particular television, are arguably the primary definers of public discourse and play a crucial cultural role in their gendered framing of public issues and the gendered discourses they present. If the flow of opinion among citizens is hindered by the use of "old-fashioned prerogative powers and new forms of image management" (Keane 1991, 94), precisely how are the media implicated in this compromised democracy and where are women positioned, as subjects and objects of the media's interest? What function do the media perform in the perpetuation of ideas and ideologies that protect the status quo and that, at the same time, exclude women? Analyses that define and examine the media as specific agencies of public knowledge and definitional power and that comprehend the viewer as citizen (Corner 1991) have generally failed to distinguish the salience of gender in these media-ted relations. Much of the critical work undertaken by the news media has looked at issues of accountability and bias, but the gender dimension has often been overlooked, although this omission is gradually being addressed, with a number of scholars now looking at the relationship of gender and media in a variety of contexts (see, e.g., Carter et al. 1998). As Byerly argues, somewhat despairingly, although there has been work that has looked at issues such as gender and representation, what has been missing has been a sustained critical political-economic analysis of women's position in media industries themselves, clearly recognizing the relationship between who is behind the camera with what is produced in front of it (Byerly 1998).

Women in News Industries

Over the past few years, the slogan "we are an equal opportunities employer" has been emblazoned across the masthead of countless media organs, but while women's claims for equality are now (mostly) taken seriously, I would argue that it is lip service when a hard look is taken at precisely who occupies positions of responsibility (see Gallagher 1981; Dougary 1994; Robinson and St. Jean 1997; Robinson, forthcoming). The power to shape media policy and to determine the nature and direction of media content remains resolutely in the hands of men. Even when women do manage to drag themselves out of the kitchen and into the media boardroom, they struggle every step of the way, and when they get there they must endure a continual sexist assault from male colleagues desperate to hold on to power. When Eve Pollard moved from the London *Sunday Mirror* to become the first woman editor of a midmarket newspaper, the *Sunday Express,* she was described as a "killer bimbo" who knew how to use her bosom as a cosh (Dougary 1994, xiii). The small number of studies that have analyzed the position of women in media organizations across Europe demonstrate depressingly similar findings. Women consistently feature less than men in news and current affairs programming, as news presenters, reporters, and journalists, but also as expert commentators (see, e.g., Women's Broadcasting Committee 1993). They make up a small percentage of technical and production staff and are rarely seen in decision-making positions (Michielsens 1991; Neves 1994). This is not to argue that more women media professionals will necessarily improve the way in which women's views are reported upon—see below—in the same way that doubling the number of women politicians in the United Kingdom at the 1997 election has not had (at least not yet) a significant influence on the shape or content of the social policy agenda. But having a broader diversity of voices is important for its own sake, not necessarily because of gender but because of difference.

Traditional feminist analyses have previously argued that mainstream news reporting has always tended to speak to men's concerns rather than to those of women and that the invisibility of women, as anchors, newsreaders, and reporters on television has often been seen as symptomatic of the lower status of women in the real world. News themes and stories reflect a male view of reality, crudely duplicating current social divisions between the public "male" world and the private "female" one. Orthodox "effects" theory would suggest that the impact on the audience of exposure to such a specifically (en)gendered view, without benefit of competing alternative visions, would reinforce the orthodoxy of women's insignificance and confirm their "proper" place (Pingree and Hawkins 1978). But changes in newsroom personnel strategies, the revolution in practice that has been brought about by developments in media and communications technology, and the increasingly global nature of mass media have all forced a reconsideration of the relationship of news to gender. For example, what is signified by the recruitment of attractive young women to newscasting and presenting in recent years? During the past five or so years, television journalism has become a much softer medium in its focus on human and personal-interest stories (see Beasley 1993; Gallagher 1995; Christmas 1997; Norris 1997; Holland 1998; Steiner 1998), taking on a more intimate tone and style of address as it blurs the lines between hard and soft news in its quest to satisfy the lazy appetite of an audience that can collectively switch the zapper if the program does not engage in the first five seconds of viewing.

But more women in the newsroom cannot be regarded *necessarily* as a significant step forward on the road to equality. As Arthurs argues, "more women in the [televisual] industry is not enough: there need to be more women with a politicized understanding of the ways in which women's subordination is currently reproduced and with the will to change it" (1994, 100). I have made precisely the same point in relation to women politicians (Ross and Sreberny-Mohammadi 1997): that more women in Parliament is not enough if they do not commit to pushing forward a woman-friendly agenda, as witnessed by the high expectations in Britain of electing 120 women politicians to Parliament in the 1997 general election and the sense of betrayal felt by many Labour-supporting women when nearly all those women politicians subsequently voted to reduce welfare benefits for single mothers.

So rather than seeing women news professionals as exemplifying the new (higher) status of women in public domains, it is possible to detect an altogether more cynical rationale underlying their employment, that is, that women (in television news at least) make news more human, more watchable, and they improve ratings. And women are less likely to be militant and can be paid lower wages. The increasing trend toward "intimidation" (see van Zoonen 1989, 1994, 1998) appears to be running in tandem with specific editorial policies to engage more with the viewer, and women newsreaders could be viewed in this context as merely modern-day versions of traditional and reactionary forms of femininity. Commenting specifically on BBC news, Patricia Holland suggested that newsreading might become a "woman's job" because the task now requires a significant element of performance and the performer should be reasonably decorative (Holland 1987).

The F-Factor

The issue of personal appearance and "fanciability" for newsreaders and other front-of-house media personnel now forms the focus of much public debate: the size and refractory qualities of earrings, the color and cut of suits, and the length of hemlines are all deemed appropriate subjects for discussion. An interest in the ability of individual women to do their job has become subordinated to questions about their sartorial judgment, and this inappropriate fixation not only targets women in news industries but is a strategy almost routinely employed in relation to women who *make* the news, such as politicians (Liran-Alper 1994; Sreberny-Mohammadi and Ross 1996; Ross and Sreberny-Mohammadi 1997). The decorative qualities of women newsreaders have now become an integral part of their perceived "rightness" for the job, and women are in danger of being pushed back into occupying traditional female territory as mere objects for the male gaze. Nowhere is this more blatant than in the pairing of the young, attractive woman newscaster with the older, more sophisticated male presenter—an obvious male fantasy.

As news programs draw closer to entertainment genres—so-called infotainment—so their highly formalized presentation strategies have relaxed. When Angela Rippon and Anna Ford were selected to read the news on BBC and ITN, respectively, in the late 1970s, it was at a time when the social status of women in British society was being questioned. "Rippon and Ford became a focus for male uncertainty about the 'problem' of powerful, attractive women" (Root 1986, 89). Decades later, women news professionals remain at the periphery of the action, attractive satellites orbiting round the male star. Newswomen are caught in a double-bind: they are viewed as sexual objects even while engaged in the serious business of news reporting, and at the same time they are criticized for trivializing the news because they are too decorative and can distract from the content of their words. Though each may not speak as a woman or for women, each has a voice that is denied authority because of her sex: each must seek a style of dress that is feminine and yet neutral. But the constraints on women in this man's world may mean that the question is less about whether women *can* speak from this position than do they want to? As Holland asks, "If the cost of being offered a public voice involves giving up the right to speak specifically as a woman, is it a price worth paying?" (1987, 149). Although media commentators have long noted the way in which women presenters on television appear to be chosen for their age and their looks rather than their ability to do the job, the take-up of a new breakfast television franchise in Britain by GMTV *(Good Morning Television)* and the attendant publicity around its new host made the crude link between sexiness and ratings entirely transparent. Fiona Armstrong was recruited to cohost the new program with Michael Wilson, following the current breakfast TV convention to always have a woman-man line-up to give the show a comfortable, family feel. Armstrong had previously worked as a mainstream news presenter and was told by GMTV program director Lis Howell to wear sexier, shorter skirts and to smile more. Howell said of her new employee:

> Like all the main presenters, she was chosen for her good looks and manners. I do want the viewers to fancy the presenters in the nicest possible way and we have enhanced Fiona's image. In her final days at ITN she was not looking good. The lighting was hard and they did not pay attention to jewelry and to things like that. The flirtatious side had died. Since being here, she has developed a million per cent. She has great legs. (Howell quoted in the *Daily Express*, 5 January 1993)

The way women look, their general physical attractiveness, and their potential "sexiness" were all seen as crucial factors that could determine their success in pursuing a television career by women viewers in a series of interviews I conducted on behalf of Britain's TV and radio watchdog organization, the Broadcasting Standards Council (see Sreberny-Mohammadi 1994; Ross 1995a).[1] "I think that they appoint women they think will appeal on a sexy or comfy sqfa basis" ("Elaine"). More specifically, one respondent remarked, "They set up a female who is thinking and intelligent . . . before you know it, the tabloids are having a go at her, saying she should shorten her skirts, she should lower her neckline. TV producers read that and they have her in the make-up room as fast as they can" ("Maureen"). The casual commodification of women as sexual objects was alluded to on several occasions in the study and it was felt that few women escape the media's fascination with sex. While some of the study's respondents thought that

Margaret Thatcher had at least provided a role model for women, others felt she had done more harm than good. Whatever their views on her politics, though, most respondents appreciated that even *she* was subject to precisely the same sexual curiosity and prurient interest that burden other women in public life. "Watching her memoirs on TV, they had to ask Cecil Parkinson if he found her sexy. Why ask the question? Nobody asked if anyone found Jim Callaghan sexy" ("Jenny"). While this chapter does not focus specifically on women as audiences for news products, there is some evidence to suggest that part of the push toward news media's increasing intimacy and informal modes of addressing the audience is bound up with a recognition that, contrary to the industry's beliefs about gendered program preferences (i.e., men do news and women do soap opera), women do indeed watch and read the news (see Mills 1990, 1997; Rapping 1995; Ross 1995b; Hartley 1996; Nightingale 1996). But what my previous study of women audiences and news reveals is that broadcast news media are still not getting it "right" if they want to retain, let alone increase, market share among women audiences. The following content analysis case study of gender and general election reporting reinforces this point.

Gender, Politics, and the Media: Reporting Strategies in a General Election Climate—The Same Old (Hi)story

The remainder of this chapter looks at a small part of a much larger project on women and the media; its scope is British terrestrial TV news broadcast during the second week of the 1997 British general election campaign. Within the generality of news items, the study focused specifically on those items that were centered on the general election. The study aimed to see where women featured in the election campaign, in what context and capacity (as presenters and reporters of election campaign items, as politicians, as members of the public, as experts, etc.), and the extent to which the principal concerns of women (identified in the Women's Communication Centre [1996] survey), such as child benefit, child care, parental leave, pay/conditions for part-time workers, the minimum wage, and poverty in older age, were viewed as political priorities and therefore included as campaign themes by parties. It is my intention here to draw the various threads of the preceding argument together in the exploration of this case study, demonstrating the synergies (or in this case, the total *lack* of relationship) between "ordinary" women's political priorities (women + policy = gender politics), the priorities of broadcast news journalists in terms of items selected for inclusion in general election campaign coverage and individuals chosen to speak (journalists + gender (male) = male agenda), and broadcast news media's use of particular media personnel for particular items (men/hard news/high profile/high salary vs. women/soft news/low visibility/lower salary = political economy). The picture that emerges is depressingly simple: men on top, women underneath, in media as in life.

Over the one-week period (4 to 10 April 1997), the election coverage contained in news programs broadcast by four of Britain's five terrestrial TV channels was monitored (the new Channel 5 was excluded from the study because reception was still very poor—and even nonexistent—in some areas). Eight separate news programs were monitored each weekday, including breakfast, lunchtime, and evening news programs across all channels, together with news roundups broadcast during the weekend. A coding sheet was used to record the sex and status (among other story attributes) of each person who had any kind of coverage during an election item story: a total of 44 programs were monitored in this way, producing 136 separate general election campaign items that form the basis of this limited analysis. Using the 136 news items as the base, a total of 374 individuals contributed to these items and the gender breakdown for these appearances was 315 men (84 percent) compared with 59 women (16 percent). Disaggregating these depressing ratios into categories, we find that the vast majority of the contributions made by women were in the context of vox pops and, more specifically, under the label "mother," although a smattering of women politicians were given a morsel of airtime to play with.

The Political Triumvirate and Assorted Others

Given the context of the study, it would be expected that politicians themselves, especially the party leaders, would feature significantly in news-programmed election coverage, but the invisibility of women politicians of any party was highly disconcerting and echoed earlier work covering the previous election (University of Loughborough 1992). Excluding appearances by the 3 main party leaders, 135 Members of Parliament were featured during the monitoring period and only 8 of these were women (6 percent), sometimes even the same women. The women politicians who did manage to attract a small spotlight were Margaret Beckett (twice—on Europe and privatization); Diana Maddoc (Europe); Mo Mowlem (Labour Party policy on selection); Clare Short (very brief appearance on women's health); Edwina

Currie, Theresa Gorman, and Margaret Ewing (all on a panel discussing Europe). Interestingly, the "Europe question" was viewed by respondents in an Independent Television Commission election study as being of little interest to voters in general—more than half the sample reported that they were either not very (35 percent) or not at all (17 percent) interested in the topic, with boredom thresholds lower for women— 30 percent of women said they were interested in the European Union, compared with 48 percent of men (Sancho-Aldridge 1997, 25). Perhaps women are just more honest? It is a hard irony, then, that 5 out of the paltry 8 appearances of women politicians focused on an issue that did not appear to be an involving one for women voters, perhaps because they/we get exasperated by the constructed and one-sided nature of so many political debates:

> Those against have been given much more airtime. In fact the only politician to have had the courage to disparage the Eurosceptics has been Jacques Santer. Not a single British Europhile has been given a voice. . . . (anonymous woman, quoted in Sancho-Aldridge 1997, 27)

The focus on the "Europe question" during that campaign has an added poignancy for me now as a committed Europhile. Beyond the millennium turn, we are now in a period of desperate voter cynicism about politics, and in Britain, at least, rampant apathy coupled with a poorly informed media combine to make the "Europe question," for the public at least, mean little more than preserving (or not) the Queen's head on our currency. In the European elections in Britain in 2000, the pathetic voter turnout of just 25 percent of potential voters provides a compelling example of voter apathy and the (non)exercise of democratic responsibility.[2] The question that needs to be asked is, why did that happen? This blatant "stay-at-home" response was blamed substantially on what could be seen as the media's collective narcolepsy in reporting on what being a member of Europe would and could actually mean or in even covering the various stances on Europe taken by the major political parties. Interestingly, as this chapter goes to press, Britain is once again in the grip of a general election campaign, and even before the official polling date was announced, media pundits were already dubbing it "the apathetic election."

It is worth noting that women politicians received the same scant press attention during the 1997 general election campaign as has been noted elsewhere (see Ross and Sreberny-Mohammadi 1997), and where they did feature, they were often trivialized. For example, five women candidates were contesting the Hampstead and Highgate constituency and were presented as "the Spice Girls" in the *Evening Standard*.[3] Twin sisters Angela and Maria Eagle were both standing as Labour candidates—Angela Eagle was in fact defending her seat and Maria was standing for the first time—and were featured in an item titled "New Labour, New Crumpet." When 101 Labour women MPs were subsequently elected, they were immediately dubbed "Blair's Babes."[4] It may or may not be relevant that both these newspapers are at the "tabloid" end of the spectrum, although even the broadsheets quickly took up the "Blair's Babes" tag. One of the key themes of the 1997 British general election campaign was, arguably, that of "sleaze" and, in particular, the controversy surrounding the standing of Neil Hamilton, an MP accused of corruption. His wife, Christine (who was either captioned simply as "Mrs. Neil Hamilton," or given no credit at all), featured in five of the news items monitored, thereby achieving a level of visibility (if only as adjunct rather than in her own right) only dreamt of by women politicians. Of the 26 appearances of politicians speaking "for the Government," none were women. Even when we look at the separate category of local politician (councillor), where a better gender balance actually exists in real life, of the 12 local councillors who appeared in news items, none were women.

Given that prior to the 1997 British general election women accounted for less than 10 percent of Britain's elected parliamentary representatives, it is perhaps not surprising that they therefore featured in almost risible numbers during the campaign coverage, although, even here, their actual appearances underrepresented their actual numbers. What is rather *less* understandable is the way in which other women's voices were similarly excluded and ignored. For example, in most campaigns, various individuals are pushed into the limelight to provide allegedly "expert" opinions on certain topics. Of the 50 "expert" commentators monitored, only 4 were women (7 percent). When we turn to the category of "academic commentator," we find that 17 academics appeared during the monitoring week, none of whom were women. Why? Are women not contributing to the social, economic, and political life of the country?

Style over Substance: The Sartorial Imperative

If we look at who presents news stories, the anchors, reporters, and journalists were predominantly male although it has become quite fashionable, as noted earlier, to use female/male anchor teams in primetime news shows, with the (nearly always) older male newsreader providing the gravitas required to report on horror and tragedy while his younger female colleague relates the infotainment items at the end—the singing donkey story or the story of the misshapen cucumber—that give rise to sniggers. In this study, women reporters and newscasters were involved in 28 of the 136 items (20 percent), although this aggregate figure disguises very real discrepancies between different channels, with Channel 4 having the highest visibility of women newsreaders and reporters. When women media professionals were involved in election items, they were accorded less prominence and status in the news line-up, often discussing more "light-hearted" election issues, especially vox pops, before delivering the viewer back into the safe hands of the authoritative male anchor.

The (relative) absence of women from political news reporting is a disappointing feature of Britain's mediascape and corresponds to their lack of visibility in jobs that entail decision-making responsibilities. Findings of the "Women in Journalism" report of gender and media employment reveal that although women have begun to be appointed to senior roles (although *below* editor level), "leader writing [editorials] and political writing remain stubbornly male enclaves" (Christmas 1997, 12). Women journalists who were interviewed for the report identify the political editor as a powerful figure in the newsroom, because those journalists consider that the reporting of politics helps define a newspaper's sense of self (and despite the increasing tabloidization of even the most respectable broadsheets, a definite political slant is still broadly apparent in news reporting), and during elections, political reporting becomes even more influential.

Those few women journalists who did cover the election report a journalistic camaraderie that was "testosterone driven" and gender exclusive (see, e.g., Coles 1997). Joanna Coles, reporting for the *Guardian,* was one of the journalists on the campaign bus, and Coles likens these journeys to a minor stag party, with male colleagues leering at pornographic material previously downloaded from the Internet, sharing cans of lager, and sniggering whenever a woman happened to wander down the bus toward them. Coles was in the somewhat unenviable position of being both excluded from this spectacle of puerile masculinity by her sex—for example, when she approached the "porno" section of the bus, the computer in question had its screen discreetly lowered—and included and expected to collude with her colleagues because of their shared professional "codes."

Let the People Speak

The one category of news subject in the study that showed a better distribution of women contributors was that of the vox pop, where we counted a total of 82 individuals, 34 of whom were women (40 percent). However, a number of women who were coded to this category were included in reports because of their status as mothers, sometimes even being captioned as such: women in vox pop contexts were rarely asked their opinion on topics other than nursery education or child care. However, overall the views of allegedly "ordinary" people were scarcely canvassed at all and only 18 out of the 136 news items studied (13 percent) used vox pops. This is not to say that the views of the electorate were not given opportunities for expression during the campaign period: in fact there were a number of TV and radio programs, including *Campaign Roadshow, Election Call, The People's Election,* and *Power and the People,* that did feature such expression. Unfortunately, though, women's particular contributions and views were not routinely sought out. For example, an extended item on "finding the nation's pulse" across the west of England found the region populated, apparently, by people of only the male gender: looking at the impact of Europe on business and employment, the so-called investigative journalist interviewed a businessman, a fisherman, a farmer, a tin miner, and two unemployed men. Women were entirely invisible. At press time, preliminary analysis of the gender of callers to the BBC's "Election Call" program in June 2001 shows the ratio of men to women as 3:1.

The 1997 British general election was supposed to be the one that would speak to "women's concerns," since it had been recognized, at last, that women voters held the key to winning elections. But the concerns that women have identified in a number of studies (see, e.g., Women's Communication Centre 1996; Stephenson 1998) appear to have been ignored again. Of those specific concerns—child benefit, child care, parental leave, pay/conditions for part-time workers, the minimum wage, and poverty in older age—only 3 of the 136 items focused on any one of them, 2 stories on child care and 1 on parental leave. The single most prevalent issue covered during the election was, disturbingly if unsurprisingly, coverage of the election itself: opinion polls, whether leaders would debate on TV, "expert" views on the outcome, who was having a good and not-so-good day, and so on occupying nearly one-third of all news coverage during the six-week campaign (University of Loughborough 1997).

The question can be asked, of course: so what? What does it matter that so-called women's concerns were not addressed during the campaign? So what that women did not get to speak, even to represent their own, if no one else's, voices? Who cares that one of the main stories concerning women voters was whether they liked Tony Blair's new bouffant haircut or whether Blair was more attractive to women voters than Bill Clinton?[5] The quick answer to these "so what?" questions is that it disenfranchises woman to be so excluded from the process of politics, however shallow and shabby it has now become. A more considered and complex response requires an engagement with notions such as justice, equity, and democratic responsibility. At the very least, even if a woman does not necessarily believe she has a special and uniquely gendered set of political priorities that she would like to see addressed, what women *do* want is to see is a variety of perspectives. In a study conducted by the Independent Television Commission on voters' reactions and attitudes toward television's coverage of the general election, women were consistently more critical than male viewers and were found to be less interested in the election coverage because they felt "it did not include issues of interest to them and because they disliked the negative campaigning" (Sancho-Aldridge 1997). Part of that dislike was perhaps the conspicuous and repetitive sporting and military metaphors used to describe the performance of the parties: this party has scored a number of points today, that party landed a solid punch; even the funds that parties have available to support their campaigns are called their "war chests." Moreover, the performative aspect of political reporting reinforces the aggressive and combative tenor of so-called political debate, reducing the decision of which party will govern the country to a matter, apparently, of which has the superior games*man*ship skills.

Conclusions

What this very small study reveals is yet more evidence, if any were really needed, that women's voices are not being heard, women's lives are not being reflected, and women's experiences are not being considered when it comes to the media's reporting of the politics of the society to which we all belong, unless they are framed in routine and sexualized ways that accentuate gender and occlude almost every other personal attribute. Even "elite" women, such as politicians, often struggle to get their message across, in the face of a coterie of (male) political journalists who ply their trade with their (male) political buddies over a white wine spritzer in the Commons Bar (see Ross and

Sreberny-Mohammadi 1997). The 1997 British general election will *not* be remembered for the promotion of women-friendly policies or the quality of political debate but for the tedious display of political antagonism vented by each party against the others. It will be remembered for the interminable array of news and current affairs programs that saw the same few (male) figures shuffling on to argue why everyone else was unfit to govern, but not owning up to what their own parties actually had to offer an electorate stupefied into apathy by the onslaught of soundbite journalism and smug rhetoric. In the ITC's study, respondents reported overwhelmingly that there was too much coverage of the party leaders, too much "soft" interviewing, too much "negative" campaigning, leading to merely 18 percent of the audience sample giving election coverage more than a passing glance and a third of viewers switching channels to avoid the coverage altogether (Sancho-Aldridge 1997). But where was gender on the agenda? A significant part of the problem (and therefore of the solution) lies with who constructs the news, who produces the news, who reports on the news.

The power to determine the nature and direction of news media content remains firmly in the hands of men: political men who make the news and media men who write about it, the latter at the invitation of the former. The journalist Joanna Coles suggests that the atmosphere at a typical press conference resembles that of a boys' public school, where a few clever girls have been allowed into the sixth form (Coles 1997). The men on the platform address the journalists in their midst by their first names: Yes, Michael, do you have a question? Richard? Andrew? The few women in the press corps are not similarly addressed, still less invited to ask their question.

I want to argue that the kinds of stories, perspectives, and interests we see and read in the media are inextricably bound up with the kinds of social and economic relations that exist in news organizations themselves, as sites of news production. In an industry dominated by men at the top who make key decisions while doing up their flies in the urinals or trading shots across the golf course, is it little wonder that the key decision that women who present the news have to make is whether to wear the pink or the blue today? The political economy of the newsroom provides a strongly gendered context in which the traditional power plays of economic relations—men on top and women underneath—are played out in alarmingly conventional (for which read sex-stereotyped) ways (see Women in Journalism 1998).

We know from our own observations [that] the news the country is given is largely what is considered newsworthy by men—produced, directed, edited and shot overwhelmingly by men. (Women's Broadcasting Committee 1993, 14)

The media, and television in particular, have a significant function to perform in helping to establish the parameters and limits that structure our thinking about the world. They are capable of triggering hopes and aspirations and are inseparable from our daily lives, involved in a continuous circuit of meaning, providing pixels of pleasure as they inform, educate, entertain, and socialize us, almost without our conscious involvement in or recognition of the seduction of that easy but potent diet of pret-a-manger info/edu/tainment. While it is relatively easy to bemoan the stereotypical way in which women are routinely portrayed by the mainstream media and to call for "better" portrayal, such a call suggests that there are shared "truths" and "realities" that could provide more authentic representations than the sex-typed fare the media consumer is usually offered. But rather what we should be arguing for is the marvelous diversity of women's lives to be represented, the good bits, the bad bits, and the bits in between. If we do not want women to be portrayed everywhere as whores or victims, neither do we want to pretend that every woman has uncompromised virtue or can repel an attacker with a well-placed karate chop. It is precisely the contradictions, the contrarinesses, and the counterpoints that need to be reflected, in art as in life (see Steeves 1987; Douglas 1994; Ross 1998).

Endnote

If the point of theory is to provide increasingly "better" understandings of the social world, then the purpose of a critical feminist theory is to question orthodox epistemological production. Here this means exposing the normative assumptions that underpin what might be called the newsroom ethos, assumptions that are socially constructed and masquerade as "routine" journalistic practice (see Skidmore 1995, 1998; Coles 1997; McLaughlin 1993, 1998). Such assumptions serve to marginalize women—both as contributors to such knowledge production in their role as professional journalists and also as chroniclers of their own history and experience as "ordinary" women—through disallowing their voices a platform, denying us/them the opportunity for that articulation. While some studies (see, e.g., Melin-Higgins and

Djerf-Pierre 1998) show that women journalists use strategies of incorporation to combat the prevailing "masculine" and "macho" norms that usually pervade newsrooms—that is, they become one of the boys—precisely the opposite strategy has also been initiated through developing specifically gendered spaces such as the irreverent Scottish magazine *Harpies and Quines* whose title neatly parodies a magazine, the very up-market *Harpers and Queen,* which places women very firmly in feminine rather than feminist space.

It seems clear that the ways in which women are *represented* in the media are inextricably linked with who *produces* those media outputs, which in turn is linked with who (or what) owns those means of production. As Carter et al. point out, "feminist and gender-sensitive studies of journalism are becoming increasingly concerned with the changing patterns of news media ownership [especially] within local, national and global contexts" (Carter et al. 1998, 3). Although space does not permit a fuller discussion of the implications of the increasing convergence and concentration of myriad small media organizations into a handful of "big" players, that one big global problem of conglomeratization (see, e.g., International Institute of Communications 1996) provides the contextualizing background to the discussion on gender, space, place, and portrayal I have sketched out here. Sex, politics, and money have always enjoyed intimate relations, and media's involvement in that triumvirate merely adds another player to the field. It will take a concerted effort of will to unravel the vested interests that are deeply embedded in that particular nexus. The hope is that as more women do succeed to positions of influence and authority, they open out spaces for different voices and different perspectives to emerge and speak in all their varied tongues.

Notes

1. This work was commissioned by the Broadcasting Standards Council and awarded to the Centre for Mass Communication Research, University of Leicester, UK, under the management of Professor Annabelle Sreberny Mohammadi.

2. During a vox pop on 10 June, "people on the street" were questioned by reporters about their voting intentions, the vast majority said they would not be voting because they did not know enough about the issues to make an informed choice.

3. Julia Hartley-Brewer, "Five Wannabes of NW3 Spice Up the Fight for Votes," *Evening Standard,* 18 April 1997.

4. Bill Mouland, "Blair's Babes," *Daily Mail*, 8 May 1997.

5. For example, three stories in late 1996 focused on Blair's attraction for women, with the following headlines: "Blair's Bad Hair Day" (*Guardian*, 11 July 1996); "Blair Woos Women Voters with New Hairstyle" (*Financial Times*, 11 June 1996); "Rogue Male Beats New Man to a Woman's Vote" (*Sunday Times*, 11 October 1996).

10. Gender and the Political Economy of Newsmaking: A Case Study of Human Rights Coverage
Carolyn M. Byerly

History is replete with evidence that those who control the media in effect control the content of the ideas that those media produce and disseminate. In that context, neither Karl Marx nor Susan B. Anthony[1]—two of the earliest to critique the owner-media relationship—was particularly revolutionary in their observations. Their central concerns, however, are as relevant today as they were in the nineteenth century. Mass media ownership for 150 years has tended to be corporate, elite, and male. In these contemporary times, we have Rupert Murdoch, Michael Eisner, and other powerful media magnates to remind us that owning more and more media industries makes one both very rich and very able to set in motion a particular set of ideas, values, and role models that become self-perpetuating in the messages their industries purvey.

To what extent, then, have organized efforts by women, over time, succeeded in getting the issues that feminism has raised onto news agendas of these male controlled media enterprises? This question motivated the present research, which examines the news coverage of the fiftieth anniversary of the Universal Declaration of Human Rights on 10 December 1998. The study sought first to determine whether and how women's human rights were specifically addressed in that coverage, given twenty-five years of feminist interventionist strategies to increase women's employment in media professions, to expand gender issues in news coverage, and, more recently, to create online feminist news magazines to expand the circulation of women's information in mainstream and specialized audiences. The study proceeded from the recognition that global feminism had framed women's oppression and marginalization as human rights concerns for at least a decade. Had mainstream news organizations been paying attention?

Second, the study sought to understand the nature of the coverage within the larger political economic context formed by women's structural relationship to the media industries. Women have had a limited role in controlling either the wealth or decision making of capitalist institutions historically. Feminist media scholarship has been limited in analyzing the political economy of media, with respect to gender, focusing instead on representational issues (Byerly 1999). Even feminist scholars who have critiqued recent laws and policies that have allowed men to consolidate their financial power through corporate mergers and acquisitions have missed the gender implications of these events.[2] The news media are among the most powerful of these corporations in their ability to influence public dialogues about things central to women's lives and status. The present study seeks to contribute to the literature on women, feminism, and the political economy of news.

Terminology

The term *human rights* refers to the entitlements specifically set forth by the thirty articles of the Universal Declaration of Human Rights. The document was adopted by the UN General Assembly by acclamation in 1948. While it lacks the compulsory dimension of treaties, the document has served as a set of guiding principles for member nations to use in refining their own statutes. In years since, the Universal Declaration has provided the framework for the writing of numerous other conventions (i.e., treaties) and declarations that provide more specific human rights guarantees. For example, the Convention on the Elimination of Discrimination against Women (CEDAW), now ratified by all but the United States and a handful of other nations, extends binding protections to women.

Human rights leaders often group the Universal Declaration's thirty articles into civil, political, economic, social, and cultural rights. These include the right to equality; a right to life, liberty, and personal security; freedom from torture; privacy for oneself and family; a right to a nationality and citizenship; the right to own property; the right to assemble; the right to participate in elections; the right to work and join trade unions; the right to an adequate standard of living; the right to cultural life and community; the right to free and full personal development; the right to participate in the making of laws and policies; the right to be free of slavery; the right to freedom from discrimination; equal recognition before the law and courts; a right to religion, one's own opinions, social security, rest and leisure, education, and a just social order.

Feminism and *feminist* refer to women's liberation movements and the individuals who lead and are identified with them. Such movements, which generally seek to advance women's social and political status, have often been intertwined with broader movements for social change, particularly in nations that experienced colonialism and/or authoritarian regimes (Basu 1995, 9). Women of the United Nations member states began soon after World War II to seek international statutes to bring about greater equality for women.

Developed and *developing nations* are imprecise terms used to refer respectively to advanced industrial nations, like the United States and Canada, and nations at varied levels of such industrialization.

Framework of Analysis

I looked to political economy and feminist theory to develop an analytical framework to examine news coverage of the Universal Declaration with respect to women. Critical scholars associated with theories of political economy provide a useful set of organizing principles to guide such inquiries. The first is to remember that ownership and decision making lie at the heart of what will circulate, be talked about, and ultimately be acted upon. The second principle, really a corollary of the first, is that media content (what some call the "text") can never adequately be examined outside its proper context, which has been determined largely by the structures, routines, and relations of power that produced it.

Feminist critical scholars concerned with the political economy of communications have expanded these tenets by factoring in gender. In the process, they provide a theoretical framework to question how men's and women's political and economic relations in the larger society enter into both ownership and message-making patterns in the media. Feminist theory also presupposes that social institutions have the flexibility to change and that marginalized groups like women have the power to bring that change about. Indeed, both radical and moderate branches of feminism have always aimed to effect institutional change. The corporate media, which collectively represent one modern "institution," have been the target of global feminist leaders since the UN Decade for Women (1975–1985). Their goals have been to increase feminist access to mainstream news through interventions that include establishing women-run news and other media enterprises, training more women with feminist identities to become reporters so they can include questions and issues of concern to women, and promoting women to decision-making posts in mainstream industries (Byerly 1995).

While deterministic in its approach, political-economic theory also accepts the role of human agency in producing a different outcome. My own recent research with Warren (1996) found that most of the seventy-two male and female journalists we surveyed at eighteen of the largest circulating U.S. newspapers identified with civil rights, feminism, and/or gay rights movements. This identification, in turn, had enabled them to work actively for more equitable personnel policies, reporting assignments, and, in some cases, story content in years since the 1970s. The study also reminds us that feminism has had an impact on the consciousness of both male and female media professionals. Meyers (1992) has also shown that journalists' social and political consciousness enter into reporting of news about economic problems.

There is also evidence that thirty years of feminist movements have left their mark on mainstream news. In my own nation, the United States, newspapers and broadcast news both routinely cover the issues that feminism has raised, many of which can be considered to contain human rights themes, most particularly those involving violence against women. Some of those stories have been high profile and high quality enough to have won Pulitzer Prizes. Among these are the *Des Moines Register*'s series on Nancy Ziegenmeyer's rape case, in 1991, and the fifteen-part series "Violence against Women: A Question of Human Rights," in the *Dallas Morning News* in 1993. Mainstream news about women matters if the public is to understand the conditions underlying women's inequality, their organized efforts to advance, and the range of ways that women participate in the social structure each day.

The "Human Rights News Moment"

Anniversary stories—built around significant dates, such as those marking the end of wars, the passage of groundbreaking legal decisions, the new millennium, and, in this case, the UN's adoption of the Universal Declaration of Human Rights—are a long-standing staple in the news business. Organizations associated with issues of human rights have traditionally used the December 10 date to create news in the form of announcements (of new campaigns or important progress someplace) and the annual ritual of public vigils to observe human rights violations around the world. In fact, 1998 was no exception, except that human rights groups tooled up early. Web sites like Human Rights USA appeared early in the year, presenting the thirty articles of the declaration, facts about human rights cases from nation to nation, recent research, and other materials. In October, Amnesty International announced its first campaign directed against a Western nation—the United States. AI's blistering 150-page report cited police brutality, the continued use of capital punishment, the execution of minors, the rape of women in prison, and a long list of additional acts in the U.S. criminal justice system in "American failure to deliver the fundamental promise of rights for all" (Crosette 1998a). The organization thereby established a two-month "news window" for its campaign to generate stories and commentaries from nearly every perspective throughout the fall.

Another dramatic development in fall 1998 was the indictment of former Chilean President Augusto Pinochet by a Spanish magistrate for crimes against Spaniards living in Chile during Pinochet's dictatorship in the 1970s and 1980s. Citizens around the world followed the daily news to see whether Great Britain would extradite the aging, ailing Pinochet from its shores to Spain for trial. News stories in every language followed the technicalities of international law and relations, while they also revisited the egregious acts of illegal arrest, torture, murder, and intimidation that Pinochet's regime reportedly committed against Chileans and others.

But women were also at the forefront of human rights news in 1998, particularly in Afghanistan, where the Taliban had seized control of government and social institutions. The Taliban imposed regulations that all but forbade women from working, going to school, or even being seen in public without being completely covered by the all-concealing *hijab*. In the fall, mainstream and women's alternative media throughout the world regularly ran stories about women under the Taliban. These events in Afghanistan created an intersection of gender, culture, and religious politics that set off other newsworthy events. One of these was the denunciation of the Taliban rulers' philosophy and behavior by the Organization of Islamic Conference, a fifty-five-nation body that challenged reporters to abandon their stereotypic reporting of the Taliban's practices as "Islamic fundamentalism" as well as to report more specifically on the ways that women's human rights were being violated (Goodman 1998, 28).

Aside from organizing to bring world attention to the violation of women's human rights in Afghanistan, feminists around the world also used the occasion of the fiftieth anniversary to step up visibility for other issues. Women in the United States lobbied Congress to ratify the UN Convention for the Elimination of Discrimination against Women (CEDAW). Feminist organizations also reemphasized the UN's special report on violence against women, originally released in 1994, which criticized the battering, rape, and torture of women in the United States and other nations by everyone from their husbands to policemen, jailers, and others in authority positions. In addition, feminists reminded their publics that only five years before, in 1993, they had succeeded in winning their international campaign to make "women's rights *human* rights" at the Vienna Convention on Human Rights (Tierny 1998; Tomasevski 1995; *International Campaign* 1993).

Women have had a long-term association with the concept of human rights. Women's rights are inextricably linked to their social, economic, and political status, and for more than a century women's movements have placed these concerns central to their goals. More-over, a modern-day champion of women's advancement, Eleanor Roo-sevelt, was a prime architect of the Universal Declaration in 1948, giving women an intimate connection to the celebrated document. In the five decades since its unanimous passage by the General Assembly, women have succeeded in getting more than two dozen measures to advance women's rights and participation in their societies through the United Nations.

During summer and fall 1998, stories about women and human rights appeared regularly in both mainstream and feminist online and published news sources. *On the Issues* ("The Progressive Woman's Quarterly," as its cover announces) dedicated its fall 1998 issue to women's human rights. As the fiftieth anniversary approached, other feminist media increased their coverage. The San Jose, Costa Rica–based feminist news service, Servicio de Noticias de la Mujer (SEM),[3] distributed stories from Chile, Colombia, and other Latin American nations that listed women's human rights accomplishments and remaining problems, both in this region and elsewhere in the world. SEM Bureau Chief Thais Aguilar said that the agency wanted to emphasize the continuing basic violations that women experience in regard to education, quality of life, work, and health (Aguilar 1999).

SEM and other feminist news sources emphasized that women's human rights are complex, as well as both local and international in nature. For instance, women's advancement and equality are hindered everywhere by the current processes of globalization, which concentrate capital and control of industries in fewer and fewer hands. Other human rights problems include trafficking in women; lack of access to education, health, and other basic services; poverty; overpopulation; religious persecution; domestic violence and sexual assault; and female genital mutilation. "Complexity" also includes an acceptance of progress on some fronts. For example, feminist movements have provided a crucial political space through the decades for females to develop new critiques of society and to demand their human rights. There have been gains—sometimes small, sometimes profound. All of these aspects of women and human rights are newsworthy. But to what extent did the mainstream media attend to them in the news moment of the fiftieth anniversary of the Universal Declaration of Human Rights?

Women and the Political Economy of News

Feminist media scholars have scrupulously documented and theorized women's invisibility and misrepresentation in news and other media since the 1970s. Tuchman's (1978b) famous essay named the problem "symbolic annihilation," but what underlies the problem is perhaps more relevant to the present discussion. Gallagher (1981) was among the first to explain women's marginality in media content in terms of the larger political economy. She observed that "despite an overall growth in world communication facilities in recent years, a large percentage of the world's population—women in particular—is not reached by the mass media at all" (25). The reasons are complex, she said, but basically have to do with a gross inequality in the distribution of resources (such as capital to buy media), educational levels, and access to political decision making (where changes in policy affecting these problems could be made). But Gallagher also reminded us that ideology plays a major role in the perpetuation of such unequal economic and political power, because (and this will sound familiar) those with the ownership and control of the media industries also have the power to silence and render invisible women's voices, ideas, experiences, problems, and achievements.

In the 1970s, women's representation in the news was in the single digits in most nations (Gallagher 1981, 77). That figure rose in most nations over the next decade, as women played increasingly more prominent roles in public affairs, sports, and other places in society (thereby becoming news subjects in traditional terms). Women also entered journalistic forces in greater numbers, despite sexist attitudes and customs toward them in many industries and locales (*Women and Media Decision-Making* 1987). In a general way, in most nations' news media, new ideas about and images of women had begun to become more of a mainstay in the news media by the 1990s, as feminism embedded itself into language, laws, and other social institutions. But such improvements are by no means uniform or complete *anywhere* (Byerly 1999).

Women's struggles to communicate more openly made (and continue to make) progress, but the data compel us to grapple with the fact that little has changed in the dominant political and economic structures that define the world today. Nearly two-thirds of the world's women today live in nations whose gross domestic product is less than $1,000 per capita per year. A still larger proportion—75 percent—live in nations where the annual per capita income is declining. Though nearly a third of women are part of the formal (paid) workforce, they are often underpaid and have little job security. Women's unemployment rates everywhere are higher than men's and that is likely to continue (UN data quoted in Chen 1995, 23–24). All of these conditions are central to women's human rights and status.

The global communications industries form the centerpost of the global political economy, both in terms of infrastructure and what is transmitted. The infrastructure—giant corporations that build and control the satellites, fiber optics, computers, and other machinery—constitutes the vehicles through which funds and investment information travel at high speed from place to place. Transmissions also, of course, include everything from scientific and government data to entertainment programming (most of it coming out of the United States). Telecommunications industries are not isolated entities, since they interface and overlap with other global corporations as mixed-conglomerates, through interlocking boards of directors and other legal synergistic arrangements.

By the mid-1990s, global communications industries generated profits of $2 trillion—more than double the $745 billion they had received a decade earlier (*World Investment Report* 1996). While there has been no research to date on the number of women who have any real part in either the ownership or profits of these industries, logic tells us it is miniscule. Neither do females have much power as employees within any of these large industries. Gallagher's (1995) recent cross-national research reveals that across all media, women hold only about 12 percent of the jobs that could be considered decision making. In some nations, that dips below 4 percent. Of the 239 media organizations that Gallagher studied across all nations, only 3 percent were headed by women (47). How do these facts affect women's ability to speak publicly through the news media?

Content Analysis

Using several online databases, such as Latinworld.com and Lexis-Nexis, I searched for stories and commentaries in English and Spanish containing the words "human rights," "women," and "Universal Declaration" that were published between 1 and 11 December 1998. To assure sufficient Latin American representation, I focused particular attention on the Buenos Aires daily *El Clarin,* a major agenda-setting newspaper within the region. This process identified approximately three hundred stories and a few commentaries out of several thousand that had circulated on the topic of the Universal Declaration in the eleven-day period. About a third were in Spanish. All articles were analyzed for the amount and kind of information that they contained with respect to women's human rights. Those that contained at least a paragraph were examined in more depth with respect to theme and perspective.

Findings and Discussion

Only about a dozen (4 percent) of the three hundred stories included at least a paragraph of information about women and human rights, and of these still fewer were focused specifically on women's human rights as a central theme. Nearly all (96 percent) of the stories and commentaries in the sample mentioned women *only* in passing, as in "a day to mark progress in men's and women's human rights. . . ." About a fifth of the stories and commentaries were about Pinochet. The remainder were concerned with scattered themes, such as demonstrations by citizens in Jakarta calling for greater human rights protections, protests in Europe against the Chinese occupation of Tibet, the work of unions in various nations to improve workers' conditions, and the Australian government's poor treatment of its indigenous people.

The coverage, overall, provided no real substance about women's human rights violations or recent efforts to address them.[4] Consider, for example, an Associated Press story by Emma Ross, datelined London, 11 December, which identified what heads of state were saying about human rights around the world on the declaration's anniversary. Ross's story referred briefly to women's human rights in its last paragraph—the paragraph most likely to be cut when editors shorten stories to fit the space allotted. Another example is found in a Reuters' story titled "Guatemala News in Brief" (with no identified author), which ran on 10 December. The story was concerned with the sentencing of three former paramilitary for the 1982 massacre of civilians at Rio Negro. Although women and children accounted for nearly half of the indigenous villagers massacred, the story made no effort to move beyond this fact, exploring, for example, why women and children might have been targeted or how often this kind of violence occurred during the years of terror.

One could say that emphasis on event coverage and on official institutions and their spokespeople—two tendencies in mainstream news— logically confines the reporter to what the authoritative source is saying. For instance, if the president says little or nothing about women in his address to the nation, who should be blamed—the president or the reporter? If the judge provides no narrative on the mass killing of women and children, what can the reporter do? But such a defense circumvents the responsibility of reporters to question their sources critically and to background their stories adequately in order to create deeper meanings and a bigger context for events and issues. What would have prevented reporter Ross from including a paragraph about women's efforts in the United States to gain ratification of CEDAW? Or to lobby for renewal of the federal Violence against Women Act (VAWA) over the past year? What could the anonymous Reuters reporter have done to provide background facts on how many women and children were murdered by official and paramilitary forces during the 1980s in Guatemala, or the extent to which Guatemalan women (like Nobel prizewinner Rigoberta Menchú) have led the movement for peace?

Even a story solely about the murder of female human rights activist Galina Vasilyevna Starovoitova, in St. Petersburg, Russia, did not place the subject's gender into the context of her human rights struggles. In his 7 December story, author Malcolm Gray, writing for the Canadian-based Maclean's wire service, remarked on every aspect of Galina's life *except* her gender. Indeed, the word "woman" appears only once, when he calls her a "woman politician." How rare is it to have a female human rights leader in the former Soviet Union die in the line of work opposing human rights violations by the Russian patriarchy? How did other women view her? Was she identified with women's equality movements? Did she do anything specific to advocate for women?

Many of the reporters in this sample were female, allowing us to ask the perennial feminist question about whether gender makes a difference in a story's attention to women's concerns. In fact, this study found little difference between female and male writers in this regard. Consider, for example, several versions of a story by Nicole Winfield at the UN, covering Secretary-General Kofi Annan's speech on the UN's commitment to human rights, circulated by both AP and its affiliate AP Worldstream. None of the versions did more than mention the "human rights of men and women." On the other hand, there was a story covering a speech by President Clinton by Cox News Service's

Bob Deans, on 10 December, which detailed Dorothy Thomas's long commitment to women's rights work around the world through Human Rights Watch and other organizations.

The absence of women in this study's sample illustrates that the news industry mostly overlooked women's lives, problems, and political activity in relation to human rights in fall 1998. However, a handful of stories *did* pay such attention to women's human rights in the same time frame and should be closely scrutinized for their content and their contributions to gender in news flow.

These dozen pieces included a range of hard news, feature stories, and commentaries, and they represented both Western and developing nations' news sources. Most concerned some aspect of violence against women, the central issue raised by women's movements everywhere for three decades. Included in this group was a story by Samaa Abu Sharar, of Worldsources, Inc., a wire service concerned with developing nations. The story, which ran on 10 December, provided a well-researched account of domestic violence in Jordan and the campaign by Jordanian women to get the state to protect them. The article made clear connections between battering and women's status and included contact information for groups providing both information and crisis assistance. This story brought a strong feminist perspective through its analysis of the problem by feminist sources, including victims of domestic violence, and through examples of how women were campaigning for change.

Two hard-news stories by Silvana Boschi, of the Buenos Aires' *El Clarin,* were concerned with the release of a U.S.-FBI report on the kidnapping of babies from women "disappeared" by Argentine military in the 1970s, and the subsequent arrest of a federal judge involved in these dealings. The stories, which ran 2 and 7 December, clearly placed women and their children at the center of this human rights issue, as both victims and leaders. The first story also noted the fact that it was the grandmothers of the disappeared who assumed the name "Madres y Abuelas de la Plaza de Mayo" (Mothers and Grandmothers of Mayo Plaza) and, wearing their white head scarves, had picketed each Friday since the early 1980s, to demand government accountability for their relatives. This group is widely credited with bringing down the military dictatorship and bringing many of the perpetrators to trial.

Another story, by Kitty Holland in the *Irish Times* on 9 December, was concerned exclusively with international trafficking in women and girls and the need for public intervention.

While all articles were not exclusively concerned with women and human rights, several included well-placed sections that helped to foreground issues and leaders. Several of these concerned denunciation of the brutality of women under Taliban rulers in Afghanistan. Among these was a story by Nancy Montgomery, of the *Seattle Times*, on 11 December, which covered a high school event where students spoke out; and Dora Priest's piece for the *Washington Post* that same day covering then First Lady Hillary Clinton's anniversary speech, in which she criticized the Taliban.

Commentaries, in the form of regular and guest columns, provided particular leeway for writers to explain the importance of the Universal Declaration to women. One by the United Food and Commercial Workers' Union in Canada and circulated on the Canada News Wire on 9 December, announced the group's initiatives for the coming year. Included in the discussion were the recommendations from its Women's Advisory Committee for workplace policies to stop sexual harassment and other problems particularly affecting women. Another, authored by Anne Hoiberg, president of the UN Association of San Diego, appeared in the San Diego *Union-Tribune* on 10 December. In her piece, Hoiberg reiterated the wide range of human rights violations suffered by women and children in the United States and explained why Congress's adoption of CEDAW would help to protect women's rights and freedoms.

Conclusion

There are several points to be made about the foregoing analysis. First, the dearth of substantial women-related coverage surrounding the fiftieth anniversary of the Universal Declaration is clearly troubling, given thirty years of global feminism that have revealed, analyzed, and redressed the wide-ranging violations of women's human rights everywhere. Are reporters not paying attention? Is one left to believe that women's lives and political activities are no more newsworthy today than they were at the dawn of modern feminism? What should we make of the fact that only about three hundred stories containing the terms "human rights, women, and Universal Declaration" surfaced in a sea of thousands of stories in news databases, and that such a miniscule number—about twelve—contained any in-depth information or perspectives reflecting feminist analyses of women's problems or solutions? Women's experience clearly did not figure prominently in news definitions of the fiftieth anniversary. That fact makes a statement about mainstream journalism's narrow and persistently sexist view of news. News today continues to have a gender-specific interest, and that interest is male. Reporting occurred within and represented the traditional "news net" of male-dominated agencies, forums, and events—defined by Tuchman (1978a) more than two decades earlier. The result is that women's real and present human rights problems, views, and political action were marginalized to the point of near invisibility. We can conclude that at least in its coverage of the Universal Declaration's fiftieth anniversary, mainstream news in English and Spanish continued its longstanding pattern of symbolically annihilating women.[5]

Second, though few in number, several excellent articles about women and human rights did emerge in this analysis. As the examples above illustrate, these articles were sophisticated in their use of copious data and real-life human dramas to illustrate the meaning of human rights in women's lives. In mainstream news industries that still clearly marginalize women in coverage, we might look to these examples of what is *possible* when gatekeepers consider the gender dimensions of "human rights" more often. The task falls to feminist media scholars to learn more about the consciousness of the writers and other gatekeepers involved in bringing these to print, as well as the role of newsroom policies and other routines (the structural factors associated with the profession) that shaped the context within which they worked. Indeed, there were both male and female bylines on these exemplary articles. At least two of the articles (those by Boschi for *El Clarín*) appeared in a newspaper owned by a female whose tenure coincides exactly with the years of global feminism. What were the gender and political consciousness of the female and male writers and editors at the other news organizations? How can human agency intervene in structures of power on women's behalf?

Even with these signs of feminism's limited intervention and the hope they convey, we must return to fundamental concerns about the role of gender in the political economy of news. None of the articles examined in this study—even those concerned primarily with women—raised larger questions about the gendered nature of political and economic structures within which human rights (women's in particular) are violated. The patriarchal context within which underpaid female union workers were exploited in Canada and females are denied the right to be educated or to work in Afghanistan went unexamined. These structural concerns, absent from news reporting in general, were particularly evident in the news and commentary on the Universal Declaration of Human Rights' fiftieth anniversary.

Feminist media scholarship can support feminist political action to strengthen women's ability to speak in the public sphere in several ways. One of these is by continuing to document the quantity and quality of news and information relevant to women so that feminists can mark progress as well as the persistence of omission. A second is by making connections between such coverage, or representation, and the financial and policy contexts within which coverage is defined and produced. In an era of globalization, where male financial and political power continues to grow stronger, feminist scholarship must expand its commitment to problematize women's marginalization within the political economy of world capitalism. A third is by deepening our research questions about the role of human agency in social change and looking to the moments and sites where smart, committed reporters and other gatekeepers have helped women to speak. A fourth is by examining the ways in which women-owned and feminist-oriented media, particularly new online listservs and news services, help to circulate oppositional analyses and information about women, as compared to mainstream print and broadcast sources. Women's new media collectively represent parallel communicative structures whose potential has not yet been examined systematically.

Radical feminist strategies to transform patriarchal world capitalism must include both intermediate and long-range objectives, with women's ability to speak more often and more forcefully a central component.

Notes

The author thanks Alejandra Ferreira-Sachero for her research assistance, particularly in the early stages of this project.

1. Marx contended that those who own the means of production also control the ideas circulated. This is perhaps articulated most clearly in his *German Ideology*, coauthored with Friedrich Engels in 1846. Similarly, U.S. women's rights leader Susan B. Anthony (1820–1906) is credited with saying that as long as newspapers and magazines are controlled by men, women's ideas and deepest convictions will be prevented from reaching the public (quoted in Gallagher 1987, 11). Such analysis subtly defines a dialectical process in which the media serve as sites of production (for ideas and meanings), as well as the battleground for control of that production. The struggle presumably occurs between

wealthy elite owners and marginalized groups, e.g., women. Feminist media critiques and agendas for reform have traditionally followed this thinking.

2. One case in point is Patricia Aufderheide's book *Telecommunications Policy and the Public Interest* (1999), the definitive analysis of the Telecommunictions Act of 1996, which omits any consideration of gender.

3. SEM was part of the New Delhi–based Women's Feature Service until April 1999 (Aguilar 1999).

4. While this study reports only those stories that did mention females and human rights, however minimally, we should acknowledge that the news media in general used the occasion of the fiftieth anniversary to generate a range of important stories. For instance, the U.S. agenda-setting newspaper, the *New York Times,* ran four stories with human rights themes between 8 and 10 December, but none of them mentioned women and only one of them quoted a female source—the conservative former head of state in Britain, Margaret Thatcher, who said she believed it was a "grave mistake" for her nation to try to extradite General Pinochet (Hoge 1998). The omission of gender is perhaps all the more remarkable when we consider that two of the four *Times* authors were female. Barbara Crossette's story from the United Nations in New York City concerned the General Assembly's decision to list antisemitism as a form of racism, and Harvard Law School professor Mary Ann Glendon's guest commentary chastised the UN for failing to punish those who had committed atrocities in Sudan. Both pieces lent themselves to inclusion of how women's human rights had been violated, but neither author used the occasion to shine a light on this dimension of her subject. None of these four items was counted within the sample examined here because they did not include women.

5. For a full discussion of the concept of the "symbolic annihilation of women" see Tuchman (1978b).

III

In the Private Sphere: Entertainment, Identity, Consumption

11. Weighing the Transgressive Star Body of Shelley Duvall
Justin Wyatt

> Economics, however, is another story, one that is just beginning for
> feminism. Wonder why. Is money, and a field mapped by numbers,
> presumed to be neutral? Or too symbolic for women? Within film,
> economic history has been written from within both market and
> Marxist premises. Rarely are these biases noted, even by feminist
> econo-historians—to say nothing of positing a feminist economic
> history of cinema.
>
> **—Patricia Mellencamp, *A Fine Romance***

Patricia Mellencamp's provocative musings draw attention to the
paucity of film scholarship addressing the intersection of film, feminism, and industry. However, as she suggests, the scholarship in the
area of industry studies is complicated even further by perceived divisions between market and Marxist models, industrial and cultural
models. The conjunction of cultural- and political-economic analysis
has created a great deal of discussion within both disciplines. Indeed, as
part of the heated *Critical Studies in Mass Communication* colloquy on
the dialogue between cultural studies and political economy, Graham
Murdock (1995) suggests that political economy "mostly works at a
structural level," yet he offers a convincing case for the viability of a
critical political economy tracing the connections between production,
consumption, and representation. Working from this perspective, I
shall investigate a case study from the film industry illustrating the ways
through which production, consumption, and representation are intertwined in the career of a second-tier star, Shelley Duvall. Certainly a
vast literature exists tracing the institutional/economic rationale and
social significance for stars, the principal form of human capital in any
commercial Hollywood film.[1] However, I am interested in Duvall precisely because her stardom is marginal, a unique case that nevertheless
illustrates the power of hegemonic and patriarchal forces within the independent film world and the manner through which identity politics
can be converted into a commodity form.

Duvall's stardom cannot be separated from director Robert Altman, who guided the actress through the majority of her films during the 1970s. While the ongoing association of male director/female star has been present throughout film history—from Lillian Gish/D.W. Griffith, Marlene Dietrich/Josef von Sternberg, to Diane Keaton/Woody Allen— most of these teams received attention for their work in mainstream, commercial entertainment. As these pairings demonstrate, gender structures the division of labor between male auteur and female actor. Indeed, the possibility of female auteur partnered with a male star is a virtual impossibility in domestic or international cinema.[2] A leading iconoclast during a period of retrenchment in the mainstream industry, Altman was able to establish a market identity partly through developing a repertory company of actors, with Duvall as the most important member. An examination of Duvall's period of stardom during the 1970s therefore reveals both industrial and representational factors of interest for a critical political economy. From the perspective of the industry, Duvall's star image, under the close guidance of Altman, demonstrates one of the structures inherent in establishing the auteur identity and, in commercial terms, Altman's "brand name" necessary for critical and at times popular support. From the perspective of identity politics, Duvall's stardom, focused primarily on her extremely thin body, mirrors the popular fascination of the time with thinness, as well as the possibility for variation within the norms of female attractiveness. If we examine the connection between these two issues, Duvall's stardom illustrates the "institutional negotiations" that Lisbet van Zoonen suggests are at play within feminist representations from the dominant media. Indeed, the categories of "independent," "ingenue," "ideal body shape," and "star director" are problematized and complicated through the curious star figure of Shelley Duvall.

Appropriating Thinness: Constructing the Star Image of Shelley Duvall

Ponder a range of descriptions attached to Shelley Duvall by journalists—"a flawed beauty, too thin, eyes too big, slightly protruding front teeth," "a bean-pole bombshell," "big, wide eyes in a narrow face, two prominent front teeth, and a Modigliani figure." "Start with two huge brown eyes. Add buck teeth and a pair of ears that, well, let's face it, they stick out. Put all this on top of a very skinny 5'8" frame, and what do you come up with? Shelley Duvall" (Lovell 1977, 191; Armstrong 1981, 121; Jahr 1977, 41; Scherman 1980, 168). In positioning Shelley Duvall, numerous popular magazines and newspapers have felt compelled to foreground her physical features in their profiles of the actress. This strategy reflects the intimate connection between Duvall's stardom and her body—more precisely, Duvall's painfully thin, tall physique and her "unremarkable" face and pronounced teeth.

During the height of Duvall's stardom in the mid-1970s, several stars, both female and male, evidenced a wider range of physical types and attractiveness than during the Golden Age of Hollywood, echoing an apparently greater acceptance for deviations from the traditional norms of physical beauty within society of the period. Nevertheless, Duvall's star image illustrates the limits of such deviations. While Duvall's physical characteristics differed from those of the typical ingenue, the threat posed by these differences became an increasingly obvious part of her star image. By 1980 the contradictory impulses—to appreciate her difference and to diminish the same difference—effectively halted Duvall's career as a leading lady. Guided by Robert Altman, Duvall's star image illuminates at least three significant features of commercial American filmmaking of the period: the passing interest by Hollywood in different body types, albeit an interest that masked an inherent hostility; the ability of the film industry to construct those of different body types as marketable through being unusual, exotic, and distinctive; and the continuing power of the dyad of male director/female star reinforcing a division of labor along gender lines. Duvall's stardom and body and the threat contained by both were ultimately contained by Hollywood within a single decade.

Duvall became a favored member of Altman's repertory company, appearing in seven of his films from 1970 to 1980: *Brewster McCloud* (1970), *McCabe and Mrs. Miller* (1971), *Thieves Like Us* (1974), *Nashville* (1975), *Buffalo Bill and the Indians* (1976), *Three Women* (1977), and *Popeye* (1980).[3] Although she did appear in a few other projects (*Annie Hall,* Joan Micklin Silver's *Bernice Bobs Her Hair*), the majority of her acting in the decade was under the direction of Altman. Accordingly, Altman was in a unique position to mold the image of Duvall as he desired. Altman's filmmaking is primarily iconoclastic, defined by the desire to break the conventions of the classical Hollywood model in design, structure, and aesthetics. Duvall functions as yet another means for Altman to break the model of classical Hollywood storytelling. Altman's experiments in genre, sound design, and narrative structure severed his connection to the classical Hollywood invisibility of style. His deeply self-conscious filmmaking continually reminds the viewer of the constructed world of the film through inversions of standard genre conventions, self-reflexive stylistic flourishes (e.g., zoom shots, musical commentary on the dramatic action), and the use of a repertory company of actors (e.g., Duvall, Keith Carradine, Michael Murphy, Paul Dooley, Geraldine Chaplin). The experimentation extends to acting and casting. Structured improvisation contributes key scenes to many films; Duvall, for instance, wrote the majority of Millie's extended monologues in *Three Women*. And, as Maurice Yacowar (1980) notes, Altman casts via a repertory company based on the director's "personal reading" of the individual actor or actress. While Altman's personal reading of Duvall may be, as Yacowar claims, located in "the tension between worldliness and naivete," Duvall functions simultaneously as "the most improbable femme fatale" at the center of a genre narrative.[4] Consequently, Duvall's physical appearance is employed for its ability to shatter one more convention of Hollywood storytelling.

Duvall did contribute to the status of Altman as auteur, a label that has meaning in both aesthetic and institutional/industrial terms. By creating a market identity (or perceived market identity) through a distinctive style and a repertory company, Altman was able to offer a differentiated product within the studio system of the early 1970s. His institutional power during this period was considerable; from 1970 to 1975, Altman directed eight films for six different studios. This prolific output is even more impressive given the lack of commercial success of these ventures (of the eight movies, only *M*A*S*H, Nashville,* and *California Split* broke even). Altman's ability to present and promote himself as an auteur derived from two major factors: the box-office triumph of *M*A*S*H* in 1970, with studios hoping for another subversive crowd-pleaser; and the economic depression experienced by the studios in the first half of the decade, leaving the door open to more experimental and unconventional filmmaking such as Altman's.[5]

Altman's frequent casting of Shelley Duvall and his perverse rendering of her star image cemented his own identity as a rebellious director contemptuous of studio norms for building stars. In Duvall's debut film, the iconoclastic comedy *Brewster McCloud,* Brewster (Bud Cort) constructs a set of wings to fulfill his dream of flying, ironically within his covered home of the Houston Astrodome. Duvall is cast as the ingenue, Suzanne Heap, a hippie femme fatale who seduces the virginal Brewster, betrays his confidences to the police, and subsequently leaves him for an upwardly mobile political assistant. Her physical appearance emphasizes the outrageous, from her ultra-mini skirts to her heavy use of mascara, which makes her expressive and large eyes pop from her slender head. Although a complete novice as an actress, Duvall explained her casting as ingenue Suzanne in the following manner: "Maybe it was that I have big teeth and big ears and the fact that I had on patched blue jeans and little bells around my waist and that I looked bird-like and *Brewster McCloud* has to do with birds" (Shalit 1977, 8). The comparison is apt for suggesting the immediate connection between Duvall's physical appearance and a certain deviation from the body shape of the traditional female ingenue. The positioning of Duvall as birdlike is strengthened diegetically through the device of a lecturer (René Auberjonois) coyly classifying each of the characters into various species of birds. As the lecturer provocatively describes Suzanne attempting a seduction, "The low-footed Booby will compete for the attention of her intended by goose-stepping in front of him, raising her bright blue feet as high as she can, and thrusting out her chest." In her film debut, Duvall is presented as peculiar, duplicitous, and highly sexual, all of these characteristics anchored by a physical dimension.

After *Brewster McCloud,* Duvall plays a bit role as a mail-order bride in Altman's revisionist Western *McCabe and Mrs. Miller* and the romantic lead, a Depression-era southern girlfriend of a small-time hood, in *Thieves Like Us.* Both roles place Duvall in a sexual context, calling attention to her body in scenes of romance and domesticity. In the richly atmospheric turn-of-the-century frontier world of *McCabe,* Duvall plays Mrs. Coyle, a young, immature widow forced to join the forces of Mrs. Miller, the town madam in Presbyterian Church. In one of the only extended scenes involving Duvall's character, madam Mrs. Miller (Julie Christie) pins Duvall's negligee, while lecturing her on the routine of sex in the whorehouse and commenting on Duvall's thin, gangly body—"you're small, just like me," Mrs. Miller concludes on inspection of Duvall. The body becomes the defining trait for the character in other significant ways within the film. Especially compared to the bubbly Suzanne in *Brewster McCloud,* Duvall's Mrs. Coyle is almost mute, petrified by her shyness and her unfamiliarity with frontier life. The remarkably quiet young whore is continually featured in group situations with the other prostitutes, who are similarly outside the range of "traditional" feminine beauty through deviations in such traits as age (old), size (very large), and ethnicity. Consequently, given the lack of dialogue and the tendency to "read" the character in terms of the other prostitutes, Duvall's body becomes even more important in establishing her character.

Three years after *McCabe*, Altman increases Duvall's visibility considerably with a leading role in *Thieves Like Us* centering on the ill-fated affair between escaped prisoner Bowie (Keith Carradine) and Keechie (Duvall). Matching Carradine with Duvall for physical similarities (thin, plain featured, awkward), the couple-on-the-run are designed to erase any illusion of glamour from the typical noir protagonists.[6] For the majority of the action, Duvall occupies her time caring for Bowie, who becomes her first lover. Altman again chooses to focus on Duvall's body, this time in a lengthy bathtub scene featuring upper-torso nudity. The bathtub scene by itself earned the film a Restricted rating from the MPAA, yet Altman refused to cut the nude shots. As he explains, in a frank and crass manner tipping the balance of power toward the male auteur and away from the actress, "I would never in a million years have done a nude scene with a girl who had big tits and all the conventional sexual equipment. But with Shelley, I was trying to point out her boyishness to underscore the innocence of their love affair" (Jahr 1977, 41). Although the nudity is placed in a domestic context, the length of the scene and the multiple front and back views of Duvall emphasize her thinness and the length of her body. The androgyny is also underlined textually with Carradine commenting that Duvall's character is "hairy," but quickly adding that he enjoys that quality.

In the second half of the 1970s, Altman continues to situate Duvall in scenes emphasizing the physical, albeit increasingly in a contemporary context. In *Nashville*, Duvall plays groupie L.A. Joan, another fish-out-of-water parallel to Mrs. Coyle. Visiting her aunt and uncle in the conservative country music capital, L.A. Joan uses the opportunity to careen from affair to affair, avoiding a visit to her sick aunt in the hospital throughout the entire film. As she arrives at the Nashville airport, Duvall's L.A. Joan exposes much skin with her tank top and hot pants. Laconic rock star Tom (Keith Carradine) exclaims, "Jesus, you oughta stop that diet before you ruin yourself!" The comment seems as much flirtation as a thinly veiled attempt to suggest that L.A. Joan suffers from anorexia. Throughout the film, L.A. Joan is presented as a chameleon, switching names (her given name is Martha) and altering identities, especially with wigs and make-up.[7] Through these various incarnations, L.A. Joan is able to remake her identity, effectively trying on different looks and styles to match different environments. Altman also equates L.A. Joan's interest in fashion with her powerful sexual desire—the character dresses to seduce, preferably one of the rich and famous. Narratively, both emphases on fashion and sexuality are treated in negative terms: the character's fascination with both blinds her to the needs of her aged uncle and prevents her from visiting her dying aunt even once. For L.A. Joan, style and sexuality take precedence over family responsibilities and obligations. The attention to the physical is underlined because L.A. Joan, like Duvall's Mrs. Coyle, is silent through much of the film: always on the periphery of action, L.A. Joan speaks through her fashion combination and choice of partner for the night.

After a bit part in *Buffalo Bill and the Indians,* Duvall gained more prominence in April 1977 with appearances in Woody Allen's *Annie Hall* and Altman's *Three Women.*[8] The *Annie Hall* role amounts to an extension of Duvall as L.A. Joan, a flaky *Rolling Stone* reporter who beds Allen, describing the experience as a "Kafkaesque experience." The match between Duvall's body and sexual experimentation is expressed more fully, however, with *Three Women.* Duvall stars as Millie Lammoreaux, a superficially glamorous therapist in a Palm Springs rehabilitation and geriatric center. Millie is constructed entirely through the media: fashion magazines, self-help books, and television talk shows combine to create a perfectly artificial character. Millie's routine at the Purple Sage Apartments is similarly carefully orchestrated with intricate recipe cards (ordered by the amount of cooking time entailed), dinner parties, and mixers at the pool, all events color coordinated with purples, yellows, and plastic flowers. Ignored by virtually all her coworkers and neighbors, Millie's facade is met on occasion with contempt: as her "friends" remark when a want-to-be chic Millie descends the apartment stairs en route to the pool party, "Watch out, here comes 'Thoroughly Modern Millie.'" Whereas Altman continues to place Duvall in scenes that emphasize her body either in a domestic or sexual context, with *Three Women* he offers Duvall a fully developed character continually humiliated by her lack of self-consciousness. By aligning Millie so clearly with contemporary fashion and sexual practices, Altman presents Duvall—and her body—derisively as a cultural model from a specific time and place.

Similarly, Duvall is reduced solely to the physical as the cartoon character Olive Oyl in *Popeye.*[9] In playing Olive Oyl, Duvall is presenting a literally flattened version of her own body—and Altman emphasizes her thinness and gangly quality by having Duvall crane her neck as much as possible, thereby stretching her body even further. As in the other Altman films, textually, Duvall's body shape orients much of the action. Consider Olive's first song, a lament titled "He's Large," listing all of her suitor's flaws and citing his physical dimensions so different from hers time and time again. The separation between Millie Lammoreaux and Olive Oyl is remarkably fine. Olive Oyl embodies all of the awkward, self-involved, and unselfconscious qualities of the *Three Women* heroine. Popeye's mumbling, incoherent musings on life offer little humor and he is presented as the straight man to Duvall's Oyl. The pratfalls and embarrassments are matched with Olive Oyl's overwhelming sense of her own desirability; as Duvall describes the character, "You're talking about someone who just happens to be one hundred and one percent woman" (Scherman 1980, 169). Olive Oyl's affections are torn between Bluto and Popeye—a battle that she heartily encourages throughout the film. Playing Olive Oyl returned Duvall to the cliché of the skinny, maladroit ugly duckling without the variations and shadings apparent in her previous roles. As a result, instead of complicating the stereotype, Duvall endorses it fully, erasing some of the contradictions present in her other roles. With *Popeye,* the physical threat of Duvall—in terms of body shape, size, and appearance—was dismantled by Hollywood through equating her with the hyperbolic cartoon body of Olive Oyl.

While all the Duvall roles emphasize the physical and the sexual, there is an increasing emphasis on humiliation and embarrassment across the decade. With the early roles, Altman remains neutral in his presentation of Duvall. The self-centered seductress of *Brewster McCloud* fits in the film's skewed world view—her eccentricity and self-absorption are just part of the framework. With *McCabe and Mrs. Miller* and *Thieves Like Us,* Duvall's presentation as a sexual being is negotiated by the physical setting (turn-of-the century frontier life, Depression-era Mississippi) and her social roles (whore by necessity, naïve girlfriend). A shift occurs, however, with the next three films. Altman begins to offer a causal relationship between the character's desire and her humiliation—she is made to suffer for her sexual feelings and her attempts to present herself as attractive.

Women's Cinema, Women's Bodies

Duvall's function as brand name and marker for Altman's auteurism correlates with the popular fascination with the thin body in the late 1960s and early 1970s. The harbinger of this trend was model Twiggy, who set the stage for the attractive ultra-thin body. In this trajectory, Duvall's stardom reflects the move toward a more diverse range of female Hollywood stars and correlates with a shift in the ideal body type presented by the media. While the 1950s were ruled by the curvaceous beauty of Monroe, the 1960s began the retreat to a thinner look for the American woman, eventually transforming into "the ultra-slender ideal" for women's body size. As the sociologist Sharlene Hesse-Biber (1996, 28) explains this change in the late 1960s, "Yet as women gained economic, social and political resources for charting their own destinies, the pressure to shrink in body size again returned. The media began to play a dominant role in this pressure." Within the media, fashion photography, television, and women's magazines served to establish this pivotal shift.[10]

Perhaps most significant as a beacon of this shift was the media explosion, circa 1967, over the 17-year-old, 91-pound, 5-foot-6-inch Cockney model Twiggy. The American media, in particular, were simultaneously confounded and fascinated by the possibilities offered by Twiggy.[11] Consider a national cover story (10 April 1967) that characterizes the figure of Twiggy in the following tortured manner: "Four straight limbs in search of a woman's body, a mini-bosom trapped in perpetual puberty, the frail torso of the teen-age choirboy" ("Twiggy: Click! Click!" 1967, 62). In reporting the assessment of Beatrix Miller, editor of British *Vogue,* that "She's exactly the right look at the right time," the writer counters with, "The right look is seventeen and starved" (65). Rated the "most beautiful woman in the world" by visitors to Madame Tussaud's London wax museum, Twiggy queried several parameters of female sexuality and attractiveness of the time through blurring the distinction between child and adult, male and female, as well as emaciated and skinny. By the early 1970s, the impact of Twiggy and the ultraslender ideal was revealed through fashion trends: as Joan Jacobs Brumberg (1997) notes, the bra top and low-slung shorts of the early 1970s responded to "an increasing tolerance for the extremely thin bodies." Within the media, the presence of Shelley Duvall echoed many of the confusions evident in Twiggy, particularly the thinness accentuated by an androgynous and youthful quality.

Both body weight and body shape are, of course, ideologically loaded, and the alteration toward a more thin figure helps to enhance the already dominant value of thin-as-beautiful and fat-as-ugly. As Helen Malson, a psychologist, explains, this normalization occurs in large part through our cultural narratives and romantic fictions that posit the beautiful (thin/slim) heroine who will be rewarded with the man of her dreams, a comfortable house, and a perfect marriage (1998, 106–07). Such discourse romanticizes the thin body, equating it with female beauty that can then be used to secure heterosexual romance and financial security. Implicitly this model offers a space only for the thin woman; those falling outside thinness cannot be assured of being attractive enough to secure an appropriate male partner. The prevalence of eating disorders among young women has been widely attributed to this media construction. Cognizant of these mass media "fables," feminists of the period countered the equation of the attractive woman as thin—consider Susie Orbach's *Fat Is a Feminist Issue,* published in 1978, or more recently Naomi Wolf's *The Beauty Myth,* published in 1991. The call-to-action became producing images within the media to combat "thin as beautiful."

How does Duvall enter into the body culture of the 1970s? Certainly her thin body capitalizes on the fascination with thinness in the larger social realm, and, at first glance, Duvall might be considered an extension of Twiggy in an American context. But Duvall's place is actually more tenuous and her star image more threatening to the norm than that of the innocuous Twiggy. Whereas Twiggy's soft features and innocence are prominently featured in magazine profiles (mentioning, for example, that she still lives at home with her parents, and showing photos of Twiggy cuddling with her soft toys), the image for Duvall is more explicitly sexual. Duvall's angular body and face are continually presented within a sexual context in scenes featuring her as the able sexual aggressor. Twiggy, on the other hand, despite her unusual physique, developed her acting career along the more traditional lines of female ingenue through debuting as the shy, yet talented understudy in Ken Russell's musical spectacle *The Boyfriend* (1971) ("The English Dream," 1972, 56). Illustrating the varied meanings of the term "model," Twiggy acts as a visual hanger for new fashion designed for the thin body, at the same time that she fulfills many of the traditional roles assigned to young women: dutiful and respectful daughter; longtime girlfriend for manager Justin DeVilleneuve; modest, devoted subject of the industry that makes her completely available for visual consumption. Duvall's position is more subversive, calling attention to the extreme thinness of her body through scanty costumes and nude scenes. In fact, she often appears as simultaneously a paradigm for the counterculture and, through the humiliation of her characters, as a critique of the same.

Duvall's incipient stardom occurred at the same time that articles were proclaiming the role of "the New Woman" in Hollywood. Critic Molly Haskell (1974, 327–28) assessed the bleak situation for women in the earlier part of the decade in the following way: "But, even these, the great women's roles of the decade, what are they for the most part? Whores, quasi-whores, jilted mistresses, emotional cripples, drunks. Daffy ingenues, Lolitas, kooks, sex-starved spinsters, psychotics. Icebergs, zombies, and ballbreakers. That's what little girls of the sixties and seventies are made of." Commercially, women commanded little respect at the box office as well: in 1976, only one actress (thirteen-year-old Tatum O'Neal) was cited on the list of top-ten box-office attractions. After a decade of male buddy movies *(The Sting, Butch Cassidy and the Sundance Kid, Scarecrow, California Split)* and reactionary crime melodramas (the *Dirty Harry* series, *The French Connection, Serpico*), leaving little room for female representation of any kind, several commercial films in the 1977–78 season addressed issues of particular relevance to women.

The emergence of "the New Woman" in Hollywood was undoubtedly a fabrication of hopeful media critics, yet the period of the late 1970s did offer a spate of films addressed primarily to a female audience: *Julia, The Turning Point, The Other Side of Midnight, The Goodbye Girl, Looking for Mr. Goodbar, An Unmarried Woman*. While feminist filmmakers such as Yvonne Rainer had been addressing issues such as female friendship, sexual experimentation, and the conflicting demands of career vs. family for several years, these concerns were debated for the first time in films from the major studios receiving saturation releases. Of course, the motivation for this inclusion was first and foremost commercial, with the major studios attempting to secure a "new" audience during a period of economic downturn. As Twentieth Century-Fox's Gareth Wigan explained the trend, "Our research indicates a large public awareness that women have been left out of movies. There are dramas, conflicts, situations that have been neglected while we've been concentrating on men and action-adventures. By leaving out women, we've left out half the world's population" (Michener 1977, 61).

While Duvall was caught up in this media frenzy, receiving a mention as one of *Newsweek*'s "New Faces of '77," several other young actresses breaking the mold of the prototypical ingenue also received significant press, including Talia Shire, who played the "ugly duckling heroine" Adrian in *Rocky*; Candy Clark, the "dizzy blonde" in *American Graffiti*; and Sissy Spacek, Duvall's costar in *Three Women*. Spacek, the cover star for the *Newsweek* article, offered a more accessible media figure than Duvall, but was trangressive nonetheless compared to the glamorous female stars of the studio era. Small (5 feet 2 inches), deeply freckled, withdrawn, and distinguished by a broad accent betraying her Quitman, Texas, roots, Spacek negotiated the space between experimental projects portraying her as a quirky child-woman (*Welcome to L.A., Three Women*) and more traditional genre-based films. Undoubtedly, her star image grew strongly from her portrayal in *Carrie* of the eponymous protagonist, a wallflower with telekinetic powers who transforms momentarily into a prom queen. Critics such as Charles Michener (1977, 63) offered caveats on her star power ("her 'girlishness' and 'Texas twang' may be too limiting to warrant the label of major stardom"). Yet the genuine transformation of Spacek in *Carrie* to queen of the prom indicated that Spacek was capable of generating adequate sexual allure in a manner that Duvall could not.

The Political Economy of the Body Duvall

At the most basic commercial level, the icon of the thin actress humbled within the narrative responds to a potent economic rationale by offering an alternative to the traditional femme fatale and by lending a coherence to the director's oeuvre for building a (cult) fan base. By creating films in contrast to the norms of the studio products, the director illuminates these norms of conventional studio filmmaking. As Peter Golding and Graham Murdock (1991) suggest, a political economy of media texts can demonstrate how specific media representations are linked to the commercial factors at play in both the production and consumption of the texts. For Altman, presenting an ingenue as painfully thin and plain augments the deviations in narrative and narration characteristic of their films. The emphasis on the body physicalizes the difference of the director's style, offering visible evidence of the auteur's unique vision of the world. Casting Duvall in roles that betray a consistent reading of the director's understanding of the actress allows the director to fully shape the image of the actress in the public realm. Consequently, the auteur director replaces the studio system by essentially entering into a long-term "contract" with the actress through casting her in roles that build in a sustained manner across time. Other actors, working for a variety of directors, have the freedom to vary their choice of roles, although a coherent public image may be more difficult to establish given a diversity of acting choices.

With Duvall, the economic motivation might also be to capitalize on the fascination with thinness in fashion, selling Duvall, as one reviewer described her, as "the Texas Twiggy." Such a reading has some merit but misses the deeper psychological dynamics operating in Duvall's star image. The combination of Duvall's height with her thinness effects an androgyny, blurring the lines between male and female. Helen Malson (1998, 114) explains that the thin woman can be read as a rejection of traditional gender distinctions: "[The female body] resists a patriarchally imposed feminine identity and can thus be 'read' as signifying a quasi-feminist, 'liberated' subjectivity of the late twentieth century." Such an anxiety is multiplied by Altman's continually placing Duvall in sexual situations, in effect forcing the viewer to consider the androgynous woman as an aggressive sexual being. Robert Self identifies the unusual spectatorial position in his description of Duvall appearing naked in *Thieves Like Us*. For Self, Duvall's presence reflects Altman's perspective of social alienation: "Unable to see her as an erotic object, the spectator experiences the social dichotomies between the pathetic body as subject and the beautiful body as object; the viewer focuses reflexively the distance between the pleasurable looking afforded by romance even in a film noir and the painful (almost embarrassed) looking afforded by the Altman text."

Is this equation to be interpreted as Altman's progressive gender politics, expanding the possibilities for sexual representation on screen? Possibly, but such a reading fails to account for many episodes in which female sexuality is interrogated and often humiliated within the Altman films (first and foremost may be the uncovering of Hot Lips Houlihan in the shower for all the cast members of *M*A*S*H*). Altman's "track record" with gay characters is even more dubious; frequently gays are offered as comic stereotypes for the protagonist's macho jokes (e.g., *O.C. & Stiggs, California Split, A Wedding*). Perhaps the most apt parallel to Duvall's presentation is the Karen Black character Joe/Joanna, in Altman's *Come Back to the Five and Dime, Jimmy Dean, Jimmy Dean* (1982): a postoperative transsexual alienated from both the straight and gay worlds given her sexual ambivalence and androgyny. Duvall, like Joe/Joanna, becomes a sexual oddity whose striking physical features become yet another label for Altman's oeuvre, just like the overlapping soundtracks and zoom shots. Altman turns Duvall into an icon of the eccentric and iconoclastic that he embraces both within the cinematic texts and through his cinematic style, yet this kind of representation is flavored by the humiliations experienced by the Duvall characters narratively. These humiliations function to distance Altman from a full endorsement of Duvall and her difference from the norms of traditional female beauty. As her career progresses, the films increasingly function to defuse this difference, punishing and eradicating Duvall's uniqueness.

Altman's usage of Duvall recalls Mikhail Bakhtin's concept of the grotesque, which is often utilized within feminist media criticism to define female figures outside the boundaries of dominant social norms. The results of these trangressions vary considerably. For Kathleen Rowe (1995, 32–34), the grotesque is invoked in the form of the "unruly woman," excessive, fat, and a liminal figure between life and death. The unruly woman—from Roseanne to Miss Piggy—inspires conflicted audience reactions of delight and uneasiness. Most significantly, the full-bodied, boisterous comic figures present an opportunity for transgression for their audience, both female and male. While Duvall similarly inspires conflicted reactions from the audience, ultimately her threat is less potent than that of the unruly woman. Gaylyn Studlar's description of Divine's functioning as grotesque in the John Waters films seems to be a more appropriate point of comparison for Duvall. Studlar (1991, 146) argues that Divine, the grossly overweight transsexual playing female roles within the narratives, actually reinforces the dominant social and sexual order through grotesque and hyperbolic appearance: "The antierotic, parodic treatment of Divine guarantees that the position of the heterosexual male viewer will not be made problematic. . . . He can safely enjoy Divine's 'feminine' outrages against social and sexual convention while using the figure of the grotesque wo/man to confirm his own perfection in masculine normality."

This devaluation of Duvall occurs at the same time that the larger culture is shifting its feminine ideal to a leaner, tougher, more athletic body. As Sharlene Hesse-Biber (1996, 45) charts this shift, "Getting in shape with exercise is now considered an essential part of a healthful lifestyle and the 1980s brought a more muscular ideal of the female body. The subcutaneous fat layer, which gives softness to the female physique, disappeared in favor of large, hard muscles." The ultraslender ideal transformed into the toned body, tight and taut rather than merely thin. While the reasons for this transformation were debated within feminist media circles, the powerful and lean body was considered to be indicative of a feminism joining physical, emotional, and psychological strength. Jane M. Ussher (1997, 51) underlines this stance by citing women stating that they are working out "for themselves" rather than to bolster attractiveness to the opposite sex. Ussher correctly points out that this shift should not be judged too positively: the possibility of sculpting the body to perfection can be just as damaging as developing a very thin body. Not coincidentally, the rise of the sculpted body correlates perfectly with the increased visibility of plastic surgery and the introduction of liposuction to help achieve these goals. Within the media, this change was realized in several ways, from the relatively minor (Barbra Streisand aerobicizing over the credits in *The Main Event*) to those culturally remarkable. In the latter category, Jane Fonda's re-creation as workout guru seems most significant. The transformation was somewhat gradual; by the time of Jane Fonda's New Workout and Weight-Loss Program, the shift was complete toward the more powerful, strong, and in-control body.[12] The new body nevertheless continued to host a series of contradictions: while fat was still anathema to the 1980s body, large breasts were once again in vogue, a problem since the worked-out body tended to reduce breast size. As Patricia Mellencamp (1995, 224) playfully suggests, "breasts now must, like Jane Fonda's, be implanted."

Methodologically, the Shelley Duvall case study illustrates issues that could be described discretely as political-economic (the commerce of the fashionable and of the male auteur) and feminist (the role accorded to the female star in the director/star dyad, the representation of the female body, and the construction of norms of attractiveness) in design. Nevertheless, joining the two approaches immediately reveals a new set of questions and concerns. Two issues appear to be critical: how gender enters into commercial arrangements and functions as a commodity within the marketplace, and how social structures impact the construction of media texts through the accommodation of industrial dictates and constraints. Both are necessary for a full understanding of both Duvall's star image and indeed the complex relationship between the star, the female body, and the motion picture industry.

The form of Duvall's containment, both within the cinematic texts and within the industry, certainly continues in contemporary media. On the other end of the body-shape spectrum, Camryn Manheim's star image illustrates just how much body size still centers media representation. While Duvall's image was shaped mainly by Altman, Manheim (1999), impassioned lawyer Ellenor Frutt from the ABC series *The Practice*, has presented herself on numerous occasions as "the poster child for fat acceptance," leading to her acceptance speech at the 1998 Emmy Awards in which she proclaimed, "This is for all the fat girls!" The *New York Times* succinctly captured the essence of her star image in the title for their Manheim profile, "Not Model-Thin, but a Role Model on TV" (Fritsch 1999, E1). While the controversy over Manheim's size is acknowledged, encouraged, and even marketed by the actress, her size still constitutes enough of a reason for the focus of a magazine or newspaper article—the acting talent and awards receive secondary mention.

As the example of Manheim illustrates, the dominant norms of society still depend on extremes to solidify the position of exactly what is attractive and acceptable for the woman. Duvall's stardom two decades ago demonstrates the same lesson. While superficially inclusion through representation is offered, this inclusion is undercut by the presentation of the character within the narrative. The motivation behind these representations does not vary by origin: with Altman as the creator of Duvall's image, one learns that the independent auteur is just as capable of creating regressive images as the anonymous studio hack. Altman's auteurism and brand identity in the marketplace depend in part on these images of Duvall, both trendy and dramatically outside the realm of conventional ingenue image and behavior. Reinforced by the popular media's focus on her body and a passing interest in addressing feminism as an ignored audience category, Duvall became a pawn for a media resolutely concentrated on a body slightly more voluptuous and an image less sexually aggressive. Duvall's fleeting period of stardom shows that, contrary to popular belief, in Hollywood you can be too thin.

Notes

1. For a discussion of the economic significance of stardom, consult Richard Dyer (1979, 10–12).

2. The single exception to this rule would be Lina Wertmuller and Giancarlo Giannini, frequent collaborators during the 1970s.

3. Duvall was scheduled to appear in Altman's *A Wedding* (1978) as well, but her appearance never materialized for reasons that are unclear. Curiously, Altman had cast her as "the girl next door," a more "normal" role for the actress. Perhaps the clash between the role and Altman's image of Duvall led to her withdrawing from the part. Eventually the role was played by Susan Norman, Paul Newman's daughter (Klemesrud 1977, C19).

4. Helene Keyssar (1991, 19) makes a similar claim for Duvall's functioning in the Altman films, stating that the actress offers the paradigm for "the tension between the glamorous and the pedestrian that causes pain for most of Altman's characters and that identifies them as undeniably American."

5. Justin Wyatt (1996) analyzes the commercial performance of Altman's films from this period against the constuction of Altman as auteur, tracing the economic determinants of Altman's auteurism.

6. As Judith M. Kass (1978, 164) commented on Altman's unusual casting,

"With their look of being permanently leggy, gauche adolescents, their promi- nent teeth and gawky/graceful movements, Carradine and Duvall are virtually typecast as the antithesis of Faye Dunaway and Warren Beatty's 1967 Bonnie Parker and Clyde."

7. In one revealing moment for the character, a physical transformation completely erases her identity: according to the script, "L.A. Joan walks out of the bathroom with a blonde 'natural' wig on and taps Bud on the shoulder. He looks at her, doesn't recognize who she is, and steps aside so she can pass. She gives him a look of disbelief, shrugs and walks off" (Tewkesbury 1976).

8. Duvall's appearance in *Buffalo Bill and the Indians* as the First Lady to President Grover Cleveland (Patrick McCormack) is also presented mainly in terms of her physical difference. Cleveland's husky physique makes his wife appear tiny and frail in contrast, an observation remarked on by characters within the film.

9. In one of the most appalling examples of the mainstream industry's treatment of Duvall, Paramount executive Don Simpson apparently tried to veto the casting of Duvall as Olive Oyl since she was not physically attractive to him. As Altman recalls, "After the [demo] reel finished, Simpson stood up and said, 'Well, I wouldn't want to fuck her. And if I don't want to fuck her, she shouldn't be in the movie'" (Biskind 1998, 370).

10. While the shift to thin-as-beautiful was significant, many of the media representations still portrayed a more conventionally attractive female figure, albeit often in narratives superficially offering female empowerment. As Susan Douglas (1994) notes, the mid-1970s were also the time of *Charlie's Angels, The Bionic Woman, Wonder Woman,* and *Police Woman.*

11. See, for example, "The Arrival of Twiggy" (1967, 33–34); "Twiggy Makes US Styles Swing Too" (1967, 99–100); "Is It a Girl? Is It a Boy? No, It's Twiggy" (1967, 84–90).

12. Hilary Radner (1995) explores Jane Fonda's shifting image and the im- plied body ideal across the range of the Workout videos.

12. Periodical Pleasures: Magazines for U.S. Latinas
Amy Beer

> What does it mean to be Latino? The answer is as individual as
> we are. . . . Being Latino in the United States means having two
> cultures, two sets of traditions and in some cases two different
> languages. But most of all, being Latino should be a great source
> of pride. All of us at *Estylo* magazine are trying to bring you that
> sense of confidence and self-esteem.
>
> —Juana Gallegos

In October 1997 *Estylo* joined *Latina* and *Moderna* in a group of new
magazines targeting women defined by their ethnic consciousness as
"U.S. Latinas."[1] While *Vandidades Continental* and *Cosmopolitan en
Español,* the best-selling Spanish-language women's magazines, aim at
Latin American women interested in the lifestyles of an international
elite, *Latina, Moderna,* and *Estylo* use bilingual editorial and advertising to address women who see themselves as both "Latina" and
"American." A typical issue of each magazine includes profiles of successful Latinas; columns and stories tailored to Latinas on health,
beauty, fashion, and careers; and articles on topics such as intercultur-
al dating, bilingual education, and raising bicultural children.

As publications "by Latinas for Latinas," these periodicals exempli-
fy and diverge from contemporary trends in the media industries. Corporate interests are increasingly aware of the consuming powers and
proclivities of U.S. Latinos, but advertisers still target Latinos mainly
through Spanish-language media. The new magazines are a long-
overdue alternative to two centuries of derogatory media stereotypes,
and they provide a forum for women excluded, not only from the
media, but also from economic and political empowerment as U.S. citizens. Yet advertiser-supported magazines are a core product of the
media industries, as commodities in and of themselves, as commodities
that generate the production of other commodities, and as products
that promote the consumption of still more commodities. In an industry dominated by transnational conglomerates, the new magazines are
published by relatively small, U.S.-based corporations: *Estylo*'s pub-

lisher is an independent firm, Mandalay Publications, based in Los Angeles; *Latina* is published by Essence Corporation, the owner of *Essence*, the first and still the most profitable magazine for African Americans; and *Moderna* was created by the publisher of *Hispanic*, the largest circulation general-interest magazine for U.S. Latinos.

Women's magazines early attracted the attention of U.S. feminists, and a number of important works interrogate the representational practices and industrial history of the medium.[2] This article places the new Latina magazines in the context of the contemporary international magazine industry and considers their production of Latinas for readers and advertisers. My analysis indicates that because the magazines define Latinas primarily as consumers, they are a limited forum for women to explore nonconsumerist identities, challenge hegemony, or express oppositional points of view.

The Contemporary Magazine Industry

The economic structure of the magazine industry encourages reader segmentation and strict control over editorial content. With few exceptions, consumer magazines generate profit mainly from advertising and not from magazine sales, but costs of printing and distribution and readers' insistence on a certain amount of editorial content impose perpetual constraints on the number of ad pages in any magazine. To maximize ad revenues, like all other advertiser-supported media, publishers must demonstrate that their products reach desirable consumers. U.S. women's magazines always segmented readers by gender, race, and class, and, later, by age, and publishers early supported the establishment of an independent agency, the Audit Bureau of Circulation (ABC), to measure circulation and invested in market research to document readers' desires and consuming habits. In addition, contemporary consumer magazines offer advertisers a variety of "value-added" promotions, such as covert ads in the form of product mentions, and, although they are loathe to admit it, tolerate advertiser input into editorial content (Pogrebin 1998a, 1998b).

The consumer magazine industry is highly concentrated. A small number of transnational multimedia conglomerates now own most of the world's magazine publishers.[3] Group publication allows magazines to pool advertising sales and marketing research resources, negotiate jointly with distributors and printers, and offer discounts for multiple advertising buys.[4] Group publishers owned by multimedia conglomerates are also well positioned to survive periodic downturns and benefit from new media outlets. Beginning in the early 1980s, when a general recession, rising paper costs and postal rates, and new electronic media threatened to erode magazines' profitability, conglomerate-owned magazines multiplied their advantages with cross-media discounting and value-added strategies using new media, such as cable television programs and, most recently, Internet channels, based on successful magazine formats and content.[5]

Conglomerates also have advantages in starting new magazines. Descriptions of the magazine industry often portray this sector of mass media as an enduring bastion of entrepreneurial heroism and attribute new magazines' success to a brilliant idea that reaches a previously undiscovered lode of consumers. Launching a new magazine, however, requires not only a good concept, but, even for a limited-circulation periodical, between $5 and $10 million in capital for market research, publication expenses, and promotion (Nuiry 1996, 55). Publishers often give away or deeply discount space to attract advertisers to new magazines; even with paying advertisers, most new magazines lose substantial amounts of money in the first three to four years. And while it might seem that advertisers would support magazines appealing to consumers' interests and identities not targeted by other media, *Folio*, the trade publication of the magazine industry, insists, "One of the best indicators of a new magazine's circulation potential is the pervasiveness of competing magazines" (Sheiman 1994, 130). In the 1970s, as more women began to remain in the paid labor force, publishers tried to capitalize on increased female purchasing power with new magazines for working women, single women, women with an interest in health and dieting, feminists, and African American women. Long-running "service" magazines, which address middle-class women as mothers and homemakers, also revamped themselves to reflect changes in women's lives, and, despite a proliferation of new magazines, these continue to be the most profitable, reaching large circulations and generating enormous advertising revenues.

Magazines for U.S. Latinos

As demographers and market researchers documented the rapid growth in size and purchasing power of the U.S. Latino population, some sectors of the media industries began to tout the untapped potential of this market. Advertiser-supported media aimed at U.S. Latinos have existed since the early twentieth century (Subervi-Vélez et al. 1997), but advertiser spending on Latino-oriented media remains vastly disproportionate to the population's estimated purchasing power, and most advertisers spend their Latino-oriented budgets on Spanish-language television. This has little to do with U.S. Latinos' language and media use and much to do with the needs of advertisers and the political economy of ownership of Spanish-language media. In the 1960s, publishers began to distribute Spanish-language women's magazines in the United States, although these magazines were always aimed at Latin American readers (Salwen and Garrison 1991, 126–27).[6] Presently, Editorial América, a division of the Mexico-based multimedia conglomerate Grupo Televisa since 1992, is the largest global publisher of Spanish-language magazines.[7] Editorial América extensively distributes and promotes its women's magazines, including *Vanidades, Cosmopolitan en Español,* and *Buenhogar* (versions of Hearst's *Cosmopolitan* and *Good Housekeeping*) in the United States.[8] Nevertheless, the company continues to aim its magazines at pan-Continental audiences and to publish only in Spanish, which it justifies based on its own research showing that "four out of every five US Hispanics prefer to speak and read Spanish at home" (Kelly 1997, 14).

Using Spanish also makes business sense because of Editorial América's corporate connections and transnational reach. Unlike most other magazine publishers, Editorial América derives most of its revenues from single-copy magazine sales, since Grupo Televisa owns numerous distribution outlets in Latin America and has preferential access to others (Phillips 1994).[9] Accordingly, Editorial América has little incentive to promote research on Latinos' use of print media, and few of its magazines are audited by the ABC. Editorial América also publishes many of its magazines, including *Buenhogar* and *Cosmo en Español,* as joint ventures, rather than as licensed versions. By publishing in Spanish, Editorial América avoids U.S. competition with partners such as Hearst and with other corporations like Time-Warner, the publisher of *People en Español,* that control U.S. magazine distributors. Moreover, as a subsidiary of Grupo Televisa, Editorial América has another important incentive to promote use of Spanish-language media to reach U.S. Latinos: Televisa's magazine-publishing profits may not depend primarily on advertiser support, but its substantial revenues from U.S. Spanish-language television do.[10]

In the early 1990s, even as the magazine trade press tried to stimulate enthusiasm for U.S. Latinos, it frequently reminded readers of problems in this market. After the release of the first syndicated study of Latino magazine readers, *Folio,* in a story titled "The Elusive Hispanic Market," reported:

At first glance, the market gleams like some vision of El Dorado. The population numbers 23 million and grows 34 percent annually—nearly five times faster than the general population. Its number of college grads and $50,000 plus wage earners is growing almost as fast, and its purchasing power has tripled over the past 10 years (Cyr 1993, 55).

According to *Folio,* although some advertisers were beginning to make "friendly gestures" toward Latino print media, many periodicals had "choked on the dust" along the road to El Dorado because of lack of advertiser support. Noting the intense competition between African American, Latino, and Asian media for limited "ethnic" ad budgets, *Folio* attributed advertiser hesitance toward Latino magazines to a "messy cultural diversity" within the U.S. Latino population; an overall lack of print vehicles and audited measurements of Latino readership; persistent confusion about whether to use English or Spanish to reach Latinos; and a widespread perception that Latinos are disproportionately brand loyal.

By 1996, publishers launched several new English-language and bilingual magazines targeted at U.S. Latinos. It is unlikely that investors would risk substantial capital without some evidence of forthcoming advertiser support. The North American Free Trade Agreement, and the possibility of including additional Latin American countries in a regional trading bloc, undoubtedly spurred enthusiasm for pan-Continental advertising campaigns suitable for a variety of print media aimed at diverse Latinos. At the same time, the U.S. media began a shift in its representations of Latinos.[11] A few Latina actors began to appear in roles that were set in "mainstream" rather than Latino culture, or that presented cultural encounters between Latinos and Anglos as positive; in contrast to past representations, these roles defined Latinas as similar in many ways to Anglo women. Television featured Giselle Fernandez as the coanchor of *Access Hollywood* and Daisy Fuentes as the cohost of *America's Funniest Home Videos.* In 1997 NBC tried out a sitcom, *Union Square,* starring Constance Marie as an aspiring actor. Actors Salma Hayek and Jennifer López became spokespersons in television and print advertising campaigns for Revlon and L'Oréal cosmetics, and Hayek starred as Esmerelda in TNT's production of *The Hunchback of Notre Dame* (1996). At the movies, López, before starring in *Selena* (1996), played a heroine who is Latina in name only in *Anaconda* (1995), an enormously successful action film. Hayek costarred with Matthew Perry in *Fools Rush In* (1996), a romantic comedy contrasting the warmth and love of a Latino family with a dysfunctional upper-class Anglo family, and Cameron Díaz appeared as an "all-American girl" in films such as *She's the One* (1996) and *My Best Friend's Wedding* (1997).

Commercial interests' endorsement of a few Latinas does not indicate that employment opportunities for Latinos in the media industries, or even media representations of Latinas, have improved significantly.[12] For advertisers and other corporations, however, these productions raise the possibility of a materially successful Latina who demonstrates few indications of "messy cultural diversity," who is as comfortable, if not more, with English as she is with Spanish, and who accordingly might be a viable target for advertising in bilingual magazines.

Marketing Latino Magazine Readers

Some new publishers of Latino magazines tried to define small subgroups with demographic similarities that ostensibly transcend cultural differences. *Si*, for example, a general interest periodical launched in 1995, targeted assimilated, affluent readers with editorial content on art and design, music, politics, fiction, and fashion. According to *Si*'s founder, education and affluence minimize differences between Latinos: "'A Cuban-American lawyer has more in common with a Mexican-American lawyer than with a Cuban-American gardener,'" she told *Folio* (quoted in Beam 1995, 42). Others distanced their readers from those of Spanish-language women's magazines. *Latina*'s publisher, Christy Haubegger, pointed out that magazines like *Vanidades* and *Cosmo en Español* had "'very little to do with life in the States'" (quoted in Beam 1995, 43) and would not appeal to young, U.S.-born women or to women who had spent most of their lives there (Beam 1996).

Haubegger, as a twenty-eight-year-old Mexican American graduate of Stanford Law School, was a magnet for U.S. Latino and general-interest media. Although *Latina* benefited from the publicity, rivals were in a difficult position. *Hispanic*, the publisher of *Moderna*, described Haubegger's efforts to create *Latina* in a lengthy article titled "Magazine Mania: Whose Media Is It Anyway?" The story begins on a positive note:

> The seed for *Latina* sprouted a couple of years ago. Haubegger set out to create the kind of magazine that she and millions of like-minded

Latinas wanted to read. Armed with a business plan, a strong editorial concept, and boundless energy, she began searching for investors in Silicon Valley and New York. (Nuiry 1996, 55)

The article next points out that Haubegger was adopted by an Anglo couple who helped her to understand "her native culture." Without mentioning *Hispanic*'s connection to *Moderna,* the article uses *Moderna*'s editor-in-chief to question Latinos' acceptance of a magazine published by Essence, a corporation directed by African Americans, and, in this piece and in several subsequent stories, criticizes other new publications for not responding to the needs of Latinos.

Hispanic's stance indicates that competition for advertisers and readers, heightened by transnational corporations' entrance into the market, constrains representations of political, class, ethnic, and racial differences within the U.S. Latino population and reinforces the exclusionary basis of advertiser-supported media.[13] *Hispanic* did not object to the idea of new magazines, and it appeared to support Haubegger's endeavors, since she is Latina and her efforts support the publisher's goal of marketing Latinos as desirable consumers of English-language media. More publications for U.S. Latinos would be good for all: Haubegger herself commented, "'I would love to see more Hispanic print for advertisers because they can't justify creating a campaign just for me'" (quoted in Beam 1996, 24). But *Hispanic*'s coverage also claims a privileged position for itself and its sister publication *Moderna,* by implying that Latino-owned and published magazines are uniquely capable of interpreting and representing Latinos' needs and interests.

Defining Latina Identity: Language Use and Cultural Diversity

Latina, Moderna, and *Estylo,* as bilingual publications "by Latinas for Latinas," must create a marketable U.S. Latina identity for investors and advertisers that offers an alternative to existing media and that also provides a pleasurable experience for readers. In their universe of "Latinas," these magazines include U.S.- and Latin-American-born women, but language and editorial slant constitute their readers as English-dominant, U.S. residents.[14] All three publish most editorial content in English, with Spanish colloquialisms sprinkled throughout, and even articles headlined in Spanish on covers usually appear with a privileged English-language text.[15] *Moderna* most overtly excludes women who are not comfortable in English, regularly running only one column (on cooking) in Spanish and translating few English-language articles into Spanish. All three magazines present use of Spanish as an option, often tied to a desire to participate in Latino cultural traditions. In "Spanish Playgroups: How to Keep Your Child's Cultural Identity Alive," for example, *Moderna* describes one woman's experience with a playgroup that speaks only Spanish as part of its focus on introducing children to "Hispanic books, songs, poems, games, and traditions" (Garcia 1998, 56). After *Estylo*, which was launched in English, began to run some articles in Spanish, a letter from the publisher noted that this responded in part to requests from readers who "enjoy reading in Spanish, to keep in practice" (Wolfus 1998, 10). In *Latina*, knowing Spanish is a personal option and not an essential part of Latina identity (Cabaza 1998, 90).

Establishing readers as English-dominant distances them from consumers of Spanish-language magazines, but, by defining "Latina" broadly, the magazines enlarge their scope of material. The magazines do cover issues and people largely absent from English-language women's magazines and run stories on problems and issues affecting materially marginalized Latinas. Their readers, nonetheless, are defined as similar in material status and aspirations to those of other advertiser-supported U.S. women's magazines. The editorial mix combines elements of women's service and fashion/beauty magazines, although it emphasizes Latinos' shared values and experiences. Fashion layouts are often tailored to Latinas' sense of style and show mostly expensive designer clothes and accessories, with prices listed only at the end of each issue, suggesting that readers are sufficiently affluent to care more about brands than prices. Travel features present destinations as places to explore and share Latino culture, but a *Moderna* article on Mayan sites gives shopping tips before describing the cultural attractions (Menard 1998b), and *Latina*'s story on tourism in Mexico centers on where to buy silver (Butler 1998). Latina-oriented career and workplace advice, as well as fashion and beauty pointers for the office, also indicate that the magazines define readers as women who earn their own incomes.[16]

Latina and *Estylo* are more overtly instructive about Latino culture than *Moderna*, although all three magazines portray positive individual characteristics as mainly derived from attributes inherent and specific to all Latinos. When articles identify the national origins of subjects and sources, these are not usually the source of personal characteristics or specific values, and the magazines minimize cultural differences between Latinos. In *Latina*'s story on Spanish-language ability and

Latino identity, for example, the "warm, familiar sound" of the voice of a Cuban-born woman reminds the writer, a monolingual English-speaker, of her Mexican grandmother (Cabaza 1998, 92). Articles on holidays and festivities treat celebrations with national significance, such as Cinco de Mayo, as pan-Latino events, and the magazines avoid religious differences between Latinos. A feature cowritten by Dr. Ana Nogales, a psychologist and author of *Book of Love, Sex and Relationships: A Guide for Latino Couples* (1998), begins

> As Latinos, we bring to our sexual relationships a unique set of cultural values, and often these are at the root of certain conflicts in the bedroom. Sexual roles and taboos promulgated by both traditional Latino culture and the Catholic Church can't help but affect our attitudes and behavior when it comes to sex. (Nogales and Bellotti 1998, 33)

The authors then interpret specific sexual problems between women and their husbands as arising from particularly Latino cultural expectations, such as the belief that women should remain virgins until they marry; Latino men's lack of understanding of female sexuality and their need to feel dominant over women; and the Catholic Church's prohibitions against masturbation.

All three magazines are critical of mainstream stereotypes of female beauty, which they characterize as tall, thin, and blonde, even if their own representations tend toward what Negrón-Muntaner describes as a construction of "ideal 'Latin' beauty . . . neither too dark or too light" (1997, 183). *Latina,* the only magazine to feature a cover celebrity whose looks indicate her African heritage, actor Gina Rivera, includes women with a wider range of skin tones, facial features, and hair color than do *Moderna* and *Estylo,* but even in *Latina,* women with darker skin or African or indigenous American features are scarce. Articles about tall, thin, blonde Latinas emphasize their cultural similarities to other Latinas. *Estylo*'s profile of blonde, blue-eyed Argentinean super-model Valeria Mazza, for instance, quotes Mazza's comment that no one believes she is "Latin" and continues, " 'I'm very proud to be Argentinean.' " Mazza explains, " 'Even though people say I don't look Latin, it's in my personality. I'm very passionate about a lot of things, and that's a quality we Latin people share' " (quoted in Figueroa 1998, 61).

Latina Labor and Gender Roles

The three magazines present readers with a wide range of successful Latino media performers, politicians, businesswomen, and professionals. This coverage contrasts sharply with the U.S. English-language media's typical representations of Latinos as limited to careers as criminals, domestic workers, or law enforcement officers. In describing Latinas' paths to success, the magazines emphasize the importance of individual determination and hard work, and they support Latinas' efforts to achieve upward class mobility and material stability on their own. Nevertheless, like all women's magazines, they imply that a lack of self-esteem is one of the principal obstacles to women's material advancement. Neither *Latina, Moderna,* nor *Estylo* overtly represents that a woman's self-esteem is developed primarily through her involvement in a romantic relationship, and they support Latinas' efforts to improve their education and work skills. All consumer magazines for women, however, inextricably tangle up self-esteem, material aspirations, and romantic happiness with diligent spending on consumer products and services. Like all women's magazines, *Latina, Moderna,* and *Estylo* represent that, to achieve her dreams and goals, a woman must work hard, not only in her job, but also in her bedroom, her bathroom, her gym, and her local shopping mall.

The Latina magazines relentlessly emphasize that determination and a capacity for hard work are defining characteristics of Latino culture. Beauty tips and fashion advice targeted at problems identified as Latina suggest that readers need to work particularly hard at their physical appearance, and Latinas' propensity to do so is overtly noted: *Latina,* for instance, points out that "Nearly half of all *Latina* readers color their hair, compared to about 30 percent of women in general" ("Did You Know" 1998). Articles instruct readers step-by-step in replicating Latina stars' looks, and even celebrities such as Daisy Fuentes, in *Estylo* (Lavin 1997b), and Cristina Saralegui, in *Moderna* (Menard 1998a), who say they reject idealized standards of female beauty, describe their physical presentation as an important part of their success and personal fulfillment. Stories about noncelebrities also demonstrate the importance of hard work and Latinos' capacity for sustained effort, as exemplified by a *Latina* feature titled "Physical Attraction." For the first of three couples, Patricia and Nelson, "maintaining their physical connection isn't just a function of being in a relationship, it's work" (Aranda-Alvarado 1998, 65). Apparently, most of the work is done by Patricia, a massage student who practices on Nelson. In the second couple, Alfredo lifts weights two to three times a week, and Sonia advises women to keep their rear ends in shape by "doing lots of walking and leg lifts." In the third, "Jimmy hits the gym at least four times a week to keep his biceps strong and Gina happy. Gina makes up her eyes simple and sexy by wearing smoky eye shadow and black mascara" (67).

Many success stories trace ambition and capacity for hard work to Latinas' families of origin, even if these maintained rigid divisions of gender roles. *Moderna*'s profile of fashion designer Carolina Herrera reports that she grew up in Venezuela among "stately old-world elegance, in which Latin machismo and aristocratic traditions regarded the role of the woman as a graceful adornment" (Rondon 1997, 23). Herrera's father did not believe that girls should even go to school; still, according to *Moderna*, Herrera's Latino roots and family inspired in her a "keen sense of awareness of her own and other women's power," and, in achieving success, Herrera's "Latina sense of self has been an essential element."

Although the magazines often more explicitly address conflicts between, in their terms, "modern" and "traditional" gender roles, they also naturalize women as responsible for housework and family by excluding males from articles about cooking, parenting, and child care. *Moderna* particularly represents gendered divisions of labor as a Latina cultural preference. In an article on Latina feminism, editor-in-chief Christine Granados begins by asserting that "Mainstream America typically portrays Latinas as a passive and oppressed group of women, dominated and beaten down by the machismo men in their culture" (1998, 37). Granados continues:

> Hispanic women are not adversarial when it comes to change—rather, they are sympathetic to others but resolute in their convictions. Through this method they have triumphed over Old World traditions. More and more Latinas are moving away from home and going to college instead of marrying, they are waiting longer to have children, and they [are] pursuing careers before getting married.

The article then describes the ability and desire to nurture as an essential Latina quality and also insists, somewhat contradictorily, that Latinas freely choose to care for family members. According to Isabel Vega, a twenty-nine-year-old video editor, "'True feminism is nurturing and creating life. Our Indian ancestors were great nurturers. . . . You can have a high powered job, and lots of money, but you'll never be equal to men, because ultimately you are a woman. And I wouldn't want to be anything else'" (quoted in Granados 1998, 38). To further define Latina feminism, Granados calls on Diana Garcia-Prichard, a research scientist and the founder of Latinas Unidas, a support group for the empowerment of Latinas, who explains:

"A woman walks in [to a meeting] late and she apologizes to the rest of us by saying 'I'm sorry I'm late but I had to make my husband dinner.' No one says a word because we all understand that it was her choice to take the responsibility to feed her husband. . . . If that were a mainstream group and someone came in late with that you would hear 'Why don't you let him cook for himself? He's got two good hands,' or 'Let him go get some fast food.' Our feminism is about respecting our sisters' choices." (quoted in Granados 1998, 38)

Latina and *Estylo* more openly encourage women to challenge expectations of gender roles, but in many stories, women transform or end unhappy relationships through discovery of their own strength and self-confidence and increased awareness of their own needs and desires. Even articles suggesting that males should participate in parenting and housework represent that it is women's responsibility to convince their men to change and to reward them when they do, frequently with sex. Outside the pages of women's magazines, Latina scholars have justifiably criticized Anglo-American feminism for its blindness to cultural difference and to the systemic power of racism and classism (see Moraga and Anzaldúa 1983; Alarcón 1991). Yet by positing Latina empowerment as a matter of individual choice and self-awareness, *Latina, Moderna,* and *Estylo* define Latinas precisely as the "autonomous, self-making, self-determining subject" (Alarcón 1991, 29) addressed by this critique.

Latinas and the Media: Consumption and Empowerment

Latina, Moderna, and *Estylo,* like many other women's magazines, devote a preponderance of editorial content to celebrities. While the magazines criticize negative media stereotypes of Latinos and decry the paucity of employment opportunities for Latinos in the media industries, they consistently represent that Latinos can redress these by demonstrating their economic power. All three magazines run entertainment columns promoting books, films, and musical recordings by Latinos, or featuring Latino artists, and they overtly urge readers to consume media to demonstrate their importance as an audience. *Hispanic,* published by the same corporation as *Moderna,* excoriated Time-Warner for exploiting the murder of Selena Quintanilla, whereas the March/April 1998 issue of *Moderna* contains a full-page ad for the

Exclusive Commemorative Edition of the *Selena* video and mentions that even though Jennifer López was not nominated for a Golden Globe award for her performance in the film, readers should "cast their votes at the stores and make the home-video version of Selena . . . one of the best-selling home video movies in the States" ("Lo Ultimo" 1998, 64). The following issue of *Moderna* also plugs the video, and its profile of Univisión talk-show host Cristina Saralegui centers on and favorably reviews her autobiography, *My Life as a Blonde,* published by Warner Books (Menard 1998a, 27–28).

The magazines avoid directly blaming media corporations for negative or inequitable treatment of Latinos. An *Estylo* feature on Latino actors in Hollywood notes that only a handful of Latinos recently have been cast in starring roles in Hollywood films and observes that most Latinos in Hollywood continue to be cast as "spitfires, maids or exaggerated ethnic characters" (Lavin 1997a, 37). The article then attributes the lack of directorial opportunities and roles for Latinos to the dearth of Latinos in the film industry and describes several organizations advocating for greater Latino employment. But according to this article, the main reason for negative media representations is that Latinos do not "throw their economic weight around": they tend to watch Latino-themed films on video, rather than in movie theaters, and they do not complain enough about unfair representations of Latinos or casting of Anglos in Latino roles (Lavin 1997a, 39).

Occasionally, an article will suggest that there is sexism in media institutions, but racism is taboo. *Latina*'s profile of Giselle Fernandez, published when she was hosting *Access Hollywood,* recounts that after graduating from college with a journalism degree, Fernandez was hired as a television reporter by a TV station in Pueblo, Colorado, that was searching for a Latina. Since then, according to Fernandez, "every time she found herself in a new place, she was embraced as a Latina" (Cobo-Hanlon 1997, 48). Fernandez admits that her career was shaped by expectations of women's roles in journalism, but she denies ever facing discrimination because she is Latina, and she in fact "believes that most major organizations are clamoring for Latinos" (49). Fernandez says "'the real discrimination comes from the fact that our communities are impoverished and the cycle of poverty makes it more difficult to get an education, to stay in school, to get to the CBS affiliates and knock on their door'" (quoted in Cobo-Hanlon 1997, 49).

It is not surprising that Fernandez is personally reluctant to condemn CBS. For *Estylo, Latina,* and *Moderna,* avoiding criticism of media corporations is also a pragmatic strategy. Celebrity covers and stories about celebrities stimulate sales, but what celebrity, already at a disadvantage because of her race and sex, would agree to be interviewed by a magazine with a reputation for unfavorable coverage of the very institutions that produce and employ celebrities? Disparaging institutions also detracts from the magazines' supportive environment for advertisers, media, and other corporations alike, and undermines the definition of Latinas these magazines promote, by suggesting limitations on readers' ability to consume because of factors outside their control, such as ethnicity. As a result, the magazines present Latina empowerment as largely a matter of individual attitude adjustment, determination, and hard work.

Conclusions

In constructing Latinas as desirable consumers, *Latina, Moderna,* and *Estylo* attempt to remedy an egregious history of negative stereotypes about Latinos. They also address a more recent confusion, on the part of corporate interests, about U.S. Latinos' language abilities, economic power, and consuming habits. These magazines do provide positive representations of successful Latinas within and outside corporate institutions. They also cover issues and concerns rarely, if ever, mentioned in other U.S. media. The ultimate survival of magazines like *Latina, Moderna,* and *Estylo,* however, depends on advertisers' needs to segregate consumers into groups defined by their similarities, rather than their differences. The magazines veil differences within the Latino population, excluding many Latinos, and their very existence arguably facilitates Latinos' exclusion from other media by providing a segmented venue for advertisers.

Like all other commercial media, the magazines neither challenge nor present readers with strategies to oppose institutional structures and relationships that marginalize not only Latinas, but all women. There is little space to confront the reality that Latinas, or any other marginalized group, are not discriminated against, exploited, and excluded from power because individuals lack self-esteem, determination, or the capacity to work hard. These magazines' self-presentation as publications "by Latinas for Latinas" ought not to obscure the relations of production and power between all commercial media products and their consumers, no matter how well-intentioned the owners. By converting the needs and desires of Latinas into commodities to be sold to advertisers, and by equating empowerment and representation with recognition as consumers, these magazines reinforce, rather than challenge, the fundamental correlation between economic and political power that contributes to the disenfranchisement of not only Latinas, but all marginalized peoples.

Notes

The author wishes to thank Jack Banks, Mimi White, and Jyotsna Kapur for their comments and suggestions on drafts of this article.

1. The use of quotation marks acknowledges that "Latina" is a construction. Negrón-Muntaner points out that "it is arguable that a Latino identity 'exists' across the United States, and that this identity has erased or displaced nationalist investments, [yet] it is also undeniable that . . . the construct, although not exhausting our complexity, has constitutive materiality" (1997, 183–84).

2. For an exemplary critique of the codes and representational strategies of women's magazines in the context of industrial relationships, see McCracken (1993). Scanlon's history of the early years of the *Ladies' Home Journal* places the magazine in the context of developing consumer culture and describes the magazine's early attempts to appeal to white, middle-class consumers.

3. Of the thirty-five largest global magazine publishers in 1997, Time Inc. received one quarter of the total revenues. Time and the three next largest publishers, Condé Nast, Hearst Magazines, and Hachette Filipacchi Media, garnered more than a third of all revenues of the thirty-five publishers ("Annual Survey" 1997). Time-Warner's 1996 magazine revenues of almost $2.4 billion were only 26 percent of its total media revenue, and even Hearst's ($834 million) were only 50.7 percent of total media revenue. Essence Communications, the only company that produces a Latina magazine for which financial data is available, was ranked the thirty-fourth-largest company, with 1996 revenues of $49 million. Even *Essence,* however, is a diversified corporation that publishes magazines, runs a mail-order catalog business, and produces special events through an entertainment division (Pogrebin 1997a).

4. Hearst, for example, sells more than half of all magazine advertising pages, accounting for almost two-thirds of its ad revenue, as part of a multiple buy (Hearst Corporation 1998).

5. Web sites and new cable ventures are oriented at transnational advertisers interested in a global presence. Hearst's "Cosmo Channel," for example, targets Latin American women, and Hachette Filipacchi's *Elle* web site, www.elle.com, offers localized versions of both editorial and advertisements for women from eight national editions (Koranteng 1997).

6. Even *Cosmo en Español,* which started as a translated version of the U.S.

magazine, in the late 1970s shifted to a magazine for "the Latin American woman" (Menard 1998a, 28).

7. Editorial América's other magazines include Spanish-language versions of *Popular Mechanics, National Geographic, Men's Health,* and *PC Magazine.* In addition to its interests in Latin American media markets, Grupo Televisa controls a substantial interest in Univisión, the most profitable U.S. Spanish-language broadcast network, and is the sole owner of Galavisión, the largest U.S. Spanish-language cable network (Grupo Televisa 1997).

8. Televisa claims a combined U.S. circulation of 700,000 and a cumulative total reach of 4.5 million U.S. readers for all its magazines (Kelly 1997).

9. In Mexico, for example, Televisa publishes 75 percent of all consumer magazines sold, and it controls over half of the magazine distribution outlets (Grupo Televisa 1997).

10. Grupo Televisa's program sales to Univisión and Galavisión generate a greater percentage of Televisa's revenue than all program sales in Latin America (Sinclair 1996, 55). These sales, of course, do not depend directly on advertiser support, but advertiser support is vital to the continued viability of these networks. In the early 1990s, Univisión and Telemundo, the second U.S. Spanish-language broadcast network, funded the creation of a Nielsen Hispanic Television Index to respond to advertisers' dissatisfaction with the lack of standardized and syndicated measurements for Latino television viewing (Wood 1993). As other transnational corporations debuted Spanish-language cable channels aimed at U.S. and Latin American viewers, Univisión and Telemundo gained powerful allies in establishing the superiority of Spanish-language media in reaching U.S. Latinos.

11. López's study of changing representations of Latinos and Latin America in Hollywood films of the late 1930s and early 1940s suggests that a contemporary shift similarly may owe not only to increased awareness of U.S. Latinos as consumers but also to the importance of Latin American markets for films and television (1993, 69).

12. Negrón-Muntaner's and Kleinhans's analyses of Jennifer López's performance of ethnicity in *Selena,* and Valdivia and Curry's (1998) study of Brazilian television star Xuxa, for example, illuminate some of the complications in contemporary production of Latinas by other segments of the U.S. media.

13. For a discussion of this tendency in the context of television programming for U.S. Latinos, see Rodriguez (1996, 72).

14. This article discusses the magazines' editorial content in issues from September 1997 to December 1998. All three magazines contain many ads visually identical to those in English-language women's magazines, although sometimes with Spanish-language texts. The relative lack of ads targeting U.S. Latinos suggests that advertisers are primarily interested in creating campaigns

that can be used in Spanish-language print media distributed in the United States and Latin America.

15. Most feature articles and columns present the English-language text first and most prominently. Translations into Spanish, which are often condensed, tend to run in sidebars or at the end of the magazines.

16. *Estylo* and *Latina* in particular, however, use examples of "real women" who have solved a problem of concern for a number of Latinas employed in relatively low-paying occupations in service industries or nonprofit organizations. This suggests that the magazines present levels of consumption that at least some readers aspire to rather than presently enjoy.

13. Born to Shop: Teenage Women and the Marketplace in the Postwar United States
Angela R. Record

> To some extent, the teenage market—and, in fact, the very notion
> of the teenager—has been created by the businessmen who ex-
> ploit it.
> —Dwight Macdonald, *The New Yorker,* 1958

In 1947 Eugene Gilbert traveled from Chicago to New York to earn his
fortune by defining and exploiting the untapped teenage market. By
1958 Gilbert had earned a reputation as a leader in his industry; he
grossed between $500,000 and $1 million annually by selling teenage
consumers as the next hot commodity. In 1945 he established Eugene
Gilbert and Company, an umbrella organization dedicated to the research of teenage tastes and buying habits. Clients willing to pay for
Gilbert's information included *Seventeen* magazine, Simplicity dress
patterns, Hollywood V-ette Vassarette bras, Mars candy, Hires soft
drinks, and Royal typewriters. Gilbert's syndicated newspaper column,
"What Young People Think," appeared in more than 325 newspapers
(Gehman 1957; Gilbert 1957; Macdonald 1958).[1] Gilbert's understanding of the rapidly evolving teenage cultural identity made him
rich, but his success had a great deal to do with timing. The United
States postwar economy produced a seemingly affluent context from
which the earnest teenage consumer emerged. Gilbert was among the
first businessmen to successfully identify and exploit this teenage demographic. Others would soon follow suit. Of course, it was primarily
the white, middle-class, heterosexual teenage consumers that appealed
to sellers in the marketplace; because of space constraints, this essay
will focus solely on these members of the majority class. Subsequent
references to teenagers and the teenage market assume a heterosexual,
white, middle-class demographic. Employing political economy and
feminist theory, this essay will illustrate how the teenage market in the
postwar United States courted the adolescent woman in a particular
way. This courtship wed consumer-based activity with dominant ideological notions regarding teenage women and domesticity; teen women
were encouraged to spend, marry, and mother.

The Postwar Economy

Employing political economy requires that "classical" Marxism inform the analysis; in other words, we must explore cultural texts and practices in the context of the conditions of their production. We need to locate these texts and practices in their moments of production and analyze the historical conditions that produced them. This essay will trace the relationship between the emergence of a newly courted teen market and the changes that had taken place in postwar capitalism, namely, the move to a "consumer-debt" society. The new consumer-debt society illustrated a huge shift in social consciousness. Americans embraced a "rent-to-own" rhetoric—an ideology that encouraged consumers to buy now and pay later. Popular culture aided in the perpetuation of this rhetoric by depicting the signifiers of material success as indicators of personal happiness. This happiness, they implied, could easily be obtained through the purchase of consumer goods. As Richard Dyer (1981) suggests, the ideals of popular culture "imply wants that capitalism itself promises to meet" (184). The "rent-to-own" rhetoric allowed consumers to satisfy their material desires immediately but at the cost of assuming consumer debt.

This rhetoric became a new ideal in the postwar United States. It seemed that few questioned the move away from a "pay as you go" consumer mentality, for "buy now, pay later" became part of the postwar ideological terrain. Much discussion has centered on the 1950s as a period of newfound affluence. This affluence, however, was illusory.[2] The affluence that seemed to appear in the 1950s—evidenced by increased consumer spending—was actually achieved through consumer loans. As such, the change in the standard of living in the postwar United States was the result of unprecedented consumer debt, *not* greater personal income. Consumer debt skyrocketed 560 percent, from $8.5 billion in 1946 to $56.1 billion in 1960. Outstanding installment credit rose 45 percent in just three years, from $23.6 billion in 1954 to $34.2 billion in 1957. In 1946, Americans paid $800 million in consumer interest; in 1960, they shelled out $7.3 billion—an increase of 813 percent.

These figures increased, in large part, because of the tremendous rise in consumer spending on housing construction and durable goods. New housing construction soared during the postwar period, reaching a high of 1.65 million new homes in 1955 and declining only slightly to about 1.5 million for the remainder of the decade. Americans assumed new mortgages in droves, vastly increasing their debt load.

Mortgage-based indebtedness jumped almost 400 percent, from $41.8 billion in 1946 to $206.8 billion in 1960. By 1960 between 60 and 70 percent of American families "owned" homes. Americans wanted something to park in the driveways of their mortgaged homes, and car ownership exploded during this period. Car registrations leapt from 26 million in 1945 to 40 million in 1950; by 1960, 75 percent of American families had purchased an automobile, many by assuming yet another monthly payment. Even the advent of television had an impact on consumer spending. In 1946, less than 7,000 new television sets were manufactured. In 1950, over 7,000,000 television sets were manufactured. By 1960, over 85 percent of American homes contained a television. These figures constitute part of the 119 percent increase in consumer spending on durable goods.

It was this increased spending on durable goods and housing construction that lent the illusion of an affluent economy, since Americans increased their burden of debt as they moved into the next decade.[3] Even when the recession hit in 1957, and the GNP fell sharply, consumer spending continued to rise. So the postwar "affluence" Americans allegedly experienced came at the cost of enormous consumer debt. This period, then, was the first time American families began—in earnest—to live beyond their means (Aaronson 1958; Coontz 1992; "How Old Is Your Audience" 1955; Palladino 1996; "TV . . . Caught" 1951; U.S. Bureau of the Census 1975; Vatter 1963).

The Teenage Consumer

From within this newfound consumer-based economy, teenagers emerged as vibrant consumers. Even the word "teenager" implied profit potential, establishing "a permanent wedge between childhood and adulthood" (Hebdige 1988, 29). This wedge meant money and, as Dick Hebdige (1988) argues, the "invention of the teenager [was] intimately bound up with the creation of the youth market (29). The sheer numbers of teenagers in the 1950s offered tremendous profit potential in the American marketplace. In the late 1950s there were 16 to 17 million teenagers in the United States, close to 12 million in the 15-to-19 age bracket alone. By 1956, 35 percent of teenage boys eligible to work after school did so (twice the number in 1944), earning an average $9.00 per week (including allowances). The average weekly income of the teenage girl was just over $6.50. With about 4.7 million teens working part-time and about 800,000 working full-time, the postwar period saw approximately 5.5 million teenagers, or one-third of the teenage population, hold jobs. Job earnings, allowances, and their parents' disposable income combined to give teenagers over $9 billion to spend, or $1 billion more than the total sales of the General Motors Company ("Catching the Customers" 1957; Gehman 1957; Macdonald 1958; "A New, $10-Billion Power" 1959; Porges 1958).

It was the spending power of these teenagers that attracted new interest. Marketers were aware of young consumers long before the postwar era, since a youth market did exist prior to the end of World War II. Paula S. Fass (1977), for example, traces the behavior of American youth in the 1920s, exploring "the relationship between youth and dynamics of social change" (9). Youth culture was certainly in place by the Jazz Age, but the emergence of the teenage consumer market in the postwar period was significant for several reasons. First, teenage consumption practices rose in earnestness and impact. The $9 to $10 billion spending money gave the teenage market newfound credibility. Second, teens spent money freely and often. Their participation in the consumer market favorably impacted the U.S. economy. Third, and perhaps most importantly, marketers and advertisers began to take teenagers seriously as a viable consumer demographic.

The teen market was, in fact, so viable that sociologist David Riesman (1950) referred to middle-class American youth as "consumer trainees" (79). Riesman certainly had a point, especially when one considers the spending habits of teenage consumers. According to *Life* magazine, teenagers owned thirteen million cameras, ten million records, and over one million television sets ("A New, $10-Billion Power" 1959). About 65 percent of teens paid for their own entertainment, from movies to the soda fountain; around 60 percent bought their own records and sports equipment; and approximately 40 percent bought their own shirts, shoes, and jewelry. Out of every dollar, teenagers spent about five cents on reading material and nine cents on music or movies. Boys spent ten cents on dates, four cents on car expenses, eleven cents on sports, and nine cents on clothes and grooming. Girls, on the other hand, spent nothing on cars or dates, six cents on sports, and a whopping twenty-six cents on clothes and grooming ("The Dreamy Teen-Age Market" 1957; Gehman 1957; Gilbert 1957; Kraar 1956; Macdonald 1958; "A New, $10-Billion Power" 1959; Porges 1958). All of this spending did not, of course, account for the merchandise that teens influenced their parents to buy. As Doherty (1988) argues, the newly nurtured teenage market "was an immediate boon to the nation's emerging consumer-based economy" (52). Teenagers did spend.

Teenagers also influenced the spending of their family. Given postwar America's increasing willingness to buy "on credit," families shelled out billions of dollars in discretionary income—and their teenagers helped them decide what to buy. At least 90 percent of teenagers chose their own shoes, although their parents paid the tab. Over 70 percent chose their own records, jewelry, sports equipment, and fountain pens; about half of all teens selected the radios, shampoos, and watches that their parents purchased (Gilbert 1957; Porges 1958). *Business Week* understood why sellers jumped at this teenage market: "for its own purchasing power and its effectiveness in making families spend; for the role it plays in family spending and its influence in the choice of brands; . . . for its rich potential as an adult market tomorrow" ("Catching the Customers" 1957, 86). Rich potential indeed.

Born to Shop: Teenage Women and the Marketplace

Political economy, although useful in exploring the material conditions of the postwar United States, can be myopic when it comes to gender. Morag Shiach (1998) asserts that popular culture "as an institutional space, and as a political concept, embodies definitions of class identity, historical change and political struggle which are often blind to the questions of feminism" (333). By focusing exclusively on the primacy of class, political economy excludes considerations of gender. Feminist theory offers a way to address political economy's shortsightedness.

Feminists have offered a wide range of approaches to popular culture.[4] These approaches share what Lana Rakow has identified as two basic assumptions. First, they assume that "women have played central roles as consumers of certain popular culture products, that they are a central subject matter of popular culture for both men and women, and that, in some cases and in some time periods, they have been significant creators and producers of popular culture" (Rakow 1998, 278). Second, they assume that feminism, "as a critique of existing social relations," presupposes "that change is not only desirable but necessary" (Rakow 1998, 278). These assumptions underlie many feminist approaches to popular culture.

One aspect of popular culture that feminists have repeatedly critiqued centers on the ideology of the ideal woman. It was (and is) the white, heterosexual, middle- to upper-middle-class woman that dominant culture held (and continues to hold) as ideal. This ideal was "based on White male values—the values of those who are empowered to make the rules" (Joseph and Lewis 1981, 159). Most importantly, the 1950s ideal woman celebrated her domesticity; as Kathryn Weibel (1977) has shown, popular culture in the United States has consistently depicted the ideal woman as "housewifely, passive, wholesome, and pretty" (ix). While for many this ideal was (and is) not our reality, popular culture courted the female consumer as if she embodied—or wanted to embody—this ideal. Women were tempted "with the promise of future perfection, by the lure of achieving ideals—ideal legs, ideal hair, ideal homes, ideal sponge cakes, ideal relationships" (Coward 1985, 13). This promise of future perfection was imbedded in the way of living held out to women—"women shopping, cooking, buying and wearing the goods produced by this society" (Coward 1985, 13). Women were taught that frequent consumption of consumer goods offered the fastest route to future perfection.

Future perfection for the 1950s ideal woman rested in the domestic sphere. Dominant ideology held that women were domestic, passive creatures valued solely for their physical appearance. This appearance was tied firmly to a beauty ideal that was white and flawless (Wolf 1991). The culture industry[5] worked to sell dominant ideological notions of domesticity and consumption to women. These ideal notions, presuming the identity of the ruling class, ignored women (and men) who were not white, middle- to upper-middle-class, and heterosexual. Popular culture worked to perpetuate the ideology of the ideal woman by wedding impossible physical standards with a desire for domesticity.

In particular, industries targeted teenage women in ways that emphasized their social roles as wives, mothers, and homemakers. Aaron Cohen, *Seventeen* research director, said that the ultimate goal for teenage women was marriage and household possessions; furthermore, "the main interests of the teenage girl today are her family, her home, her education, her career, marriage, and a home of her own" (Macdonald 1958a, 83). *Seventeen,* however, focused on the teenage woman's role as a wife, mother, and homemaker rather than on her role as an educated career woman.

Seventeen's focus mirrored the postwar effort to return women to the domestic sphere. After the war ended, women who had entered the workplace as part of the war effort were urged to leave their jobs and return to their roles as mothers and housewives. Women did oblige, marrying younger and starting families. Almost half of postwar brides married while they were still teenagers. For example, in 1954, 48 percent of new brides were under 20. In 1956, 500,000 teenage women married, one-third of the national total. Gilbert claimed that the age at which women married in the United States was "lower than in any peasant country abroad" (Macdonald 1958a, 84). One million new mothers were teenagers. Birth rates increased after the war, reaching a high of 25.2 births per thousand in 1956–1957 but decreasing to 23.7 in 1959–1960. The 1950s birth rate far exceeded the 18.4 births per thousand in the 1930s (Coontz 1992; Vatter 1963). With more teenage women entering matrimony and beginning motherhood, it is no surprise that *Seventeen* focused on the teenage woman's domestic role in society. Postwar women married and mothered at a younger age than their predecessors. Whether these women assumed a domestic role because they wanted to or because they felt they had to remains open to argument.

A poll by the Institute of Student Opinion, sponsored by *Scholastic* magazines, probed about 50,000 students in 500 U.S. high schools in 1950–1951. The survey asked students what career they expected to follow. Less than 5 percent of the teenage women thought they would find themselves in business or industry, government or military service, or farming. About one-third anticipated a profession in medicine, law, teaching, or nursing. But almost half of the women responded that homemaking was in their future. In another survey, only 2 percent of women indicated that they *wanted* to be a homemaker but nine times as many said they *expected* to do so ("Do Students Expect" 1950; "Results of Recent I.S.O. Poll" 1951). Marriage and motherhood were on their horizon.

Obviously, popular culture nurtured these expectations. Even in high school classrooms, *Scholastic* emphasized stereotypical gendered roles. An advertisement for the Household Finance Corporation offered filmstrips dedicated to the emerging consumer housewife; titles included "Managing the Family Income," "Mrs. Consumer Considers Credit," "What Shall I Wear?," "Spending Your Food Dollars," and "How Does She Do It? Cleaning a Refrigerator" ("Filmstrip Lectures" 1950). General Mills sponsored the Betty Crocker All-American Homemaker of Tomorrow Contest, which awarded $125,000 in prizes ("General Mills" 1954). Even *Seventeen* encouraged the young woman's domestic role by depicting the 1950s teenage woman as domestic first, everything else second: "She recognizes her responsibilities as a woman. She is very interested in the art of homemaking. . . . Today's girl thinks that homemaking is a creative and fulfilling process" (Jones 1984,

162). Indeed, homemaking was particularly fulfilling for a consumer-based economy; women spent money on products geared toward a domestic life.

Unfortunately, magazines "have consistently glamorized whatever the economy, their advertisers, and during wartime, the government, needed at that moment from women" (Wolf 1991, 64). After World War II, dominant culture needed women to return from the work sphere to the domestic sphere. Women were encouraged to celebrate their domesticity. This created what Betty Friedan calls the "feminine mystique" or "the fulfillment of femininity through women's roles as housewives" (Rakow 1998, 279). In interviews Friedan conducted, she found "a schizophrenic split between what [women] believed should be a fulfilling role in life and the actual isolation and despair they felt about their own lives" (Rakow 1998, 279). In the end, "the really crucial function, the really important role that women serve as housewives, is to buy more things for the house" (Friedan 1963, 206). If teenage women relied on popular culture to determine the course of their lives, they would find their options rather limited.

Sixteen Going on Seventeen: Targeting Teenage Women

Popular culture emphasized women's allegedly restricted options by creating a domestic norm. The interest in perpetuating this norm was further fueled by the postwar increase in marriage and birth rates. In the publishing industry, *Seventeen* magazine—and others like it—provides one example of how advertisers and publishers exploited the young female market by affirming mainstream feminine stereotypes. *Seventeen,* the first magazine to offer fashion and beauty tips to teenage women, sold out its first 1944 edition of 400,000 copies in two days. In less than two years, subscriptions reached one million. The success of *Seventeen* helped legitimate the adolescent female market; the magazine maintained its dominance in the industry for years.

Seventeen rarely questioned the status quo; rather, it contributed to its perpetuation. Editors embraced white, middle-class heteronormativity and encouraged readers to do the same. *Seventeen* focused primarily on the young woman's domestic role and her need to spend money in order to achieve domestic bliss. As part of their domestic training, *Seventeen* guided adolescent women through diets, skin and haircare regimens, cooking recipes, social tips, dating do's and don'ts, and fashion knowledge. It told women where to buy the proper skin cream, the right shampoo, the perfect make-up, and the trendy fashions; it marveled at how the right product could help young women obtain the "proper" image necessary to attract a husband. In other words, *Seventeen* instructed young women on everything they needed to know to make good wives and mothers. And, most importantly, a good wife and mother knew how to shop.

Seventeen illustrates how dedication to domestic ideology could prove profitable. The magazine devoted articles to the teenage woman's "happy future . . . [how to shop] for china, silver, glassware, and table linens" (*"Seventeen's* Treasure" 1956, 127). Advertising dedicated to household equipment and furnishings increased over 450 percent from 1946 to 1956. By 1958, *Seventeen* had more advertising for luggage, silver, and engagement rings than any other magazine. Issues of *Seventeen* illustrated the tremendous advertising efforts of merchandisers, carrying ads for Gorham sterling silver, Bali bras, Keepsake diamonds, and Chanel No. 5. Macdonald (1958a) claimed that the average teenage woman owned "eight slips, three crinolines, two girdles, and seven bras. . . . Thus equipped, she is in a good position to get a husband at 18" (84). After all, according to the psychologist George Lawton (1951), "most women find their greatest happiness in the role of wife and mother" (113). It is no wonder, then, that teenage women started hope chests (sheets, blankets, bedspreads, towels, and tablecloths) by the time they were fifteen. They were certainly encouraged to do so ("Admen Don't Impress" 1954; "Catching the Customers" 1957; Gilbert 1957; Kraar 1956; Macdonald 1958; Palladino 1996; *"Seventeen's* Treasure" 1956).

Teen women were also encouraged to spend. According to Riesman (1950), "women are the accepted consumption leaders in our society" (81). As such, young women were inculcated into consumerism as early as possible. Teen women did their part to participate, spending money on products designed to enhance their appearance, to increase their odds at finding a husband and securing their future as a housewife (or so mainstream America would hope). Each year teen women spent over $800 million on school wardrobes, $300 million on toiletries and cosmetics, $20 million on lipstick, $25 million on deodorants, and $9 million on home permanents. Teena Paige Fashions, Inc., earned $118 million in the teen dress market. These revenues were remarkable since about 90 percent of teenage women influenced their parents' buying decisions for blouses, skirts, dresses, lipstick, and lingerie. About one-third of all teens bought these items wholly on their own (Gehman 1957; "A New, $10-Billion Power" 1959; Porges 1958).

By spending so much on clothing and grooming items, teen women demonstrated their awareness of a beauty ideal. They used their purchasing power to try to achieve it.

Merchandisers salivated at this opportunity. Helene Curtis Industries' sales of beauty and grooming products to teen women tripled in the postwar period. Hires Root Beer geared its $1 million advertising budget toward the teenage demographic; one promotion hired female students to demand Hires on dates, plug the soft drink at dances and games, and throw root beer parties. Cosmetics companies capitalized on Elvis Presley's popularity by marketing lipsticks—Hound Dog Orange, Heartbreak Hotel Pink, and Tutti Frutti Red. Other corporate promotions included a joint venture between Schrank Dreamwear, Canada Dry Ginger Ale, Coty, and RCA Victor to promote pajama parties that feature pajamas, ginger ale, perfume, and records; a Kraft Foods jingle contest that awarded one year's free personal telephone service to the winner; and local talent shows that showcased Breck hair products—leading to $1 million in increased sales (Gilbert 1957; "A New $10-Billion Power" 1959; "Teen-age Consumers" 1957).

And the commotion over teenage women and hosiery demonstrated the importance of the teenage market. A group of teen women complained that the reason they refused to wear nylons was because they couldn't "help getting runners on those school chairs" ("Teen-Agers' Refusal" 1950, 11). The hosiery industry was up in arms when the teens opted not to wear nylons due to potential runs. The Hosiery Workers Union was concerned enough to consider making suggestions to furniture manufacturers on how to remedy the problem. The union expressed concern that if women refused to wear hosiery as teenagers, then they would surely refuse to wear hosiery as adults. Promotions were created to entice teen women to buy hosiery. Glen Raven Knitting Mills used advertising and department stores to promote Glen Raven hosiery, as worn by June Allyson, Arlene Dahl, and Lauren Bacall in the film *Woman's Work*. Advertising placed in *Seventeen* encouraged teens to wear stockings like the stars—in other words, be a lady ("The Dreamy Teen-Age Market" 1957; "Glen Raven" 1954; Kraar 1956; "Teen-Age Consumers" 1957; "Teen-Agers' Refusal" 1950).

'Til She Drops: Negotiating Self-Esteem

If domesticating teenage women into their roles as wives, mothers, and homemakers proved profitable for marketers and merchandisers, then creating and perpetuating a feminine beauty ideal solidified their revenues. As Naomi Wolf (1991) argues, beauty "is a currency system like the gold standard" (12). Merchandisers were primarily responsible for engineering an unachievable beauty ideal and advertising products specifically geared toward attaining this ideal. Unsurprisingly, "assigning value to women . . . according to a culturally imposed physical standard" involved negotiating women's self-esteem (Wolf 1991, 12). In opinion polls, 40 percent of teenage women admitted they needed to develop self-confidence and 60 percent wanted people to like them more (Remmers and Radler 1957). Over 40 percent of teenage women were concerned about improving their figure, and over one-third wanted to improve their posture and body build. Anxiety manifested itself in food issues. The U.S. Public Health Service reported that over 50 percent of teenage women had poor diets; one out of three skipped breakfast entirely, perhaps in an attempt to achieve the feminine ideal (Honor 1957). *Parents' Magazine* warned that the teenage woman's moody behavior had "nothing to do with her clothes and everything to do with her inability to accept herself and her own body" (Farnham 1951, 76). Of course, the diet industry profited greatly from the teen's low self-esteem; Slenderella, a diet-reduction program, claimed one in eight Boston clients was a teenager, and teenage consumption in New York and Philadelphia increased between 50 and 150 percent (Gehman 1957).

So teenage women spent money on those goods alleged to improve their self-esteem, spending over 25 percent of every dollar on clothes and cosmetics (Gilbert 1957; Macdonald 1958). Since the "beauty myth is always actually prescribing behavior and not appearance" (Wolf 1991, 13), magazines like *Seventeen* advised their readers to be charming, poised, and, above all, well-groomed. They advised women on faulty bosoms, embarrassing blemishes, diets for the figure, and dressing to scale—tips for the too thin, too fat, too short, too tall (Ivens 1951). They even devoted entire issues to women's appearance; the implicit idea in fashion and grooming tips held that women needed to look good to land a husband. So *Senior Prom,* formerly *Calling All Girls,* claimed to be "the teenage girl's favorite, because of its sparkling stories and novelettes, and fascinating articles on the latest fashions, dating, etiquette, and the development of charm and poise so important to them now" ("Perfect Magazine" 1949, 139). *Compact* magazine promised to "inform, inspire, and enlighten" the teenage woman "with important data on dates . . . careers . . . college . . . clothes . . . budgets . . . behavior" that would help "her prepare for a better tomorrow" ("Designed for Teen-Age Living" 1951, 130). Even *Scholastic* partnered with fragrance company Lenthéric to produce a "Personal Check Chart for Girls—a Guide to Perfect Grooming and Popularity." The chart offered recommendations for the teen's lipstick, teeth, nails, clothes, hair, deodorant, posture, jewelry, and shoes ("Filmstrip Lectures" 1950; Gilbert 1957). After all, a woman's charm and appearance, they suggested, were the gateway to her popularity.

Advertisers appealed to the teenage woman's desire to be charming and popular. Advertisers in *Seventeen* bombarded readers with products aimed at maintaining appearances—cosmetics, clothing, hair- and skin-care products, jewelry—and achieving the beauty ideal. This ideal was instilled at a very young age. Consider, for example, an advertisement for Listerine Antiseptic. The ad depicted a child dressed in her mother's clothes and admiring her appearance in a mirror. The ad copy encouraged the girl's fixation:

> Dressing up like a mother . . . mimicking her manners . . . practicing mother's good-grooming routines! Yes, this youngster has already learned an important secret of feminine charm. This little lady knows what no lady ever forgets . . . that daintiness is the first step to popularity. ("First Aid" 1949, 5)

By the time the little girl became a teenage woman, she understood that a woman's worth in dominant culture was literally based on face value. Popular culture helped perpetuate such stereotypical ideologies, and advertisers helped determine the definition of feminine perfection, or the beauty ideal.

This beauty ideal constituted one aspect of feminine stereotypes; behavior models constituted another. Part of the feminine ideal nurtured in the postwar United States included "ladylike" behavior. Charm courses became increasingly popular as teenage women flocked to learn about posture, grace, and grooming. After all, "girls want[ed] the best chance at marriage" and their chances allegedly increased if they embodied the feminine ideal (Honor 1957, 81). Merchandisers offered products and services aimed at achieving this ideal. Helena Rubinstein employees conducted mini–training courses that taught basics in skin- and hair-care, make-up, fashion, and grooming. One participant, elected from each monthly course, competed in Helena Rubinstein's "American Look Girl" contest. Each winner appeared as a model in a full-page advertisement placed in *Seventeen*. Wonder School, a New York Fifth Avenue salon, offered tips on grooming and homemaking, suggesting, for example, how bedmaking, dusting, and vacuuming could prove beneficial to a woman's figure if performed with a proper posture and stretch (Gilbert 1957; Wambold 1949). *Parents' Magazine* encouraged mothers to raise their "daughter's standards of cleanliness. Now is the time to dramatize baths with gifts of bubble bath, pretty soap and bath powder" (Nichols 1951, 92). It was almost as if looking good was a woman's birthright, and the perfect product could help any woman claim what was rightfully hers: beauty, marriage, and motherhood.

Many Birds, Few Stones: The High Price of Teenage Exploitation

In his book *Advertising and Marketing to Young People,* Gilbert stresses that the "youth market is of enormous value to industry and reaching it is essential. Every year this market has many billions to spend on itself. It represents another great financial potential to manufacturers because of its influence upon the purchases of the adult market" (1957, viii). Thus, "capturing the mercurial tastes of youngsters is an excellent method of 'hitting two birds with one stone'" (50). Gilbert's exploitation of teenagers earned him great notoriety and wealth, while simultaneously exposing the tremendous profit potential of the teen consumer market. For teenage women, this exposure heavily influenced the development of their self-worth. While middle-class teenage women learned that they were valued for their purchasing power, they also discovered that their worth tied directly to their well-groomed appearance and their domestic potential as future wives, mothers, and consumers.

This connection between consumerism and domestication illuminates the importance of employing political economy and feminist theory as analytical methods. For while political economy offers an excellent means of exploring economic relations within a particular context, its focus on the primacy of class obscures the importance of gender. Conversely, while feminist theory provides an exceptional means with which to explore cultural power, too often it privileges gender over the equally important social categories of class, race, and sexuality. It is thus extremely useful to blend the two theoretical strains in order to illuminate the various intersections between gender and class.

This brief essay has illustrated the benefits of utilizing feminist theory and political economy to explore the contexts of a particular historical moment, revealing how teenage women were encouraged, through social and economic discourses, to participate in the postwar U.S. economy. This participation particularly illuminated women's preoccupation with grooming and appearance—a preoccupation fabricated and nurtured by popular cultural artifacts and merchandising schemes. These schemes revealed how the teen market was, in many ways, created by those who sought to exploit it. Social, economic, and ideological discourses thus vied for the teenage woman's attention, wedding the ideological expectations of the domestic woman with the economic demands of a capitalist marketplace.

Notes

A version of this paper was presented at the National Communication Association conference in Chicago in November 1999. The author wishes to thank Louis Curiel, Eileen Meehan, John Nerone, and Ellen Riordan for their wisdom and guidance on previous drafts of this essay.

1. McDonald's essay ran in two parts in *The New Yorker*. By necessity he repeats in the second part (1958b) much of the information he presents in the first (1958a). Wherever possible I reference the specific part in which the citation appeared. If, however, the reader can locate the information in either part, I reference only the year, 1958.

2. Several factors reveal postwar affluence as a false notion. First, it was the first half of the decade that experienced moderate affluence; the second half saw a significant economic decline, even experiencing a recession in 1957–1958. Second, 25 percent of the American population could be considered poor; a depressing 60 percent of the elderly population earned $1,000 or less annually. Third, although the gross national product (GNP) increased 56 percent in the postwar period, this translated to only a 3.2 percent annual growth rate. The period between 1950 and 1955 experienced solid growth; the GNP rose 4.7 percent. The period between 1955 and 1959, however, saw half the growth of the preceding years; the GNP increased a modest 2.25 percent (Coontz 1992; Jezer 1982; Palladino 1996; Vatter 1963; U.S. Bureau of the Census 1975).

3. The postwar period did see a 20 percent increase in per capita income, and a 22 percent increase in personal consumption expenditures. But compare this to the 27 percent rise in per capita income during World War II, with only a 5 percent increase in personal consumption expenditures. Despite the 7 percent *decrease* in per capita income growth from World War II to the postwar era, personal consumption expenditures growth *increased* 17 percent during the same period (Marchand 1982; U.S. Bureau of the Census, 1975; Vatter 1963; Walker and Vatter 1996).

4. See, in particular, the work of Ien Ang, bell hooks, Michèle Mattelart, Angela McRobbie, Patricia Mellencamp, Tania Modleski, Meaghan Morris, Constance Penley, Tricia Rose, and Lynn Spigel. This listing is hardly exhaustive, but these feminist scholars offer excellent and insightful examples of the study of gender in popular culture.

5. The Frankfurt School (which included Theodor Adorno, Walter Benjamin, Max Horkheimer, Leo Lowenthal, and Herbert Marcuse) saw mass culture as predictable, uniform, and transparent to the trained participant. Adorno and Horkheimer coined the term "culture industry" to refer to the culture that "the masses" passively consume, thus revealing their passivity. This culture industry manipulates consumers and indoctrinates them into consumer capitalism (and, I would argue, white-supremacist patriarchy). Conversely, "authentic" culture offers a utopian space free of capitalist constraints. While I like how the term "culture industry" links material conditions to popular culture, I disagree with the notions that mass culture is uniform and fixed, and that "the masses," or consumers, are passive. Subcultures alone suggest otherwise.

14. Advertising and the Political Economy of Lesbian/Gay Identity
Fred Fejes

Homosexuality is "a pathetic little second-rate substitute for reality, a pitiable flight from life. As such it deserves fairness, compassion, understanding, and when possible, treatment. But it deserves no encouragement, no glamorization, no rationalization, no fake status as a minority group, no sophistry about simple differences in taste—and, above all, no pretense that it is anything but a pernicious sickness."
—"The Homosexual in America," *Time,* 21 January 1966

IBM, DKNY, American Express, Waterford, Dockers, Tattinger, Nieman Marcus, Circuit City, Virgin Atlantic, Smirnoff, Movado, Rockport, Bacardi, Versace, *New York Times,* Air New Zealand, Calvin Klein, Hennessy, Camel, Grand Marnier, British Airways, Eyeworks, Chivas Regal, Armani, Stolichnaya, Parliament Lights, Dr. Martens, Finlandia, Seiko, Freixnet, Lindemann's, Graham's Port, Beaulieu Vineyards, Clos Du Bois, Coors, Life Fitness, Verge, Creative Jewelers, Noa Jewelers, Tzabaco, Southern Comfort, Lucky Strike, Absolut, Kitchen Company, Prado, Tommy Hilfiger, Nautica, Hugo Boss, Diesel Denim, Tanqueray, Wilke-Rodriguez, Andrew Fezza, Dolce & Gabbana, Skyy Vodka, Moschino, Sauzo Tequila, Barneys, Solgar, Remy Martin, Aussie Hair, Kata Eyewear, Neptune Records, John Fluevog Shoes, Beverly Hills Institute of Aesthetic and Reconstructive Surgery, Bud Light, Propecia, Wilson Leather, Freshave, Metroman, Alize, Miller Light, Louis Vuitton, Baccarat, Gaultier, Benson and Hedges, Gianfranco Ferre, Bombay Sapphire, Nature's Recipe, Merit, Tropica
—Companies with full-page advertisements in the fall 1998 issue of *Out,* a national lesbian and gay magazine

If the struggle for legal and social equality for lesbians and gay males is still being fiercely fought (and often lost), the struggle to treat them as full and equal citizens in the republic of postscarcity, postmodern hyperconsumption is all over but the shouting. The good guys (and some of the girls) won. While it is typical to think of lesbians and gay males in terms of their sexual identities, with their emergence in recent years as economic subjects—self-conscious identities produced within the structure of commodity relationships—they have achieved an equality far greater than that found in the political or social realm. Indeed it seems the acceptance of lesbians and gay males as sexual/ political subjects is predicated on their acceptance and importance as consuming subjects. While in the past other marginalized groups have attained political power through the marshaling of economic resources, for lesbians and gay males it is not in their role as producers or controllers of capital, but in their role as consumers, particularly as a defined market niche attractive to advertisers, that they are offered the surest route to equality. Perhaps in the history of social movements this represents a pioneering political strategy in which pulling out the American Express Card has replaced the raised fist. An additional irony is that even while the commodification of lesbian/gay identity represents a pioneering political strategy, in many ways it reproduces the same old gender disparities. Lesbians and gay males may have achieved equality, but because of their more attractive income profile, advertisers decided early in the game that gay males are more equal than lesbians. Even in the Republic of Hyperconsumption governed by advertisers and marketeers the iron law of politics still applies: *plus ça change, plus ça rest le même.*

Although at the birth of the gay liberation movement in 1969 homosexuals were perhaps one of the most marginalized, stigmatized minorities in the United States, it did not take long for advertisers to ask about the potential of selling to the homosexual market. Mindful of the stereotypic image of gay men as upscale, high-spending consumers interested in the latest in fashion (then as now, lesbians figured very little in these discussions), *Advertising Age* in the early 1970s began running periodic reports about the possibilities of marketing to gays. The first report in 1972 was not very hopeful. Noting that most advertisers were reluctant to have their product identified with a gay market, many media outlets would not use the word "gay" in an advertisement, and in any event most gay men were very closeted (Baltera 1972). Three years later *Advertising Age* reported that advertisers were becoming more aware of gay men as a separate market niche, yet, fearing a backlash from heterosexual consumers, they still were very reluctant to have their product identified as a "gay product." Moreover they argued that they could reach the gay consumer through the regular advertising aimed at the straight market (Baltera 1975).

A more practical reason why advertisers and marketing companies were hesitant to take the gay market seriously was lack of reliable marketing data about gay men. If gay media were serious about attracting mainstream advertising dollars, they first had to construct a statistical picture of the gay consumer. The first marketing survey of gay men was conducted in 1977 when the *Advocate,* at that time the only gay publication with a national audience, hired an independent marketing research firm to conduct a survey of its readers in an attempt to attract major national advertisers. According to results, the typical *Advocate* readers were gay professional men between the ages of twenty and forty with above-average incomes. Free of the financial burden of supporting a family, they could afford to spend their large incomes on themselves, particularly on high-priced liquors, clothes, and travel. According to the magazine's publisher, gay men were not merely trying to prove that we can "live as well as the Joneses, (but) we live a damn sight better" (Stabiner 1982). By picturing the gay market as one composed of upscale gay men with high-priced habits of consumption, the survey seemed to confirm what was thought about the gay market, and by extension, the gay community. By 1980 *Advertising Age* noted that national advertisers such as Seagrams, Simon and Schuster, and the major film companies were beginning to place ads in national publications like the *Advocate* and in local gay newspapers (Pendleton 1980). Advertisers were also becoming aware of how, particularly in urban areas, the consumption habits and fashion tastes of gay men were being imitated by straight men, particularly in clothing designs that emphasized a highly eroticized masculinity. Rather than being an isolated marginalized niche, gay men were seen as both hyperconsumers and powerful trendsetters for new designs and products (Stabiner 1982).

Yet reaching the gay market was problematic. In the early 1980s there was as yet no slick glossy publication that explicitly targeted gay men. Publications that did exist, such as the *Advocate* and local gay newspapers and magazines, did not have the high production quality required by major national advertisers, particularly fashion advertisers, and their content—heavy with photos of half-dressed or nude handsome young men and advertisements for erotic, pornographic videos and sexual services—was too explicitly sexual for most mainstream advertisers. Moreover, many advertisers, particularly fashion advertisers, were still reluctant to have their products too closely associated with the gay market. Some fashion designer advertisers such as Paco Rabanne, Marlboro, Levi Strauss, and Calvin Klein got around this problem by utilizing the "gay window advertising" approach, con-structing ads with homosexual subtexts very obvious to gay readers but unnoticed by straight readers and then placing these ads in main-stream men's fashion magazines (Stabiner 1982; Holland 1977; Merret 1988; see also Sender 1999).

In order to attract national advertisers, gay publications like the *Advocate* in the late 1980s and early 1990s upgraded their production quality and changed their format and editorial focus. The *Advocate*, for example, cordoned off its classified and other sexually explicit ma-terial into a separate publication—"We wanted the magazine to be something gay men could leave on the coffee table when their mothers came over" noted the publisher (Pogrebin 1996)—and redesigned itself as a news magazine with a focus on national events of interest to the gay community and cultural and feature stories about art and enter-tainment. Its strategy was successful and its ad revenue doubled from $1.9 million to $3.8 million between 1990 and 1992 (C. Miller 1992). In the early 1990s a number of new gay national magazines, including *Out, Genre, 10 Percent, QW,* and *Deneuve,* appeared. With the excep-tion of the lesbian magazine *Deneuve* (which later changed its name to *Curve*), these publications were aimed at gay males. In an effort to at-tract national advertisers, particularly fashion advertisers, they all had the similar strategy of printing on high-grade glossy paper and empha-sizing "lifestyle" content of general feature stories about fashion, ce-lebrities, travel, and current events to target the upper-income segment of their markets. As these new publications were competing among themselves, and with the *Advocate,* for national advertising dollars, most had short lives. Among these new lifestyle entrants, *Out* emerged as the clear victor and by 1996 was the leading gay magazine with its 119,000 circulation topping the *Advocate*'s 74,000 (Wilke 1996).

With the explicit sexual material gone and market-survey data about gay consumers beginning to appear, by the mid-1990s most ad-vertisers had overcome any reluctance about advertising in gay publi-cations. As *Advertising Age* reported in bold headlines on its front page in 1997, "Big advertisers join move to embrace gay market" (Wilke 1997b). As the head of Rivendell Marketing, a gay and lesbian media placement company, noted, "Ten years ago we had a tough time get-ting an appointment at any agency. Now everybody will see us" (Pogre-bin 1996). In addition to fashion designers such as Gucci, Versace, and Yves St. Laurent, traditional major advertisers like Aetna Life and Casualty, General Motors, Chase Manhattan Corporation, Johnson and Johnson, United Airlines, Merrill Lynch, and American Express began to take pages in gay publications. More recently even advertisers like Chesebrough-Pond's (Mentadent toothpaste), Bristol-Myers Squibb (Excedrin), and McNeil Consumer Products (Motrin) began advertising in gay media (Wilke 1998).

Moreover, many local and regional gay periodicals, noting the success of the *Advocate* and *Out,* have undertaken a similar strategy of getting rid of sexually explicit material, improving production quality, and using market research to produce a statistical profile of their readership in an effort to attract nongay local and regional advertisers. For example, to improve their marketability to nongay advertisers, the ten major gay newspapers of the National Gay Newspaper Guild commissioned Simmons Market Research Bureau in 1991 to undertake a major market study of their readership. Data were produced about the gay readership in Miami, Los Angeles, Boston, San Francisco, Philadelphia, Washington, D.C., Dallas, New York, Houston, and Chicago that matched the results of the studies done for the national gay publications (Fejes and Lennon 2000).

There is little mystery as to why advertisers are very interested in the gay market. As the advertising director of *Out* explained, "Imagine going to an advertiser and saying 'above average income, highly educated, travels a lot, buys all the new electronic toys and gadgets'" (Rosen 1994). In 1994 the major marketing research company Yankelovich Partners conducted what was at that time the most sophisticated study of the gay and lesbian market. In contrast to previous studies, which were based on the readers of various periodicals who voluntarily responded to mail-in questionnaires, this study was based on a random sample of the general population, taking from that sample those who had voluntarily identified themselves as lesbian or gay. Interestingly, this study did not find lesbian and gay consumers to have incomes significantly greater than the general population. However, what was significant was the way the income was spent. The study, which received attention on the front page of the business section of the *New York Times* and the results of which were incorporated later in a book on how to reach the gay consumer, showed gay males and lesbians to be more educated, more technologically oriented, and more likely to be self-employed than the average heterosexual consumer. As a group they were seen as far more "cutting edge," more likely to spend their money on new products. To advertisers, they were a very desirable group of innovative consumers (Elliott 1994; Lukenbill

1995). But while advertisers and marketers talked of a "lesbian and gay" market and lifestyle, the picture generally called to mind was that of a gay male. In advertising the results of its readership study to advertisers, the National Gay Newspaper Guild used the photo of a young white man in a business suit (Fejes and Lennon 2000). For a moment in the early 1990s it seemed that a "lesbian chic" was achieving a mainstream currency, that in terms of style and fashion lesbians would perform the same function for heterosexual women that gay men do for heterosexual men, and that lesbians would be "broken out" as a separate market category (Clark 1991). Yet that moment quickly passed as the advertisers decided that lesbians were not an attractive, identifiable market niche and could moreover be reached through ads aimed at women generally.

Trying to reach a "gay" market is not easy. The effort to construct a market profile of lesbians and gays is fraught with a number of major problems. As with all surveys, the construction and size of the sample determine how representative the results are of the population being measured. The one survey that used a randomly selected sample had a sample size of less than 150 (Wilke 1996). Many of the studies that utilized larger sample sizes obtained their respondents from subscription lists of gay periodicals and direct-mail lists. As a result of this process of self-selection, the samples were highly skewed. A good example of this was the 1991 Simmons study of the readership of major lesbian and gay newspapers. The sample was predominantly male (9:1) and predominantly white-Anglo: in Miami, with a 50 percent Hispanic/Latino population, only 5 percent of the gay readership identified themselves as Hispanic/Latino; and in Washington, D.C., with a 66 percent African American population, again only 5 percent of the readers identified themselves as African American (Fejes and Lennon 2000). In contrast, in what is the most comprehensive study of sexual behavior in America, the sociologist Edwin Laumann and his colleagues found that the ratio of gay males to lesbians was 2:1 (Laumann et al. 1994, 303–05) and that more African American males engaged in same-sex behavior and more Hispanics/Latinos identified themselves as homo- or bisexual than Anglos. (Comparable data for females were not given.)

Beyond these technical problems, a basic conceptual problem is involved in these surveys. There is no established method or standard for defining a lesbian or gay person. For example, Laumann and his colleagues found it necessary to break down the category of homosexuality into three dimensions: desire, behavior, and identity, each yielding a different number of homosexuals (Laumann et al. 1994, 292–97). Generally the most common method of categorization is self-identification—it is also the most conservative one. According to Laumann, only 2.8 percent of the men and 1.4 percent of the women identified themselves as homosexual or bisexual. Given the fact that same-sex acts are still outlawed in most states and open disclosure of one's homosexuality can often lead to job loss and other harmful consequences, many lesbians and gay males are reluctant to respond to questions about sexual orientation posed by a census questionnaire, telephone marketing survey, or interviewer. Perhaps it is no surprise that marketing and consumer surveys often show lesbians and gay males as having higher incomes, being self-employed, having higher levels of education, and living in major urban areas. These individuals most likely enjoy a greater sense of personal, professional, and economic security and are thus more willing to be open about their sexual orientation. Finally, the terms "gay" and "lesbian" themselves are not without ambiguity. To many of the pre-Stonewall (pre-1969) generation, the preferred term is "homosexual"; to some of the younger generation, the term is "queer." Furthermore, such studies totally ignore emerging bisexual and transgendered identities.

Nonetheless, in spite of these difficulties, studies of the lesbian and gay consumer continue, as advertisers, marketers, and gay media try to get an accurate picture of what they are dealing with. In the process, advertisers construct identities for lesbians and gay men. As can be discerned, the results of the various studies provide odd and often conflicting information. Studies based on the readership of lesbian/gay periodicals that generally set the pattern have produced a picture of the lesbian/gay market as one consisting of affluent, well-educated individuals with upscale consumption patterns. For example, a 1996 study done by Simmons Market Research Bureau utilizing a sample of almost 4,000 respondents found that 28.6 percent had annual incomes exceeding $50,000 and 21 percent of the households had incomes above $100,000. Close to 60 percent of the respondents held management positions, 48 percent were college educated, and 61 percent had taken a foreign trip in the twelve months preceding the study (Wilke 1997b). However, the sample was drawn from subscription lists of gay periodicals and direct-mail lists. The studies based on samples other than subscription lists for lesbian/gay periodicals, such as the 1994 Yankelovich study and a 1998 study by the New York marketing consultants Spare Parts, tend to show lesbians and gays as having only marginally higher incomes than heterosexuals (Wilke 1998). The two scholarly studies of income among lesbians and gay males—the first using data from the 1990 census, which counted households with unmarried partners of the same sex, and the second using data from the General Social Survey of the National Opinion Research Center—both found that lesbians and gay males actually made less money than their heterosexual counterparts, even when the sample was controlled for profession, education, and region (Klawitter and Flatt 1998; Badgett 1995).

In spite of the problematic aspects of these studies, one can argue that they still represent a marketing process that culminates in more media representations of lesbians and gay males. To lesbians and gay males, after decades of invisibility and marginality and stigmatization, being aggressively courted by advertisers and the media can be a sign of progress. Rather than being portrayed as pathetic, mentally ill sex perverts and child molesters who are threats to religion, home, family, and the state, they are now portrayed as young, healthy, fun to be with, and having a lot of disposable income. Although this marketing campaign is not explicitly political, it fits very well into the broader "assimilationist" strategy advocated by major mainstream lesbian and gay political organizations such as the Human Rights Campaign. Indeed, gay writers about media and marketing—for example, Marshall Kirk and Hunter Madsen, authors of *After the Ball: How America Will Conquer Its Fear and Hatred of Gays in the 90s* (1989), and Grant Lukenbill, author of *Untold Millions: Positioning Your Business for the Gay and Lesbian Consumer Revolution* (1995)—see the proliferation of "positive" (read young, healthy, attractive, mainstream, affluent) gay and lesbian images in the media, be they on television shows or in advertising, as the surest route to political equality and power.

Yet the political benefits of this marketing attention are not all that clear. As Urvashi Vaid noted in her critical study of the problematic nature of the assimilation strategy, *Virtual Equality: The Mainstreaming of Gay and Lesbian Liberation,* being highly valued by marketers means nothing politically unless there is also a strong political movement that presses for political rights and equality. In the 1970s and 1980s the single woman with her own income and life became a standard image in advertising and the media. Yet this did nothing to abate the growth of a strong conservative religious movement demanding that women be "restored" to their traditional role as subservient to their husbands. Racist media images are for the most part a thing of the past, and the inclusion of images of African Americans, Asians, and other people of color in advertising and media products is so common as to be unnoticed. Yet the efforts to scale back affirmative action programs and deny social benefits to immigrants are just one example of how racism is still very much a part of American life. For lesbians and gay males, all the attention that advertisers began to accord them in the late 1980s did little to temper the virulence of the opposition to giving lesbians and gays the right either to serve in the military or to have their relationships legally sanctioned.

Indeed, one can argue that the marketing studies and subsequent advertising and media attention have hurt the lesbian and gay community politically. While these marketing studies do not present a realistic or representative portrayal of the lesbian/gay community, what they have done—lacking any comprehensive demographic information—is to present a picture of the lesbian and gay community that has become very much part of the political discourse about that community. Indeed, in the various political debates about the political and legal status of lesbians and gays that form part of the ongoing "culture wars," the information provided by these marketing studies is often used as an objective description of lesbians and gay males. The professional, affluent image of lesbians and gays created by market research conforms well with the notion that the "homosexual lifestyle" is a choice made mostly by white, well-educated, middle-class males. More importantly, a claim frequently made by religious and conservative opponents of measures to ban discrimination on the basis of sexual orientation is that lesbians and gay males are not victims of discrimination; rather, if anything, they represent a privileged minority, particularly in terms of income and education (see Concerned Women of America 1991; Knight 1994). In the Supreme Court deliberations in *Romer v. Evans*, over the constitutionality of a Colorado state constitutional provision banning any laws protecting lesbians and gays against discrimination, Justice Antonin Scalia used this argument in voting to uphold the Colorado law ("Excerpts" 1996).

If the political consequences of marketing and advertising to the lesbian and gay community are problematic, so too are the consequences for the lesbian and gay community itself. It has been frequently noted that lesbians and gays often take advertising directed at their community as a sign of validation and legitimation (Penaloza 1996). If they have not yet achieved the status of citizens with full and equal rights, they at least have achieved the status of desirable consumers. For lesbians and gay males, consumption is often an act with political overtones (Kates 1998). They are aware of those companies that advertise in lesbian and gay media and that have lesbian/gay affirmative policies and benefits, and they tend to be loyal to those companies. Conversely, companies that have a reputation for being homophobic are avoided or even actively boycotted.

More significantly, media images and consumption play a more important role in the construction of a definition of the lesbian and gay community and lesbian and gay identity than they do in the process of identity formation of individuals in other groups. In contrast to people of color and other marginalized groups, youths and young adults with primarily same-sex desires and orientation have little or no help in understanding or defining themselves as gay or lesbian. Sexual orientation is fixed early in life, if not at birth, but a lesbian or a gay male develops, or "comes out," in an environment offering little information or role models (Savin-Williams 1990; Herdt 1989). Although the negative stigma attached to homosexuality is reinforced through interpersonal contact, persons who are coming out search both the interpersonal and media environment for clues to understanding their feelings and sense of difference. Thus media images, whether in advertising or other media products, become very powerful in helping one to develop a sense of identity.

In the past the images available to lesbians and gay males in the mainstream media were highly negative. Since the late 1960s, however, the lesbian and gay community began to develop its own community media, which presented alternate and affirmative images (Streitmatter 1995). The pages of these community media tended to be open to a diversity of viewpoints and experiences. For young lesbians and gay males coming out and beginning to define themselves both individually and as members of a community, the community media were very important in providing information and images that they used to construct their identities. However, in the 1980s this community-based nature of the media began to change as various publications decided to pursue the advertising dollars of mainstream advertisers. The publications became more professional and their focus became less the expression of the community's diversity than the shaping of a readership that would attract advertisers.

Today, if a gay male who is coming out turns to the gay media, most likely what he will find is that to be a homosexual in today's society is to be a masculine young white male, with a well-muscled body and handsome face, a good education, and a professional job. Moreover, he will learn, all the members of the gay community are alike. There may be a few African Americans or Asians, albeit with very Caucasian features, and a few women, but aside from their race or gender, there is very little difference. They all live in a gay-friendly environment where there is no sexism, racism, homophobia, or poverty. To be "gay" in this sense the gay male needs an annual income of at least $50,000 so that he can drink top-brand liquors, wear designer clothes, vacation in exotic places, go to the gym, and ride in an SUV. Whereas in the past coming out was chiefly about sex, today it is as much about consumption.

For a young women coming out, the situation is even more problematic. While the major national magazines like *Out* and the *Advocate* define themselves as serving the entire lesbian and gay male community, in practice the gay male market is their target audience, and thus women are marginalized, if not made invisible. This was made clear in late 1997 when the female editor and cofounder of *Out* magazine was dismissed; the major complaint was directed at her strategy of taking the magazine in a "multifaceted direction . . . which [was] very inclusive of both gay and lesbian issues . . . [but was] not working in the eyes of money people." The new editor was expected to steer "the magazine toward gay men's issues at the expense of coverage of lesbians," as the men have higher incomes (Pogrebin 1997b). Because of their smaller readership, the few publications geared primarily toward lesbians, like *Curve* (formerly known as *Deneuve*), have to try even harder to attract an upscale audience in order to attract mainstream advertisers. These magazines also experienced the need to move away from sexually explicit and political subject matter. The West Coast magazine *Girlfriends* did away with its centerfold and began to concentrate on stories dealing with parenting and breast cancer. The erotic lesbian magazine *On Our Backs,* which symbolized a rebellious assertion of female sexuality, went out of business (Pogrebin 1996). And as is true with the other gay magazines, the concerns and images of the white, upper-middle-class Anglo woman strongly shape the construction of lesbian sexuality.

Social and sexual identities that do not match the desired audience profile are minimized or made totally invisible in these publications. With improvements in printing technology making the publication of small magazines relatively easy, and now with the proliferation of specialized web pages, marginalized desires and identities are allowed some exposure. There is, for example, a magazine for people—primarily gay males—with AIDS *(POZ)*; a magazine for African American gay males *(BLK)*; *Transgender Tapestry* for transvestites and transsexuals; and numerous magazines for the different sexual communities existing within the lesbian and gay male community, such as the leather and S/M community. Yet the existence of these other publications also reflects the fact that these identities have little place in the dominant gay and lesbian publications. The centuries-old underground gay and lesbian culture—in which people with strongly stigmatized identities blurred class and race boundaries and risked much to affirm their own desires—has been repackaged with its "rough edges" trimmed away. The commodification of gay and lesbian identity has resulted in the construction of a "straight" gay/lesbian identity. As Sarah Schulman notes, "A fake homosexuality has been constructed to facilitate a double marketing strategy: selling products to gay consumers that address their emotional need to be accepted while selling a palatable image of homosexuality to heterosexual consumers that meets their need to have their dominance obscured" (1998, 146). Updating Foucault, it would seem that today the consumer-based media, and not the state, the church, or the scientific professions, are the far more effective creators and regulators of identities and desires.

Furthermore, the consequences of such narrow representation in ads can go beyond the issue of images and identities. With the introduction in the 1990s of protease inhibitors, which significantly slow the progress of the AIDS virus in the body, pharmaceutical companies marketing these new drug therapies became big advertisers in magazines with large gay male readership. Typically their ads showed young, healthy, handsome, affluent, mostly white males engaged in strenuous physical sports or activities like mountain climbing or cross-country biking and encouraged readers with the HIV virus to talk to their doctors about trying the advertised drug. According to drug companies, ads that put such a healthy and happy face on AIDS "motivat(ed) patients to talk to their doctors about treatment options." What the ads did not show was that the drug therapies did not work for all patients and that, for people for whom the drugs did work, there were often significant side effects, such as liver damage, increased cholesterol, reshaped facial structure, and redistribution of body fat, resulting in bulging stomachs and necks and fatless legs and arms. In reality very few people taking the drugs resembled the men in the ads. Such ads minimized the consequences of AIDS, according to a spring 2001 survey by the University of California, San Francisco, of gay men in health clinics. The overwhelming majority of those surveyed thought the ads promoted unsafe sex. Following the study's release, the U.S. Food and Drug Administration ordered the pharmaceutical companies to change their ads to reflect more accurately the consequences of contracting the AIDS virus (Kirby 2001).

In spite of advertising's open welcome to lesbians and gays, the "gays in the military" and "gay marriage" political firestorms of recent years show how tenuous is the political position of lesbians and gay males. Virulent homophobia is still very much a part of today's landscape, as witnessed by the October 1998 murder of Matthew Shepard, the young gay college student in Wyoming who was ferociously beaten, his skull literally cracked, and then tied to a fence, in a manner similar to ranchers displaying slain wolves, as a warning to others of his kind. Or as witnessed by the February 1999 murder of Billy Jack Gaither, a thirty-nine-year-old rural Alabama gay man who was lured to a deserted spot by two men who bludgeoned him to death with an axe handle and then set his body afire on top of a pyre of old tires. The charred remains of Gaither and the crucified figure of Shepard stand in stark contrast to the images of happy and healthy gay men and lesbians found in heavily ad-saturated magazines like *Out* and the *Advocate*. Homosexuality ignores class, race, ethnic, and regional boundaries; most lesbians and gay men are not twenty-six years old and do not live charmed, protected, and carefree lives in trendy urban centers, earning high incomes in glamorous white-collar professions, going to the gym daily, wearing the latest fashions. The situation of typical lesbians and gay males is much closer to that of Matthew Shepard or Billy Jack Gaither—living in an environment quietly antagonistic at best or at worst openly hostile to their existence, being careful as to whom they disclose their sexual identity, and often at risk in the expression of their sexual desire. To these people, the advertising-filled magazines now filling the lesbian/gay magazine sections of chain bookstores like Borders and Barnes & Noble represent a reality in which their lives and experience are once again invisible.

15. Gendering the Commodity Audience: Critical Media Research, Feminism, and Political Economy

Eileen R. Meehan

Throughout the 1970s and 1980s, media scholars sorted the field into the categories of "mainstream" versus "critical" research. These adjectives instantly communicated where one stood in terms of the root assumptions and valuations undergirding one's work—as well as which side you rooted for at the staged debates where administrative researchers like Elihu Katz or Wilbur Schramm debated some representative of the opposition—perhaps James Carey, or Herbert Schiller, or Stuart Hall (Meehan 1999; see Poole and Schiller 1981). At the time, the administrative paradigm so dominated the field that its practitioners often assumed it was the only way to do research, rejecting other approaches as subjective, unsystematic, and impractical—as "armchair theorizing" little better than wishful thinking. Thus George Gerbner underplayed the intellectual hostility associated with the paradigmatic debates when he titled his special 1983 issue of the *Journal of Communication* "Ferment in the Field." Glancing back, I am struck by the "mainstream" paradigm's ability to unify its opposition—to place Carey, Schiller, and Hall on the same side. But I am also struck by the absence of feminist work in that benchmark publication, despite the *Journal*'s openness to feminist work under Gerbner's editorship (e.g., Busby 1975; Cantor 1977, 1979; Lemon 1977; Poe 1976; Streicher 1974) as well as the tremendous outpouring of feminist research across media studies in the 1970s generally (e.g., Arnold 1976; Brabant 1976; Holly 1979; Janus 1978; Marzoff, Rush, and Stern 1974–1975; Morris 1973; Ogan and Weaver 1978–1979; St. John 1978; Tuchman et al. 1978).

One decade later, in two issues of the same journal, Michael Gurevitch and Mark Levy published essays addressing "the future of the field," which were republished under the title *Defining Media Studies: Reflections on the Future of the Field* (1994). The book organized its forty-eight contributions into seven categories (disciplinarity, new directions, influencing public policy, audiences and institutions, critical research, history of the field, and academic curriculum and legitimacy). Administrative research dominated the volume and critical scholarship was sprinkled across four of the categories. In the critical category, two essays focused on political economy (Meehan, Mosco, and Wasko 1994; Schiller 1994); the other two on cultural studies (Grossberg 1994; McChesney 1994). Overall, only one essay offered a feminist perspective: H. Leslie Steeves's "Creating Imagined Communities: Development Communication and the Challenge of Feminism" (1994) in the public policy category. Yet, in describing the collection, Gurevitch and Levy state:

> The paradigmatic debate (or "dialogue") that dominated communication scholarship in the '70s and early '80s has been replaced by new and different intellectual nudgings, by the injection into communication scholarship of *recently emergent perspectives such as feminism,* postmodernism, and neofunctionalism. (1994, 7, emphasis mine)

As a political economist, trained during the period leading up to "Ferment," and as a coauthor of an essay in *Defining,* I find this all rather disturbing, yet oddly unsurprising.

That contradictory reaction motivates this essay. As a political economist, I have focused my research mainly on the internal structures of media-based corporations—which shape the form and content of cultural commodities (e.g., Meehan 1991)—and the external relationships between such corporations—which also shape cultural commodities and which construct media markets (e.g., Meehan 1990). Working at this level of abstraction generally has meant treating large-scale, impersonal institutions as agents with little reference to the actions, struggles, or alliances of human beings. Much of the feminist scholarship in communications takes a less abstracted point of entry: women working in the industries (Martin 1991); women's use of mediated artifacts (Radway 1984; Steeves et al. 1988); the fictional men and women offered as role models by the media (Byars 1991; Byars and Dell 1992); or some combination of these concerns (Andersen 1995; Stabile 1995).

Connections between feminist lines of research and institutional lines of research may not be readily apparent. The conditions of people's work and leisure, and the artifacts that they employ in each sphere, may seem fairly remote from the impact of transindustrial conglomeration on blockbuster films or the structure of markets in the broadcasting industry. Yet political economists and feminist scholars understand that patriarchy and capitalism have been historically intertwined in the United States from the nation's founding. This suggests that important connections between patriarchy and capitalism can be discovered by scholars who synthesize feminist and political-economic approaches to media research. It also suggests that our research heritages can be taken as one starting point from which to articulate that synthesis.

To test this, I return to a defining moment in political economy—the Blindspot Debate over the commodity audience, which raged in print in the *Canadian Journal of Political and Social Theory* (Smythe 1977, 1978; Murdock 1978; Livant 1979) and in person (Smythe, Murdock, Garnham) at the 1978 conference of the International Association for Mass Communication Research in Poland. After summarizing the Blindspot Debate, I then return to my own analysis of the commodity audience in national television. I review that work to tease out the dynamics of patriarchy and capitalism that undergird the markets for commodity ratings and commodity audiences. This particular intersection of feminism and political economy suggests that much can be gained by such revisionist exercises, which, in concert with new syntheses and new approaches to research, may generate an intellectual rapprochement between feminism and political economy in media studies.

What Do the Media Make?

This seemingly innocent question drove the Blindspot Debate. Having posed the question, Smythe (1977) suggested that most critical researchers of the period would respond thus: the media were consciousness industries that made texts (films, television shows, etc.) embodying the dominant ideology, which was absorbed by the average audience member as naturalized, common sense. Hence, media were best studied by decoding texts to uncover the ideology that produced consciousness. Smythe dismissed this as a blindspot of Western Marxism, caused by academic Marxists' overriding concern with ideology and their rejection of both political economy and political action. Smythe next posed his own, then-startling, answer: the media manufactured only one commodity—audiences. By this, Smythe meant that all media assembled, packaged, and sold audiences to advertisers. Content was secondary—a free lunch at best. Media industries were neither dream factories nor consciousness industries: they were hunter-gatherers of the audience.

These bold claims generated considerable debate, with Murdock (1978) taking the lead. Murdock offered a series of differentiations to scale back Smythe's claims. For Murdock, media earning revenues from advertisers were clearly different from media earning revenues directly from audience members. This separated movie studios, book publishers, and recording labels from television networks, newspapers, and magazines. Only advertiser-supported media produced commodity audiences but, for Murdock, even those media could not be reduced to transactions between corporations. He argued that any media artifact operated at two levels: economic and cultural. While the economic level was of greatest interest to media companies, it was less relevant to audiences being processed for sale. The images, ideas, visions, narratives, characters, and performances embodied in the media artifact, and the people comprising the audiences for such artifacts, also needed study. Murdock called for research recognizing the economic and cultural dimensions of commercial media.

Smythe responded by critiquing Murdock and reasserting his central claims. Over the years, other scholars engaged these issues, shifting the focus and testing the claims of the original debate (D'Acci 1994; Jhally 1982; Livant 1982; McCormack 1983; Meehan 1984; Wasko et al. 1993). The phrases "audience commodity" and "commodity audience" entered the critical lexicon. That such a commodity existed and played a crucial role in advertiser-supported media generally became axiomatic in political-economic research on media. Further, as advertising ("product placement") increasingly shaped content in movies and books, the demarcation between advertiser-supported and audience-supported media artifacts thinned. However, for scholars working on reception or representation, the significance of the audience commodity in their decoding of texts or reconstruction of readers' reactions was little appreciated, as pointed out by such critical cultural scholars as Stabile (1995) or Budd, Entman, and Steinem (1990).

Case Study: Broadcasting and Ratings

As Smythe's notion of the audience commodity became established, it also became a focus for research. In my case, that meant exploring the audience commodity in the U.S. system of national broadcasting. My research focused on the corporations that oligopolized network broadcasting (RCA's NBC and CBS in radio; RCA's NBC, CBS, and ABC in television) and in the market where those networks sold, and advertisers bought, the audience commodity. These transactions were highly routinized. The employees who made the deals relied entirely on the ratings book, which specified the number of people in the audience and described them in rough demographic categories. These employees were not executives; they were relatively low-paid and generally female. Yet their labor put together the basic transactions from which networks earned revenues.

These crucial transactions were routinized through dependence on the ratings. This suggested a structural dependence between the market for the audience commodity and the market for ratings. From 1929 to the present, advertisers and networks had typically purchased ratings from a single provider. The buyers' apparent willingness to allow a monopoly suggested that the dynamics in this market deserved closer inspection. Rather than rehearse my research into the history of the ratings industry and the rating market's structuration, I will focus on the results of that research. Four elements that emerged from it are relevant for this discussion.

The first element was shared demand: advertisers and networks demanded measurements of bona fide consumers. Bona fide consumers had the disposable income, access, and desire to loyally purchase brand names and to habitually make impulse purchases. This consumerist caste expanded and contracted in response to capitalism's boom-and-bust cycle. To accommodate the shared demand for consumers, the ratings monopolist selected methods that discriminated against mere listeners or viewers. For example, during the Great Depression, the C. E. Hooper Company used telephone interviews to measure the commodity audience; in the 1975–80 recession, the A. C. Nielsen Company (ACN) based its sample on cable households. In both cases, the measurement method ensured that the sampled households had the funds, desire, and location that allowed them to subscribe to nonessential services. This clearly differentiated the methods and reports of such ratings "research" from social-scientific studies of audience behavior. In ratings, unified demand for the consumerist caste shaped measurement practices.

The second element was the connection between demand and price, which revealed a discontinuity between advertisers' and networks' interests in the size of the commodity audience. The larger the number of bona fide consumers viewing, the higher the price charged by networks. Conversely, the smaller the number, the lower the price. This discontinuity allowed the ratings monopolist to play networks against advertisers, and corporations to form alliances across industries. During the early 1960s, NBC tried to restructure the market by persuading advertisers to shift demand from "how many viewers overall" to "how many viewers between 18 and 34." ABC joined in the campaign and the two networks persuaded advertisers that 18-to-34-year-olds were better consumers. By 1963, ACN was shifting its sample to emphasize the new demographic; the networks followed by replacing "old favorites" like *The Beverly Hillbillies* and *Petticoat Junction* with "youth-oriented" and "socially relevant" programs like *Mod Squad* and *Storefront Lawyers*. Similarly, in the early 1970s, cable channels used this discontinuity to insert themselves into the relationships among advertisers and networks, and to persuade ACN to measure cable audiences. Discontinuity in demand, then, was used by "players" to renegotiate relationships and restructure the market, thereby changing how the commodity audience was defined and measured.

The third element to emerge was the cybernetic nature of the commodity audience (Mosco 1996). The commodity audience was knowable only through the ratings that measured it and those ratings were the outcome of corporate rivalries, alliances, and manipulations.

This led to the fourth and last element: television's commodity audience had nothing to do with the people who watched television.[1]

These four claims emerged from my institutional analysis of the long-term, impersonal relationships between corporations constituting the markets for commodity ratings and commodity audiences. Building on these claims, I then organized "television" into three markets. The market for commodity ratings served as the fundamental market that set the parameters within which the market for the commodity audience and the market for programming worked.

Three of the Markets Constituting Broadcast Television

The ratings monopolist balanced continuities and discontinuities in demand through its selection of measurement practices. The monopolist responded to continuities in demand by targeting the bona fide consumers demanded by advertisers and broadcasters; unless demanded, the rest of the viewership was unimportant. Discontinuities meant that either the ratings monopolist or blocs of buyers could attempt restructuration of the market for commodity ratings; the monopolist's methods and its definition of the commodity audience responded to shifts in market structuration and participants' power.[2] Given its monopoly position and the pricing conflict that separated advertisers and networks, the ratings monopolist exercised some agency in selecting its methods, thereby controlling costs of production. All of these economic concerns shaped the ratings reports and ensured that they were commodities— not research.

Based on the ratings commodity, advertisers and networks set to work low-paid, female employees relying on ratings to conduct the transactions in which networks sell their portions of the commodity audience to advertisers. This market and the routinization of its transactions depended entirely on the power relations embodied in the market for commodity ratings. Ratings became the proverbial floor upon which this market rested. And, although ratings were widely dismissed as misleading or inadequate in the trade press, they were treated as absolute truths in this market.

Upon that market was erected yet another structure: the market for programs in which networks, their internal production units, and independent producers negotiated over programs. Decisions here relied on track record, that is, on previous success in the ratings. A proven track record meant either that the production unit's previous series had earned high ratings or that elements of the proposed show had been featured in last year's top-rated programs. Elements included the proposed stars, type of cast, typical plot, genre, and "twist" in the genre's formula.[3] Networks assumed that past success was a predictor of future success—always defining success in terms of the ratings. The ratings, then, shaped decisions about contracts for new series and employment, about casting and plots, about routine and innovative representations.

With track record as the main prognosticator of success, no network would accept—and no producer would propose—a series without a track record.[4] But even the best prognostications go wrong. Historically, most new series are canceled due to poor ratings. Indeed, a tenth of a rating point can mean the difference between retention and cancellation. Thus, commodity ratings set the limits of broadcast programming in the present and the future.

Engendering Markets

For broadcasting, then, Smythe was both correct and incorrect. His analysis revealed that the main product manufactured by networks and sold to advertisers was the commodity audience. But his belief that the ratings monopolist exercised no agency misled him. The political economy of ratings, as summarized above, demonstrated the key role played by the market for commodity ratings and traced the structural forces that constructed ratings as truly *manufactured* commodities whose content depended on changing power relations within that market.

Returning to the main concern of this essay, I now ask: what does a feminist perspective illuminate about these ungendered markets and the ungendered corporations operating within them? My answer is twofold: taking a feminist perspective reveals that societal divisions of labor based on gender, plus prejudicial assumptions about gender, played a significant role in defining and differentiating the commodity audience. To see this, let us return to industrial concerns about the demographics of the commodity audience.

Although age grade became a central concern in the 1960s, the demographic category of gender was an industrial concern for the rating monopolist, advertisers, and broadcasters from at least 1929. Indeed, the female commodity audience had a special place in network schedules: in the daytime, doing housework, listening to talk shows and episodic serials. Both forms of programming were geared toward advertising, whether indirectly using product placements in the script or directly as commercial interruptions. Episodic serials were called soap operas as much for their content as their ownership: soap manufacturers produced the shows and contracted for broadcast time on NBC or CBS to run them. The ratings monopolist[5] treated female audiences as the normal, naturally occurring listenership for daytime programming. During the Great Depression, there was no interest in households without telephones, women who worked outside the home, or men who did not. This carried over into the 1960s and was reflected in Neilsen reports on daytime viewership by women, which carried such titles as *Where the Girls Are.*

Opposite daytime and its female commodity audience was "prime time" and its highly prized male commodity audience. However, prime time was not "where the boys were" but rather where *the* audience was. Networks that couldn't draw *the* audience counterprogrammed for niche audiences, meaning women, or women and children, or African Americans, or Hispanic Americans, or some combination thereof.[6] This subtle shift in language gendered the commodity audience as male and assumed its descent line to be European. Thus the commodity audience was differentiated into the valuable and desired audience of white men produced by the network that won the ratings contest versus the niche audiences begrudgingly produced by networks that lost the ratings contest. As *the* audience, the white male commodity audience had a "higher quality" for which advertisers willingly paid.

The industrial definition of "higher quality" shifted when NBC and ABC succeeded in joining age to gender as the crucial markers of *the* audience. That commodity audience narrowed to the white men aged 18 to 34 within the ACN sample. As cable channels squirmed their way into the mix, cable subscription was added to the industrial definition of *the* audience, yet again narrowing the commodity audience, this time to white male cable subscribers 18 to 34. With two further modifications in this industrial definition, ACN adjusted its ratings to take into account social status and women's employment outside the home. The long recessionary cycle that spanned 1975–1989 coincided with second-wave feminism. Through the same period, the Reagan and Bush administrations' monetarist policies effectively transferred wealth from the general population to the elite, promoted the exportation of heavy industrial operations, discouraged wage increases for workers of middle or lower social status, and encouraged companies to replace employees with temporary contractees (Bluestone and Harrison 1982). Among other things, these synergistic policies brought more women generally, and more college-educated women specifically, into the documented workforce. In such two-income households may be seen one effect of second-wave feminism: these women generally retained some control over their earnings.

In any case, ACN expanded its demographic categories to include "working women" as well as the terms "upscale" and "downscale" to identify the social status attached to occupation and income. For advertisers, upscale white male cable subscribers aged 18 to 34 watching television during prime time became the most valued and demanded commodity audience. Daytime remained women's time, although upscale women 18 to 34 and upscale working women 18 to 34 using videocassette recorders to tape programs were more highly valued than mere housewives. Among the new niche audiences for prime time, the category of upscale white working women aged 18 to 34 and subscribing to cable had sufficient attraction for advertisers that networks designed programs blending elements of soap operas into action-adventure programs.[7]

This periodic narrowing of *the* audience demonstrates the difference between the commodity audience and the people who actually watch television. It also suggests that noneconomic assumptions undergird beliefs about what sorts of people *ought* to be *the* audience and that those assumptions follow familiar patterns of discrimination on the grounds of gender, race, social status, sexual orientation, and age. Given limitations of space, I will discuss only the assumptions about gender.

Such institutionalized sexism might be dismissed as pragmatic given certain assumptions about gender and money: most of the workforce was male; men earned more than women; thus more men had more to spend than women regardless of women's occupations. Advertisers wanted spenders, so networks and cable channels had to target men to meet advertisers' demand for spenders.

According to these assumptions, the three markets operated rationally by discriminating against women. The market for commodity ratings necessarily placed greater value on measurements of males than on measurements of females. The market for the commodity audience rationally preferred buying the male commodity audience in prime time and treated the female commodity audience as a special niche with limited and time-specific appeal. When some of that latter commodity audience gained and controlled income, they become a very special niche—one that could be attracted through the manipulation of subtexts in male-oriented programming. That left the market for prime-time programming gearing production for the male commodity audience, but with female-friendly elements to attract the subniche of upscale women. Television was largely in the business of men—counting them, characterizing them, selling them, and programming for them. As long as "society" defined men as the proverbial breadwinners, that social reality governed the decisions of advertisers, networks, and the ratings monopolist.

Of course, that argument could be countered on its own stereotypical grounds: a sexist society may have defined men as breadwinners, but it also defined women as spenders. In the patriarchal division of domestic labor, woman's work included shopping for the household's general needs, for her own needs, and for the man's needs. The idealized version of that division of labor sent men outside the home to work for wages and women to spend those wages by shopping. Through their shopping, women assembled the materials necessary for men to rest and recuperate. If advertisers wanted to reach spenders, then they needed to target that category of people socially designated as spenders: women. Could advertisers have been blinded by sexism?

That question, posed ironically, has played out concretely in the history of two cable channels: ESPN and Lifetime. ESPN was launched in 1979 as a twenty-four-hour sports channel. It quickly gained acceptance from advertisers and cable operators. Now 80 percent owned by the Walt Disney Company, ESPN has added three more sports channels (ESPN-2, ESPN Classic, and ESPN News) and a chain of restaurant/ entertainment complexes called ESPNZone. While ESPN attracts mostly male viewers, it has not been categorized as a narrowcaster—that is, a channel serving a niche audience with highly defined and delimited tastes (Disney 1998).

In contrast, since its launch in 1984, Lifetime has consistently been treated as a narrowcaster reaching a small niche audience—women. As part of ABC's and Hearst's joint ventures in cable (A&E, Lifetime), the channel enjoyed success in terms of inclusion on cable systems but struggled to attract advertisers (Byars and Meehan 1994). Eventually, Lifetime reorganized its prime time schedule in an attempt to attract upscale heterosexual couples.[8] That seemed to turn the trick for Lifetime, which now carries extensive advertising for everything from aspirin to cars.

With Disney's acquisition of ABC, Lifetime seemed poised to launch a second channel targeting women in their teens and twenties, but nothing came of it.[9] Although Disney's 1998 annual report extolled the transformation of ESPN from cable channel into franchise, no similar plans seem to be on the horizon for Lifetime (Disney 1998). While audience gender is not the only variable differentiating the corporate histories of these two channels, this sketch suggests that being a "channel for men who love sports" places a company in a position significantly different from being "television for women."

Feminism and Political Economy

When reanalyzed from a feminist perspective, my case study of broadcast ratings yielded an unexpected finding: a structural contradiction between patriarchy and capitalism embodied in a fundamental market in the television industry, and effecting the structure of two derivative markets. The structure of the market for commodity ratings assumed that men controlled both wages and spending, making them *the* audience. But the market structure ignored similarly patriarchal assumptions about the domestic division of labor that assigned the household's shopping to women. While men as breadwinners and women as shoppers fits into the patriarchal division of labor that was idealized in the 1950s, the fact remains that women have always worked in this country. Not only have women been allotted a considerable share of the caretaking and household purchasing, but women have sought and secured paid work.

Paralleling the social status of men's blue-collar occupations have been women's pink-collar jobs: grocery clerk, secretary, domestic worker, telephone operator, nurse, farm worker, court reporter, teacher, etc. These occupations typically offered lower wages than those paid for blue-collar jobs, regardless of the levels of skill—suggesting that the patriarchal devaluation of women was echoed in capitalism's wage structure. For the market in commodity audiences, that would make male earners a better buy, but only if they adhered to a nonpatriarchal division of domestic labor. With a patriarchal division, an audience of female shoppers was the better buy. Because this contradiction was not articulated in the demand for commodity ratings, the ratings monopolist had no reason to investigate or to resolve it.

One might expect that contradiction to emerge and be resolved in the 1980s as political-economic changes forced more women into the workplace and into white-collar occupations. As women achieved greater—though not perfect—economic equality, they would seem likely candidates for inclusion in *the* audience. Yet, despite the ratings monopolist's adoption of categories to sort viewers by occupational status, women remained marginalized as niches. Males remained the object of the rating firm's art, with upscale males the most prized trophies.

This makes little economic sense. In capitalism, money is supposed to be the great leveler. Arbitrary social distinctions that unfairly oppress individuals are supposed to evaporate when people enter the market for goods and services as consumers, or when they offer themselves as labor. The logic of profit should drive advertisers to demand shoppers regardless of the gender, social status, race, age, ethnicity, sexual orientation, etc., of the particular people buying the bars of soap, rolls of toilet paper, or cans of beans. Why, then, do such distinctions persist in the markets for commodity ratings and commodity audiences—in markets where companies essentially trade in people?

A feminist political economy allows us to answer that question in terms of both gender and social status. The overvaluing of a male audience reflects the sexism of patriarchy as surely as the overvaluing of an upscale audience reflects the classism of capitalism. Each practice is rooted in the illogic of prejudice, that is, in the ideologies naturalizing the oppression of women and of working people.[10] Those ideologies shape corporate decisions such that corporations structure markets as instruments of oppression and not as liberatory spaces. Indeed, restructuring markets to foster the liberation of women and working people would actually undermine the interests of individual capitalists and of capitalism, which profit from disparities in income and oppressive social relations. From this perspective, television is structured to discriminate against anyone outside the commodity audience of white, 18-to-34-year-old, heterosexual, English-speaking, upscale men. This

recognition is crucial to scholarly work on television. Whatever ameni-
ties or pleasures television offers to viewers outside *the* commodity audience, television is an instrument of oppression.

Notes

1. Because Smythe assumed that the audience commodity and the viewership were identical, I use commodity audience to differentiate the manufactured audience from the viewership.

2. Other possibilities may exist; these are the two that I have identified.

3. "Twists" are minor innovations in plot, character, props, setting, etc.,
that are used to differentiate among series building on similar track records.
Twists and track record are typically balanced. For example, the more recent
series *Nash Bridges* was derived from *Miami Vice.* Both starred Don Johnson;
both were crime dramas about an ensemble of undercover police officers who
wore stylish outfits, talked tough, raced about in luxury cars, and were frequently lectured by a senior officer. In *Miami Vice,* the authority figure was
the unit's enigmatic captain; in *Nash Bridges,* an internal affairs officer investigating the unit. Here the twist is gender: the investigator was cast as a stylishly
dressed woman who also served as Bridges's love interest. Where officers in
Miami Vice experienced considerable moral ambiguity, *Nash Bridges* maintained a clear division between cops and robbers. Where *Miami Vice* specialized in a brooding, enigmatic atmosphere, *Nash Bridges* struck an upbeat
note through the use of bright lighting for indoor scenes. Where Johnson's
character and his partner drove through Miami at night, Nash and his partner
raced around an eternally sunny San Francisco. On *Miami Vice,* Johnson's
character lacked stable and fulfilling relationships outside his work. On *Nash
Bridges,* Johnson's character had good relationships at work and at home: he
easily led his unit, had established a personal friendship with his investigator,
acted as a loving and protective father to his daughter, and seemed to be a dutiful, if skeptical, son to his father.

4. This has encouraged producers "pitching" innovative shows in terms of
old shows; the best-known example, perhaps, being Gene Roddenberry's attempt to persuade network executives that a science fiction drama targeting
adults should be thought of as a Western: *Star Trek* was really *Wagon Train*
set in outer space.

5. The American Association of Advertising Agencies and the Association
of National Advertisers owned the Cooperative Analysis of Broadcasting,
which provided ratings only to those AAAA and ANA members that sub-
scribed to the service. CAB conducted telephone surveys with a long list of
questions asking respondents to recount every fifteen minutes of radio listening
done the day prior to contact. Unsurprisingly, CAB reported low ratings. The
C. E. Hooper Company capitalized on the networks' discontent while offering

advertisers and agencies results from telephone surveys that asked for a report of current listening and of listening during the previous fifteen minutes. Greater accuracy combined with a lower cost from expanding the buyer base worked: CEH monopolized broadcast ratings throughout the "golden age" of radio. ACN achieved monopolistic control over network radio and television in the 1950s. It maintains its monopoly over television ratings to the present day and has extended operations into web site ratings.

6. Little if any interest has been expressed in Native Americans or viewers descended from immigrants from Asia or the Pacific Rim.

7. For example, in *Miami Vice*, the melodrama centered on whether Johnson's character would recover from the death of his previous partner, form a bond with his current partner, and sort out his love life. In *Nash Bridges*, the melodrama focuses on the continuing story of one man's family. Johnson's character must deal with the romance between his daughter and one of his subordinates, maintain his relationship with his father, and transform the woman investigating his operations from antagonist to friend and, perhaps, lover.

8. Personal interview with Judy Girard, head of programming, Lifetime, New York, 1995.

9. Personal interview with Douglas McCormack, Chief Executive Officer, Lifetime, New York, 1995.

10. Although the particular dynamics shift as demographic categories shift, I believe that the basic analysis holds for people of color, speakers of languages other than English, people younger or older than the valued age grade, gay men, lesbians, etc. One would look for dynamics rooted in colonialism, ageism, heterosexism, etc., and trace the connections to patriarchy and/or capitalism.

16. The Thrill Is Gone: Advertising, Gender Representation, and the Loss of Desire
Robin Andersen

The designers of commercial culture have long been using sex to make a sale. We are enjoined to buy, on a daily basis, a vast array of products because a connection has been forged between them and sex. That simple proposition, selling sex, is in fact not so simple, however, because it implies a staggering amount of expertise, psychoanalytic theory, research, development, and of course money, all of which have been directed toward attempting to commodify that complicated mix of biology and culture that constitutes human sexuality.

But it is not enough to assess the representations of sexuality, or any connections those social constructions may have to human sexuality, without constantly reminding ourselves that these representations are not designed to provide gratification. Instead, they are motivated by a very different set of commercial demands, and therein lies the key to understanding them. They are created to sell products. Such advertisements are artifacts of market relationships; in essence they are manifestations of the political economy of late consumer capitalism. It might be argued that, precisely because sexual imagery is designed to make the sale, it must, in some way, fulfill the passions it promises. But when one examines contemporary advertisements that depict gender and sexuality, many seem to demonstrate a surprising lack of passion. I have taught advertising criticism for over a decade. Every semester students survey and critique a vast number of ads, with representations of sexuality attracting particular interest. We have noticed recently a trend toward a particular type of ad, increasingly more focused on sexuality, yet done with a tone wholly devoid of affect. Looking at these images one might correctly observe that after almost a hundred years of selling sex, the thrill seems to be gone. After analyzing numerous magazine advertisements targeted to young people of both genders in magazines such as *Details, Spin, Rolling Stone, Cosmopolitan,* and *Glamour,* among others, this paper argues that the representation of sexuality for the purposes of profit has reached, at least for the time being, a dead end. I will argue that there are basically two lines of analysis that will help explain this loss of *desire, affect, passion* in the representations of sex, and necessarily, gender, in the advertising of late consumer culture. Textual analysis of several advertisements is interwoven with the theoretical perspectives developed here.

The first point to be made is that advertisements that associate sexuality with commodities, especially ones that contain at least the implied promise that sexual pleasure can be bought along with the product, must always disappoint. With the commodification of sex, the basic proposition is untenable. In terms of human passions, sex ads fail to satisfy because they confuse sexual gratification with the possession of objects. They attempt to substitute a state of *being* with the promise of *having* (Haineault and Roy 1993). Only in rare cases, demonstrated long ago by Freud, is human sexuality literally tied to a fetish, where the libido actually cathects to the object form. Therefore, because of their inability to satisfy, the commodified sexuality of the images exploited in advertising, tied to commodities, designed so obviously for profit, has over the years come to display a more mannered, distanced tone. The hip, cynical style of these contemporary images is at once self-referential and at times self-mocking, yet they cannot break the habit of trying to exploit sexuality for profit.

The second line of inquiry useful for understanding sexual representation in contemporary advertising is really a combination of the historical legacy of patriarchy together with the economic engine of consumer capitalism. It is the intersection of patriarchal social relationships with, for example, the $20-billion-a-year cosmetics industry, which has produced the relentless cultural attitude that continues to value women based on their appearance. Regarding women's sexuality, advertisements habitually assert that women are sexy and desirable when they deliberately and self-consciously compete to attract the male gaze (Berger 1972) . While it is true in some advertising specifically targeted to female markets, most notably for sports gear, that women are depicted in roles that assert independence, the greater tendency in consumer culture is to portray women as objects designed to attract the gaze, not only of men, but also of other women invited to emulate them. Most ads are a complex mix of the woman of old who lingers just under the contemporary gloss of a more liberated image.

Many sexualized images targeted to a male market segment demonstrate a prominent feature of patriarchal social relations, placing women in subordinated positions. The long historical habit of presenting women as objects of sexual desire for men, when taken to its ultimate conclusion in consumer culture, offers men personal power over women. Contemporary media marketing targets men and women with different messages (Turow 1997), but as we will see, the promise of sexual power is a feature of the strategies of persuasion targeted to both male and female markets. However, there are important distinctions between the psychocultural dynamics of those different messages. Indeed, the consequences are much more severe in this society when men claim that power over women. I will argue further that these desensitized and, as I hope to show, dehumanized objectifications are part of a culture that celebrates gender wars, the dislocation of erotic desire, and the loss of human compassion. There are social consequences to reducing the human psyche to a commodity for the benefit of profit through persuasive marketing. Such a culture only makes it more difficult for young men and women to find fulfillment through relationships based on mutual respect, equality, and affection. This essay explores these issues and, in general, the relationship between sex and the sell, as it is manifest in contemporary advertising. It offers some formulations as to the complicated ways in which the culturally pervasive representations of sexuality function as one of the dominant features of consumer culture.

Izod and Strip Poker

Let's begin with an ad that ran in the men's magazine *Details* toward the end of 1997, promoting a line of clothing called Extreme Leisure by Izod. A group of young people, three women and three men, are playing strip poker. In contemporary surreal style, the colors are exaggerated and intense. Aquamarine walls are mixed with deep red curtains. Hot pink, purple, and gold splashes of color mark the carpeted floor. Through the windows the sky is bright yellow. Florescent fish are contained in a huge aquarium. The young, perfectly formed people are all in various stages of undress, the women down to their bras and panties. But one woman has lost all her clothes, save her provocative high-heeled gold slippers, and is walking out of the room. As she walks away from the game, she looks alluringly at us, the viewers of the ad, as the other players stare toward her back. Our view of her is only partially obscured by the fish tank.

At one level we might say this ad is a perfect example of the long history of using sex to make a sale. The ad is directed toward men. It features gorgeous women wearing very little—much less than the men. They are placed in an alluring setting, engaged in a provocative activity. The fantasy narrative created by the ad could certainly find its way to a sexual resolution. And all this is associated with the clothing. A sports jacket and cap hang prominently on a clothes rack in the left foreground. As visual persuasion, the image provokes sexual associations without having to state anything explicitly. The quality of *syntactical indeterminacy* (Messaris 1996) allows the photograph to speak without having to make promises. There is no logical cause-and-effect relationship guaranteed—buy the clothes, get the girl—only the more compelling visual evidence that the clothes are unarguably part of the same setting occupied by beautiful, invitingly naked women.

But this ad is much more than the simple implied promise of sex. More curious than even the strip-poker game and its setting is the gray-haired couple standing outside in the yellow sky peering in, their mouths agape in expressions of shock. More curious still is the small white text on the left that reads, "Did you know? STRIP POKER attracts spectators. Charging them a fee to watch means money for more beer. More beer = more EXTREME LEISURE enjoyment." The situation depicted invites the male viewers of the ad to think not only of sex and clothing, but of selling the view of the naked woman to spectators in order to finance their leisure activities, as it would appear the young men in the ad are doing. The poker-playing women are being turned into objects of exchange. The view of the female body becomes the commodity. The male consumer, like the ones in the ad, is invited to participate in the sale so they can continue consuming. For Extreme Leisure is an extremely commodified leisure. The young men must get the money to purchase beer, then they can have more Extreme Leisure. The commodity exchange is the more striking aspect of the ad, as it takes the simple sexual association into another, more titillating realm, one of sex in exchange for money—prostitution.

Looking at this ad, some might argue that the women are willing players and certainly participants in the Extreme Leisure enjoyment. Looking more closely we see that one of the men is holding a bottle of beer, but the naked woman in the gold slippers is sipping through a straw from a purple glass. Since she is not drinking beer she is not the one in control of the exchange relationship, rather she is its object. It is the sight of her being sold that buys more beer for the men. While she may be a willing participant, she is subordinated and dehumanized as the object of exchange. Here we might ask, how is it possible for the ad to be believable? Men looking at the ad are asked to believe that a beautiful young woman would willingly accept the demeaning role of being reduced to an object of sight in a monetary exchange for the pleasure, not only of the young men, but of the older couple looking in. Setting aside the reading that she aspires to prostitution, what aspects of patriarchal commercial culture make such a seemingly absurd proposition plausible?

First, it is the self-mocking nature of the text and the cartoon style of the visual that turn the ad into a joke. It is therefore not rejected, but accepted as humorous. As a joke or cartoon, the ad can be interpreted as a somewhat silly stereotypic male fantasy, but one that includes women having fun too. It is therefore not rejected either as unbelievable or as too demeaning to women. Thus, the humor works by allowing the basic suppositions of the message to stand unchallenged and reinforced. The hip tone that reinforces conventional values is a strategy commonly used to target Generation X-ers, as Nicholson argues:

> The advertiser hopes to win the hearts of Generation X by the use of "the wink." By employing the blatant use of stereotypes, the advertiser is admitting to relying on this traditional form of advertising. However, because this new audience is so sharp and wise to the ways of advertising, these techniques are reemployed "nostalgically" for the amusement of the reader. The overt function of the stereotype may have been changed, but these tongue-in-cheek representations will serve the purpose of conveying the messages the stereotypes were traditionally meant to express (1997, 189).

For the male, the ad invites him to accept the values of a particular kind of commercialized sexuality, one that is for sale, something to be used for making a profit that can then be turned back into the purchasing of products. The basic supposition about women is that they find worth in their ability to be physically alluring and attract the male gaze. If women object, they will be unhip, unable to take a joke, and relegated to the position of outsider with regard to mainstream culture. In this way the ad simply adds a hip new contemporary gloss to a set of very old traditions.

The Object of the Gaze

To examine the parameters of such old patriarchal conventions, let's look at the ways in which women are addressed by the culture of advertising. The legacy of patriarchy meshes with cosmetics and fashion because they both judge women by virtue of their appearance (Mulvey 1975), not by their success or merit (Coward 1983). Advertisements attempt to persuade would-be female buyers by convincing them that they will, and should, look better, more like the models featured, if they use the same set of products. Cosmetics and fashion emphasize, by their nature, appearance (Jacobson and Mazur 1995). Patriarchy, too, insists that women must, above all, *look* good. Historically blocked from full participation in the public sphere, women have had to deploy their ability to be attractive as their primary vehicle for acquiring social status (Wollstonecraft 1995). In Victorian times the highest goal was to marry well, and that type of social mobility was based primarily on appearance (Berger 1972). We all know that some things about the bad old days of patriarchy have been transformed. Women's demands for and successes in acquiring equal status in socioeconomic spheres are apparent in the world of images that reflect our lives back to us. But even by the end of the twentieth century, social, economic, and political equality had certainly not been fully achieved, and the legacy of patriarchy lives on. These transitional social forces have led to a complicated mix of imagery with multilayered meanings. Most images of women are complex negotiated constructions of the woman of old and the new "Woman of the 90s"—a phrase that came of age at the end of the century—expressed these contradictions. It came to mean that women must be the best, the brightest, the smartest, the most successful, and still look smashing at all times. Many images of women's sexuality in advertising in general are striking throwbacks to utterly (un)(re)constructed patriarchal representations as the image strategies persist.

The glamorous women of consumer culture with the perfect faces and skinny bodies who wear the clothes and makeup promise results. After all, they use the commodities, and because of them they have been personally transformed into objects of beauty, the cultural ideal able to attract the gaze. (Or, in the case of Izod, they don't wear the clothes but are presented as the object of the desire, the sight that attracts the gaze, the commodity that attracts the buyer.) "Maybe It's Her. Maybe It's Maybelline" is a clever line with plausible deniability that nevertheless implies that the model, though naturally beautiful, has really achieved her ideal appearance through the use of the product. And the product will help the would-be buyer achieve the same appearance. Tapping into the legacy of a patriarchal culture that constantly reminds us that we will be judged on the way we look is imperative for the cosmetics industry, because it sells products that alter appearance.

Along the way we are also told that we do not look as good as we could, we need to be better. Take a Clairol hair color ad that simply features the face of an attractive woman, with the bold text at the top, "You, Only Better." The unspoken assumption is that you are not good enough the way you are; you need to be better. The words of John Berger (1972) still hold true, that consumer culture steals the love of ourselves from us and sells it back to us for the price of the product. On the one hand, advertising is an inviting world of fantasy where we can all achieve the ideal if we only have the product, but behind that world lies the unspoken threat that we do not measure up. Anxieties and feelings of inadequacy are also powerful motivations for consumption (Andersen 1995). Only by constantly hearing that we are not good enough will we be compelled to keep buying the products. Hoping to acquire the look, measuring ourselves using the models of perfection as the standard, in the words of Stuart Ewen (1988), is always an "invidious comparison." We will never measure up to those perfect representations because photographs are touched up, eliminating eye bags, age lines, and soft jaws. But the commodified desire (Andersen 1995) to emulate such images does propel the engine of consumption. And this is also true with images of the body.

Wasting Away

The standard cultural ideal for women has steadily grown thinner. Images of women are literally wasting away. The bony, pale, gaunt, ill look made fashionable by Calvin Klein's use of Kate Moss is now the norm. The haunting looks of the emaciated waifs at the peak of fashion stare out of magazines, catalogs, billboards, and television. The shrinking standard of thinness for women is an ideal impossible to achieve for the vast majority of females. The average height for a model is 5 feet 11 inches, and she weighs under 120 pounds. The proportions of the Barbie Doll are also extreme and bizarre. If Barbie were a human being she would be 6 feet tall and weigh about 110 pounds.

This impossible standard is propelled by market relations. It is precisely because such "perfection" cannot be achieved that it has become the commodified ideal. An ad for Philips television sets reveals this strategy. Three models in skin-tight clothing accentuating their extreme lankiness are pictured with the new TV set. So narrow is the new set that one of the models can straddle it. The text at the top announces, "A television so thin it will give regular TVs a complex." Just like the other TVs, women not as thin as the models will also have a complex, but one that will keep them striving to achieve the imposed prototype. The scrawny look is nearly impossible, therefore scarce, and that scarcity is used to fuel demand precisely because it is, for the most part, unattainable. We might say then, that thinness for women is a manifestation of the political economy of patriarchal capitalism.

The most insightful cultural critics have always tied the meanings derived from textual analysis to the hegemonic assumptions that undergird the images. Dyer (1982) and Frith (1997) have offered systematic approaches that incorporate such an analysis into the deconstruction of advertisements. As layers of meaning are peeled away, the ad reveals basic attitudes and assumptions existent in the wider cultural milieu, the "philosophical persuasions" that are "unconsciously qualified" and condensed into advertisements (Dyer 1982). Images of women constitute a body of representation that continually reinforces a set of social assumptions about the way women should look. Throughout the twentieth century, modern industrial society has ratcheted down the acceptable amount of bodily flesh permissible on women (Ewen 1988).

Commercial pressures have also functioned to create a standard for women that grows thinner by the day. As advertising increasingly influences media content (Andersen 1995; McAllister 1996), the female characters on television are also shrinking. One of the more disturbing views of advertising attitudes seeping into TV is the case of Calista Flockhart, known to millions of Fox viewers as Ally McBeal. As we watch her waste away, she illustrates a growing (or diminishing) trend in the size of women on the small screen. The costar of *The Practice*, Lara Flynn Boyle, along with *Mad About You*'s Helen Hunt, have also been shrinking. Elizabeth Crow, an editor for *Mademoiselle,* observed, "It was the norm in print but not the norm on TV. Suddenly there's a very skanky look coming in there" (Jacobs 1998). The skeletal look is the consequence of turning actresses into models for the fashion industry, promoting the clothes they wear in the pages of *TV Guide,* in the fashion layouts of magazines. "The gap between actresses and catwalkers has never been narrower," says *Vogue*'s Katherine Betts: "People are really judging them by what they're wearing. They feel a lot of pressure to look good" (Jacobs 1998). What looks good to the fashion industry are women who resemble hangers. With the penetration of advertising influences, cultural assumptions informed by market relations become more socially pervasive, and this has been a major factor in women growing thinner. A generation ago "a typical model weighed 8 percent less than the average woman; more recently she weighs 23 percent less. Most models are now thinner than 95 percent of the female population" (Jacobson and Mazur 1995, 77). What is designed to sell is not an image of plump fulfillment. There is no profit motivation in that.

Power

Many times, especially in high fashion, the emaciated look is an anti-female aesthetic in which every reference to the female body is erased, as in the high-fashion photo layouts where the thin, barely covered torso of the model reveals no curves. Like Calista Flockhart, the woman pictured has no breasts, no hips, no thighs, no belly, nothing left really, no physical characteristic of sexuality. Ironically, in this instance, no adult female physical power. But ironically, though the look aesthetically is one of powerlessness, there is power in achieving the look. In fact, it is power that is offered to both the male and female markets. Marketing research demonstrates in numerous ways that people feel powerless in this society. They are not in control of their working environments, their lives, or their emotions (Andersen 1999). Mastery over the world through products is a standard enticement (Williamson 1978). Women are offered control over the germs in their bathrooms and men are promised command over the open road when they drive Sport Utility Vehicles. When it comes to representations of gender, power also plays a key role. When such mastery is offered in this culture, it is often at the expense of the opposite sex.

For women in consumer culture, power is the ability to attract. Because they have been impeded from achieving socioeconomic power equivalent to that of men in patriarchal culture, women have found their realm of achievable power constrained to the domestic, interpersonal, and consumer spheres. While those sociopolitical forces have begun to change, advertising culture is mired in the legacy of patriarchy. When women are offered power in advertising culture, it usually revolves around a product that guarantees attractiveness. Once again, the logic of patriarchy is employed as it mirrors the logic of marketing strategies. Take, for example, an ad for Lovable Bras, which assigns powerful, almost magical attributes to the product. The reader/buyer is assured that the product will "increase his pulse without cutting off your circulation." But the product comes with a warning— "our bras have been known to cause rapid heartbeat and shortness of breath. In the opposite sex, of course." The promise of the product is so profound it can actually stimulate metabolic reactions associated with arousal. As objects of desire able to evoke great passions, women are then summoned to use that attraction to assert control over men. The appeal is obvious: everyone wants to be in control of their relationships and their sexuality, especially in a culture that tries to control that sexuality. But this is power confined to the realm of emotional control, not real political or economic power, the type of power that might lead to equality in relationships in the long run. While sexual power is often for sale to the female market, it comes at a costly price for women.

Fragmentation and Objectification

As the objects of desire women become just that, objectified, and this is expressed in many ways. Visually, women are frequently represented in parts. They are fragments, not whole beings. Feminists and cultural critics have long understood the consequences of such depictions. As Judith Williamson (1978) noted, selling makeup often involves separating and isolating one part of the face from another. Thus divided, one part of the body can even work against another part. It is easier to objectify a fragment of the body. It is no longer a person able to express humanity. The whole person is lost when she is cropped, chopped, and incomplete and becomes simply an illustration of an objectified physical feature—whatever feature needs to be emphasized to sell the product.

Fragmented Sexuality

One recent advertising image for Bongo shoes illustrates the way fragmentation functions to create highly sexualized images of objectified body parts. Different sets of women's legs intertwine across the page. A man is on the floor, horizontal, perched on one elbow, woven inbetween the extremely thin legs adorned by the shoes. Only the body parts associated with male sexual desire need be included. Legs are also featured in a Nine West ad layout, this time only one pair, terminating about midthigh. They are surrounded by three men enraptured by the skimpy sandals that bedeck the feet. The separated fetishized parts are detached, standing only as objects. As such they exist to fulfill the erotic fantasies of the males who watch and objectify them. The depiction of legs on their own, eliminating the rest of the woman's body, particularly the face and eyes, leaves no humanity to confront the male spectators.

These images are striking throwbacks to the legs on a pedestal noted by Marshall McLuhan in 1951. McLuhan (1967, 99) referred to them as "commercially sponsored glamour." Such ads, he argued, encourage a "strange dissociation of sex not only from the human person but even from the unity of the body."[1] The persistence of such imagery over the years raises questions about the consequences for male and female sexuality. Why is it easier to represent male passions by presenting women as desecrated objects of sexual pleasure for them, not as whole beings who have their own passions to be shared?

Advertising imagery must be immediate and summon instant desire. Such representations have a long history, tied to pornography, in which men find pleasure in viewing two-dimensional images of women. Objectified body parts are the blunt instrument of persuasion. When such visual captivation is used to make the sale, the result is often a complex and pernicious scenario that raises a variety of disturbing attitudes toward women.

And what of women readers/buyers? Do the ads convince female consumers to buy the shoes and become dehumanized? For women, the ads make a powerful promise in return. They pledge to the would-be buyer that her legs too, thus embellished, can be the objects of desire. Her gratification is highly constrained, however. It comes through being desired, through controlling the passions of the male gaze. But what of her own passions? Is she really fulfilled just by being the object of desire? Has the female consumer so internalized the male gaze that she finds satisfaction by looking through the eyes of the man, fulfilled by his desire for her, which is now also her desire? Or do consumer representations promise her future gratification once she successfully becomes the object of desire? Then will her passions be fulfilled? These questions of culture and sexuality intersect in complicated ways in advertising representations, but they do not usually result in challenging dominant conceptions of female sexuality. Power and pleasure are so closely fused in advertising that pleasure is assumed from the promise of power and control, not allusions to sexual gratification. And as Savan (1994, 226) points out, ads that promise power "let women vent steam while clamping them into traditional stances toward men."

Those traditional stances often have negative consequences for female consumers. First, as noted, it is extremely difficult to achieve the standard look of ornamental beauty promoted in advertising imagery. The look that affords psychocultural sexual power is almost impossible to achieve without destroying one's health. Problems with body image abound, and appearance anxiety sends women far in their quest to fix the problem. The diet and exercise industry is a $75 billion annual financial windfall. On any given day 25 percent of American women are dieting, and another 50 percent are finishing, breaking, or starting diets. One survey found that 50 percent of respondents used diet pills, 27 percent used liquid-formula diets, 18 percent used diuretics, 45 percent fasted, 18 percent used laxatives, and 15 percent engaged in self-induced vomiting (Jacobson and Mazur 1995, 78). Numerous surveys of young women demonstrate their displeasure with the way they look. A survey of 494 school girls found more than half thought they were fat, yet only 15 percent were medically overweight (Jacobson and Mazur 1995, 78). Almost 40 percent of women who smoke say they do so to keep from gaining weight (Jacobson and Mazur 1995, 77). Women who internalize a cultural standard are never able to measure up, to satisfy the gaze, leaving them no way to find psychic well-being, emotional fulfillment, or cultural belonging.

In addition, women's sexuality is in flux and is constantly being negotiated in our culture. Positive expressions of a woman's sexuality asserted for her own pleasure are rare in consumer culture. (On occasion, sexual pleasure is offered, sublimated through a shampoo, a gourmet coffee product, or a chocolate snack.) But sexuality not immediately satisfied through a product is rarely affirmed. Drawing out the implications of two advertisements will illustrate these points.

The first is an advertisement for Diesel Jeans that appeared in *Rolling Stone* magazine, in which an old woman grabs the crotch of her elderly partner while he is snoozing. She has been looking at a pornographic magazine positioned on the side table, her tongue between her teeth in a lusty gesture. In addition to the way the characters are portrayed, the dark setting suggests a seediness that evokes shock and embarrassment. The text reads, "Only the finest quality 12½ oz. denim is good enough for Diesel. This is overdyed, then washed, and finally distressed. The result is antique dirty denim which has an aged, vintage appearance. A bit like your grandmother." This self-mocking Gen X–style ad is another image at once hip, humorous, and dehumanizing. Because of the setting and sexuality, the dirty old woman is like the dirty old denim. The representation must be understood within a culture that relegates women who express pleasure in sex to immoral status, after much name calling and condemnation. The message of this philosophical persuasion condemns the expression of female sexuality by associating it with "a dirty old woman."

But there are women worse than those who simply like sex. There are those who use their sexuality to frustrate men. In a two-page ad for Sauza tequila, a line of seductive beautiful women, all with blonde hair, all dressed in red, stand in a variety of enticing positions. Some show the smooth tan skin of their stomachs, some lick their lips, some cross their legs at the knees and throw their heads back. These sexy women are attention grabbers, but a truly retrogressive logic is summoned to connect that excitement to consumption. Across the middle of both pages, printed along the midsections of the women, a small line of text reads, "We can say with 99.9% accuracy that there is no possible way whatsoever in this lifetime that you will ever get a date with one of these women. Life is harsh. Your Tequila shouldn't be." This ad depicts the antithesis of the male fantasy; it is a man's worst nightmare. Here, evoking then denying sex is used as emotional manipulation to sell alcohol, substituting the product to ease the pain of lost gratification. The ad features the highly unethical sales strategy of using the substance as an escape, one associated with substance abuse. The pitch blames women for the need to escape, releasing the ad from the responsibility of the manipulation. In this cultural context, what could be worse than women enticing, then denying, men sexual pleasure? And these women are so clearly enticing. The ad reflects the attitudes of a culture obsessed with controlling women's sexuality and claiming that it exists only to satisfy men. In doing so, it taps into and encourages hostility toward women by claiming their use of sexual power against men.

Violence

But the consequences of this type of imagery—and for women who attempt to control their own sexuality or use sexual power to control men—are dire in patriarchal culture. Women are reminded of this habitually, through commercial representation. An ad for the men's cologne Smalto pictures a woman falling back with her elbow raised in a protective gesture. The text reads, "You make me weak." The confused expression can be read as passion and/or fear. This ambiguous image conflates passion with terror, "no" with "yes." The image offers men sexual power, just as other images offer women sexual power. However, it is a grisly affair in a culture where the use of violence against women persists, as does the legacy of patriarchy. In fashion layouts women are easily reminded of the threats of violence against them, and those threats are often glamourized, as, for example, in the depiction of a doll thrown against the wall in an ad in the *New York Times Magazine*'s fashion issue. Or, in another ad for expensive Italian shoes, where the model appears to have been sexually assaulted and abandoned. She crouches on all fours, behind some bushes, covered only by her bra, panties, and expensive high-heeled Italian slippers. In another ad the model is choreographed to look like a corpse, the eyes vacant as in a police-style photograph, legs twisted to the side, and a limp arm stretched out to the symbolic white lilies of a funeral. The studded black leather around her neck suggests strangulation. The variety of dehumanizing, commodified representations of sexuality have nowhere to go but into ever more shocking and titillating views trying to stimulate consumption. Robbed of the humanity that sparks emotional compassion and emulation, this style of imagery invites violence.

The Thrill Is Gone

The path of commercial imagery of sexuality has led to a dead end. Recent Gucci advertisements demonstrate the result of such trends. One is a portrayal of a sexual dalliance between atomized, alienated, confused, and fragmented people. The woman stands in front of a bed, facing away from a young man. Her body is cropped at the neck, a simple black dress covers her torso. The young man tugs at his zipper in a daze. Neither one of them appears to be having any fun. Another ad in this dark series is particularly disturbing. It is an explicit portrayal of oral sex, probably in the back of a car. The woman, on all fours, leans down, encouraged by the man's hand on her hip, but she is utterly disinterested. The young man, though possibly aroused, is emasculated in the photograph, as his crotch is a blank void covered by the black underwear, erased by the commodity.

In another fashion ad for Massimo, a young couple sits intertwined, possibly in a bar, or in a car after a night of drinking. His tie is loosened and she is in what looks like underwear. Her shoulder, turned away from him, indicates her disinterest, even as her leg is positioned across his. His vacant look completes the despondent tone.

The negotiated terrain of women's sexuality and patriarchal relations together with the necessities of commodity persuasions have led to a type of representation that is no longer satisfying to either men or women. The promise of being transformed by the product into the cultural object of desire rings false and unattainable. Many representations of sexuality no longer even attempt to portray physical or emotional gratification. At its worst, the imagery turns dangerous and violent. Susan Faludi's (1999) recent study of masculinity underscores these trends. She illustrates the cultural dynamic between commodity relations, the loss of sexual desire, and objectification of women when she discovers the attitudes of young male gang members. Members of the Spur Posse acquired status through their sexual exploits with young girls. They earned one point for each encounter; the more sex, the more points, the higher the status. In a few notable cases such sexual aggression resulted in members being prosecuted on sexual assault charges. But gang members admitted to Faludi that having sex was often "boring." When she asks one boy why he had sex with a girl who bored him, he responds, "For the points. I was developing my reputation. I was developing my name" (110–11). Another member of the Spur Posse told her, "These girls are no-names. We've got a name. That's why you're talking to us. It's all about brand names" (110). Relegated to the role of acquisition for brand-name status, sex was no longer "a turn on." Such is the loss of desire when sexuality is urged not for pleasure but tied to a system of exchange. Considered only as commodities in a system of status acquisition, the girls, as young as ten years old, were little more than interchangeable currency. But when the Spurs decided to make a porn videotape, they were excited by watching themselves. As Faludi notes, "there was a strange affectlessness to the way he and other Spurs told their sex stories, a boredom that seemed to drop away only with the introduction of a video camera" (111). When they watched themselves, they felt as if they were "in the movies," and this they found exciting. She observes, "Their sexual exploits evidently had less to do with the act itself than with being themselves, an act" (111). Their satisfaction came not from sex, but from seeing themselves reflected back in culturally mediated forms that conferred status, giving them "brand-name" recognition.

For women the disease of anorexia nervosa is the extreme expression of dysfunction. It nevertheless reveals much about the culture that gives the dysfunction its particular form. The commodity system and loss of desire of the Spur Posse, like anorexia, exist within a set of sociocultural and economic relations that direct such maladies into particular psychocultural expressions. The case also illustrates the ways in which young men in consumer culture now view and evaluate themselves through the eyes of ornamental culture, commodifying their own desire in much the same way that patriarchy has traditionally directed young women to view themselves, through the desire of the observer. Many contemporary ads have adopted the same objectifying visual, and persuasive conventions to depict men that were once consigned only to female representation.

Conclusion

Contemporary advertising images illustrate the mannered posing of disturbing scenarios, done with little affect and less satisfaction. The result is a hip emotional cynicism that I believe stems from a history of representation within a complex of consumption, profit, and patriarchy. Even though focus-group research must certainly reveal authentic longings for intimacy and psychological well-being, the legacy of patriarchy and the need for emotional manipulation is pervasive in advertising and has led to a set of images that cannot reflect fulfillment. Conservative critics who condemn Calvin Klein for abandoning repressive sexual conventions by pushing the envelope toward more sexuality explicit content have missed the point. In place of defying social conventions with erotic images, we see the vacant dispassionate stares of the women who have been or are about to be abused, or of the men who should be getting aroused, but are not. The images openly admit that the world of consumption is not a world of erotic pleasure but a bankrupt manipulation of emotional anxiety.

The lack of affirmative portrayals of women's sexual passions leaves representations of female fulfillment impossible. The commodified, fragmented, often victimized image offered as the epitome of male desire is so far from being able to represent intimate fulfillment that it has become a joke, or a dispassionate cynicism. As one of my male students put it, "I'm insulted that they think I would want a woman like that." At worst, these images reinforce a patriarchal predisposition to disrespect women and do violence against them.

In thinking about the relationship between sex and advertising, and the ways in which that relationship is expressed in end-of-the-century capitalism, it seems that advertising is so constrained by the twin taskmasters of patriarchy and profit that its representation of sexuality is now far removed from human pleasure—it reflects and promotes a new form of emotional cynicism that is extremely reactionary and ultimately debilitating, for both men and women. It is also a complete turnoff. But that jaded attitude now defines the very essence of hip. This is a hard culture to negotiate, especially for young men and women trying to establish the bounds of intimacy. As at least one of the cultural influences on interpersonal relationships, these images must be the focus of media literacy discussions that deconstruct and expose their persuasions and articulate alternative conceptions, enabling emotional fulfillment and more authentic and equitable gender practices.

Note

1. While McLuhan made note of the practices of objectification and fragmentation in the depiction of women's bodies, he did not place his analysis within the context of patriarchal social relations. His analysis, at times, assigns blame to women for such depictions. For a more detailed discussion of McLuhan's Mechanical Bride, and its influence on advertising criticism, see Andersen (2001).

17. Xuxa at the Borders of U.S. TV: Checked for Gender, Race, and National Identity
Ramona Curry and Angharad N. Valdivia

Except for a few English comedy shows, the occasional international film, and some English-dubbed Japanese "anime" cartoons that currently play on Saturday morning, virtually all of the vast quantity of television programming available to U.S. audiences via broadcast and cable is "Made in U.S.A." This virtual national programming monopoly stands in sharp contrast to the situation for many other national television markets, which play a mix of regional, national, and international fare, whereby "international" programming most often translates as U.S.-produced TV shows and movies with dubbed soundtracks. Thus, U.S.-made programming not only monopolizes U.S. TV screens but also comprises a large share of Latin American programming. The marked trade imbalance in media programming not only promotes contemporary North American cultural and political values, but also supports specifically U.S. media economic forms, notably the increasing commodification of television internationally through increased private/corporate ownership and commercially determined content.

Given the well-recognized value of commodified sexual representations in U.S. media, we would hardly be surprised to find "sex and money" to be recurrent themes or embedded aspects of much TV programming running internationally. However, it may yet be surprising (especially to TV audiences outside the United States) to discover just how narrow are the U.S. programming parameters for *acceptable* sexual commodification. A case study we present demonstrates how the unwritten rules for successful U.S. broadcast programming encode not only standards for language, production quality, narrative styles, and genres, but also a very limited and limiting range of allowable racial, gender, and sexual representations. Specifically, we examine why the Brazilian TV and recording star Xuxa (pronounced "shoo-sha"), a youthful, sexy, internationally popular female performer whose colorful, fast-paced TV programs have achieved unprecedented international distribution, marketing support, and popularity, could not manage to "break into" regular U.S. TV programming even on an

English-language program made by a U.S. television producer in the United States.

By extension, we consider how Xuxa's image and television programs articulate with established patterns in popular culture's international circulation and yet appear deviant in the U.S. Euro-American context. The "Xuxa phenomenon" both confirms and challenges standard U.S. media practices and cultural assumptions, particularly about Latin American women. With particular reference to "sex and money," our case study reveals that not only economic issues, but also U.S. norms for gender, racial, and national images (which is to say, values deployed primarily around the sexualized body, along with those produced more explicitly around "money") figure crucially in the global communications trade imbalance.

Xuxa's "Globo"lization

Before examining why Xuxa remains scarcely known in the United States, we should consider how and why she has managed since the mid-1980s to become an international media celebrity and TV and recording superstar. Initially a fashion model named Maria da Graça Meneghel, Xuxa began in 1983 to host a children's show on the then-third-largest of four Brazilian television networks, Manchete. In 1986 she introduced an expanded program on the largest network, Rio-based Rede Globo, the fourth-largest broadcasting system in the world. Her *Xou da Xuxa*,[1] carried on Globo affiliates throughout Brazil from 7:30 A.M. to 12:15 P.M. every Monday through Saturday through the mid-1990s, soon won its host recognition and acclaim throughout Brazil. It also enhanced Globo's daytime domestic market share beyond all expectations, consistently leading audience ratings for daytime programming; and, quite exceptionally for a program aimed at children, it stood high in overall ratings, behind telenovelas, the news, and sports broadcasts (Millman 1991, 300; Basas 1992, 82; Blount 1992, 9–10; Simpson 1993, 65).

Within a few years Xuxa's popularity extended far beyond Brazil through her producing a daily one-hour Spanish-language children's program at the Telefe network studios in Buenos Aires, which was carried throughout Latin America and subsequently on a number of channels in Europe and Asia. By 1991 an estimated fifty million viewers in seventeen countries watched Xuxa regularly, and she had personally reaped such profits from global sales of her syndicated programs, recordings, and extensive ancillary and licensed products (like dolls and comic books, yogurt and sunglasses) that *Forbes* listed her among the year's forty top-earning entertainers—the first Latin American, male or female, ever to make that list, which is dominated by musicians and actors working in the North American entertainment industry (Millman 1991).

Xuxa's exceptional international successes arose in part from the size of Brazil's economy—it ranks as the world's eighth largest—and its media market, for Brazilians consume more television sets and programs than any national audience outside the United States. Brazil is a leader in media production as well as consumption: in the mid-1980s, when Xuxa was its rising star, TV Globo held a 60 to 70 percent—and sometimes more than 90 percent—share of national Brazilian viewership across class lines, with programming that was approximately 70 percent Brazilian-made. Like the huge Mexican network Televisa, the Globo network managed, beginning in the mid-1970s, to transform a pronounced dominance in its national media market into global expansion through export and purchase of media outlets, to attain not only transnational but transcontinental impact. Globo has over the last decade emerged as a multinational, multimedia enterprise that has held its own even in the face of leading North American–based media conglomerates' aggressive consolidation of media power.[2] Further, as a Globo superstar whose program regularly attracted high ratings, Xuxa arguably helped to secure and expand Rede Globo's domestic media dominance and its capacity to expand globally into the satellite age.[3]

While traditionally the Brazilian television audience has not been as highly differentiated or demographically structured as in the United States, in the 1980s media marketers in Latin America began to acknowledge children as a lucrative television audience (Straubhaar 1996, 232–33). Xuxa's programs in both Brazilian and international versions stand out for integrating children onstage and in the studio audience into the show's action and spectacle. Shots of children interacting with the star or jumping, singing, and playing games occupy significant screentime in all of Xuxa's shows, whatever their overall duration; the balance is taken up by guest stars, cartoons or short educational films, and close-ups of Xuxa. Both the original *Xou da Xuxa* and her much shorter Spanish-language *El Show* drew on educational, game, and variety shows, all television genres developed in a number of places but elaborated in Latin America in a new form called a "show de auditório," with a charismatic host overseeing a long, originally live, program incorporating games, music, interviews, and news

(Straubharr 1996, 222). Yet hyperkineticism was probably its most immediately striking aspect. The fast and fluid pace of her show may well be Xuxa's—and TV Globo's—international contribution to televised formats. Other notable characteristics of Xuxa's original show were the fluid setup of the stage and audience as one, rather than separate locations and entities, as well as its intense textural excess: the vivid and strikingly designed costumes and props exhibited by Xuxa and her many onstage assistants.

Like most mainstream television, Xuxa's original show was formulaic in that it simultaneously broke new ground while incorporating familiar elements. Since Brazilian television in general and Xuxa in particular have not been impervious to North American cultural models, U.S. television programming formulas undoubtedly influenced the *Xou da Xuxa*. However, the unprecedented level of freneticism in Xuxa's original show, combined with textural overload, was not matched even by Nickelodeon shows such as *You Can't Do That on TV* that relied heavily on kid participants, slime, volume, and a quick tempo. In fact, the Nick shows may well have been modeled after the original Xuxa show, which predated U.S. versions of frenetic children's programming. In sum, the *Xou*'s systematic, even ritualized, use of bright colors, rich sartorial styling, lively carnival spirit, and Xuxa's own energetic performance drew on—and even engagingly exceeded—stereotyped Brazilian cultural traditions. In the view of Amelia Simpson, a U.S. scholar of Brazil, the combination of dynamic spectacle, consumerist emphasis, and focus on the glamorous host in *Xou da Xuxa* and its spin-offs has yielded a style of Brazilian programming that has proven "unbeatable in the ratings contest": "the new formula is part discotheque, part amusement park, part party . . . with the latest pop songs and dances and fashions on display" (Simpson 1993, 65, 90). Clowns and other costumed figures, especially a group of blonde teenaged girls called Paquitas, multiply Xuxa's bright, energetic presence. The Paquitas look and dress like Xuxa, help herd the onstage children around, oversee games, and otherwise join in the incessant movement and aura of fun. Simpson further notes that the original *Xou* served the dominant Globo programming aim to present a clean, modernist, consumer-oriented image of Brazil (65).[4] The *Xou da Xuxa* contributed to such an image, Simpson argues, with its "glossy, cosmopolitan look," extensive use of generic-sounding disco and pop music, and central emphasis on the fashionably (and often sexily) dressed star (63–65, 81–85).

Beyond her television appearances for Globo, Xuxa early demonstrated her own expertise in media- and self-commodification. In 1986 she began to produce albums of pop-style songs aimed at the children's and early-teen market; these have made her Brazil's top-selling recording artist. For example, her 1990 album sold sixfold the number of copies that Madonna's new album sold in Brazil that year, despite the advantage that Madonna's album had not only in Warner Brothers Records' general international marketing apparatus, but also in the introduction of MTV in Brazil that same year, which heavily promoted Madonna. Xuxa's albums benefited, of course, from their promotion on her own daily program, which also very successfully helped market a number of comic books, a handful of movies featuring Xuxa and structured around her image, and many ancillary products bearing the "Xuxa" brand name, including bicycles, surfboards, cosmetics, clothes, and prepared foods (Brooke 1990; Simpson 1993, 4). Throughout the 1990s, Xuxa continued to produce recordings in Portuguese and Spanish: her 1996 Spanish-language dance compact disc *Xuxa Dance*, produced in Los Angeles, "went platinum" in Chile and Argentina within a few months, and in 1997 her compact disc *Tô de bem com a vida* was a big hit in Brazil. Xuxa's concert tours continue regularly to sell out large stadiums throughout Brazil and neighboring countries.[5]

Xuxa's successes engendered powerful facsimiles especially in Brazil and Portugal, including former Paquitas who not only produce their own CDs but also appear in both Xuxa-sanctioned spin-offs and competing children's programs. The most striking instance of Xuxa's impact in commodifying and standardizing Brazilian children's programming is younger TV star Angélika Ksyvickis, who was Xuxa's successor in hosting the Manchete children's program *Club da Criança* after 1986, but who followed Xuxa to Globo to appear every weekday morning in part of the early morning time slot that *Xou da Xuxa* occupied from 1986 to 1994.[6] Xuxa herself has continued to restyle her own performances and overall image, essentially "growing up" with her audiences of the first decade. In 1995 Xuxa began making *Xuxa Park*, a Saturday morning program targeted at a teen audience; in 1997 she added the Saturday afternoon show *Planeta Xuxa*, a combination talk and variety show set on lavish stages. Besides making programs that address an older demographic group than originally, Xuxa has allowed her "gamine" image to mature, including, for example, integrating into her public image her independent "Madonna-style" motherhood of a daughter she gave birth to in 1998. She also funds several charities, including a community for orphans on the outskirts of Rio de

Janeiro. Almost two decades after her TV debut, Xuxa remains a programming regular on Brazilian screens.

Xuxa's U.S. Ventures

While Maria Meneghel had worked in the United States in the early 1980s as a Ford Agency model, she made her first U.S. public appearance as TV and recording star "Xuxa" in April 1991, at the Fiesta Broadway, the annual downtown Los Angeles street festival. The appearance was well-timed as advance publicity for *El Show de Xuxa*, scheduled soon to be carried on the largest Spanish-language network in the United States, Miami-based Univisión. Beginning that summer, Univisión affiliates in Miami, Los Angeles, New York, and ten other U.S. cities ran episodes of the one-hour program on Saturday and Sunday mornings. The show was "a sensation," with a reported 80 percent share of Latino viewers aged two to eleven watching Xuxa by February 1992 (Cerone 1992).[7] That fall, building on this initial U.S. success, Xuxa signed an agreement with MTM Television to produce an English-language half-hour daily version of her show for syndication through CBS. After taking accelerated English lessons, Xuxa and her manager spent five weeks in Los Angeles taping sixty-five episodes on a CBS soundstage, enough for a thirteen-week season (Gray 1993, 27). MTM spent reportedly more than $2 million constructing the show's large, elaborate set, with its international theme (mock-ups of iconographic tourist sites like the Eiffel Tower), fantasy elements (a smoke-breathing dragon), bright colors and multiple moving parts (including the stage centerpiece, a blue and pastel globe that opens to reveal a staircase down which Xuxa descends). The cost of each week's production was estimated at an unusually steep $150,000 to $200,000—well above the budget for *Mister Rogers*.

Although the latter is a low-budget U.S. public TV children's program, that difference had not precluded previous implicit comparisons in the press between *Mister Rogers' Neighborhood* and Xuxa's productions. Mainstream U.S. newspapers had taken note of the Xuxa phenomenon in Latin America and the U.S. Latino reception of *El Show de Xuxa* on Univisión, sporadically commenting on it in articles given headlines like "Brazil's Idol is a Blonde, and Some Ask 'Why'" *(New York Times)*; "Meet Brazil's Queen of Kid TV" *(Christian Science Monitor)*; "Brazil's Tot-to-Teen Idol" *(Washington Post)*; "Xuxa's Very Big Neighborhood" *(Los Angeles Times)*; "Xuxa's Newest Neighborhood" *(Boston Globe)*; and "The Brazilian Bombshell's Neighborhood" *(New York)*.[8] The latter three hint at the *Mister Rogers* program.

Generally, although some of these articles question Xuxa's blondeness (accounting for it with mention of her immigrant German-Polish-Italian parentage) and its relation to race in Brazil, overall the reports valorize Xuxa as a sexy innocent who is also an astute businesswoman.

The English-language program, called simply *Xuxa*, aired in September 1993 on 124 affiliates across the United States (Freeman 1993; Gray 1993). In a North American variation on the onstage assistants, two English-speaking male helpers costumed as a giant panda bear and an athletic jaguar (called "Jelly" and "Jam") explain the competitive games' rules and see to it (in another innovation for the litigation-conscious United States) that the participants are equipped with goggles and other safety gear before jumping into vats of Jell-O or being doused with purple liquid goo. Xuxa herself wears, in contrast to her often rather revealing costumes on the Brazilian *Xou*, "chaste if somewhat eccentric" outfits: "one yellow-and-black number looks like a cross between a Renaissance page-boy and a bumblebee," opined Tim Gray in a largely promotional *TV Guide* piece on the program's national premiere (1993, 26). The English-language Xuxa offers its approximation of the popular Paquitas in the four teenaged girls ("Pixies") who sing and dance in back-up to Xuxa and lead the children in cheers. On the L.A.-taped program, in contrast to Latin American versions, these girls are not all blonde, but come from diverse racial/ethnic backgrounds; they are, however, all slim and long-legged, as their majorette-style costumes in some episodes amply display.

Paradoxically, despite previous North American press interest in Xuxa's unusual Latin American programs and image, U.S. television critics now scarcely remarked on her debut on mainstream U.S. television. In a singular *Chicago Tribune* review, one of the few that appeared, Jennifer Mangan (1993) first observes how, having heard of Xuxa's popularity and fame in Brazil and France, she had eagerly anticipated watching the "Olivia Newton John look-alike." She then adopts a barbed, dismissive tone in criticizing the program's focus on the star's singing and the inclusion of educational film "snippets," but she especially ridicules Xuxa's imperfect English and famous "sign-off" gesture of kissing the camera lens. Mangan concludes, "[N]ot only do I think we are not ready for Xuxa, but Xuxa isn't ready for us."

The dearth of media coverage countering such an evaluation may have influenced MTM's decision to pull the program at the end of the season, in January 1993, after stations reportedly "showed little interest in renewing the expensive show" (Tobenkin 1994). No further episodes were taped, but MTM managed to deploy its investment else-where from 1994 to 1996 by rerunning the original episodes repeated-ly in the daily early morning slot on the Family Channel, which, like MTM, is a subsidiary of International Family Entertainment. In an in-terview for a trade journal, the sales manager of the parent company implicitly criticized the original syndicating stations for having inade-quately promoted the show, remarking, "It's an excellent vehicle that can help promote our kids block . . . we can generate new energy with the right type of promotion" (Tobenkin 1994). Still, so-called Fam TV did not itself undertake any major promotional campaign, either of the show itself or of the auxiliary products. Indeed, a further consequence of Xuxa's short-lived attempt to cross over into U.S. English-language TV is that Univisión agreed to stop offering the popular *El Show* and has not resumed its scheduling.

Interestingly, some ancillary Xuxa products did get successfully marketed in many countries where *El Show* ran. In Puerto Rico, for example, a chain of toy stores began featuring "Xuxeria boutiques" in 1991, and sales there of Xuxa dolls soon exceeded those of the then-popular Ninja Turtles. Even in the United States, half a million pairs of plastic sandals emblazoned with Xuxa's name sold in the first year dur-ing which advertisements for them ran over Univisión, along with *El Show*.[9] The marketing of these licensed products fostered Xuxa's suc-cesses locally and regionally and yielded her ever-broadening bases for expansion. At the same time, in many cases, the show itself probably got exported more easily than Xuxa's licensed products. It is difficult enough to span as many sectors of the economy as Xuxa has managed in Brazil, but it is nearly impossible to duplicate such a feat in other market economies, where Xuxa-brand soups and soaps come into di-rect competition with other internationally and some locally produced items.[10]

For all her national and regional popularity and influence, as a Latin American performer—and a woman—Xuxa had to fight a pitched battle to establish global presence in the face of the dominance of male-dominated U.S.-based media conglomerates. Although she achieved legendary national and to an extent global success, Xuxa met with bar-riers to entering particular markets, for however commercialized her own shows and products, both represent a countermovement in the world of electronic communications and popular cultural artifacts in geographic and gendered terms, as we argue further below. By 1996, Barbie-style Xuxa dolls, complete with audiocassette, lipstick, and comb, had been marked down to less than ten dollars, half the price of a Barbie, at a midwestern U.S. Toys R Us store, and a brightly colored palm-top electronic game featuring a prancing Xuxa trying to catch balloons while dodging birds was selling at Big Lots, a cut-rate chain. In short: Xuxamania did not reach the U.S. heartland.

It was certainly no shoddy accomplishment for a figure who first became famous outside the United States and whose original program was not in English to have gained a daily half-hour program for even one season on U.S. broadcast TV. But Xuxa's foray into U.S. mainstream media managed neither to interest television critics nor ultimately to "sell" (to) many regular viewers. We have suggested that political-economic analysis (of structural inequities in media ownership and ancillary marketing, for example) can partially explain this outcome, whereby a capitalist media giant like Rede Globo, and Xuxa herself, works as a dominant force in some markets, yet remains historically marginal in the United States. But the complex imbalances in global media exchange that this case study illustrates emerge clearly only when we bring to the phenomenon additional textual and cultural approaches meaningfully underpinned by feminist and postcolonial theory.

Stopped at the Border?

Accounting for why Xuxa failed to cross over into U.S. English-language TV is unavoidably more speculative and difficult than explaining why her Brazilian and Spanish shows have enjoyed unprecedented successes around the world. However, such analysis can begin to reveal how the status quo of domestically based U.S. programming dominance gets maintained even in those instances, as for *Xuxa,* when U.S.-based media corporations decide that investment in internationally derived programming might serve their own interests. Not only Xuxa and her manager Marlene Mattos but also MTV/International Family Television executives and marketing staff had concluded that the energetic, attractive Brazilian superstar could successfully negotiate the crossover into U.S. children's television.

On the face of it, the star potentially resonated with contemporary Euro-American popular culture; some U.S. TV critics writing about her Brazilian or Spanish-language shows had described her as a cross between Madonna and Pee-Wee Herman. But Xuxa's performances and image also generated cultural dissonances and consequent institutional resistance to her breaking through into mainstream U.S. TV. Why, then, did the show and its star fail to translate cross-culturally for English-speaking North American media audiences?

One obvious and frequent explanation, suggested also in the Mangan review, is, of course, language. Xuxa's command of English at the time of taping, though fluent, was not secure enough for her to ad-lib during a show and thus to project her trademark personality verbally. Yet this observation explains little, given that the English show's target audience was children aged two to eleven. Unlike adults, younger children may not really care or even fully register how well Xuxa or another figure speaks English—or any other verbal language. Karen Miller, a television programming executive, made that point to *TV Guide*: "[Children have] got a big yellow bird talking to them, a purple dinosaur, ninja turtles—you think they're going to have a problem with a woman with an accent?" (Gray 1993, 27).

Less promotionally, media scholar Marsha Kinder argues that preschoolers regularly ignore large portions of TV's audiotrack, for they are tuned in primarily to music and sound effects, and to TV's visuals, especially lively action, graphics, and animation (Kinder 1991, 30–31).[11] While the English-language Xuxa show had animation only in brief educational segments (unlike the longer versions, which integrate cartoons throughout), it partook of the innovative colorful sets and graphics that characterize Xuxa's Brazilian show and supplied lively action and music aplenty to draw the eyes and ears of many children, North or South American.

But young children could watch *Xuxa* only if their caregivers allowed. Another explanation some observers have offered for Xuxa's reportedly lukewarm U.S. reception is that many parents found the star too "sexy" as a children's TV host, both in appearance and in interactions with the children who appeared onstage as audience and game participants. Cast from another perspective, the latter is also a favored explanation in Brazil for U.S. resistance to Xuxa: that puritanical Anglo-Americans can't handle her sensual charm in childlike play (Simpson 1993, 141).[12] Simpson suggests that Brazilian audiences saw Xuxa as "the embodiment of the ideal woman, fully dedicated to courting male interest through behavior designed to be sexually stimulating, and at the same time deeply devoted to the task of caring for children" (7). Cultural differences between Latin America and the United States, including distinct religious traditions, influence the image of the maternal and of women more generally, and thus the production and reception of a specific icon like Xuxa.

Although her appearance in the United States was subdued in comparison to her other shows, Xuxa's thigh-high boots and bouncing blonde locks still resemble Miss Piggy (whom creator Jim Henson claimed to have styled on Mae West) far more than Mr. Rogers. And such auxiliary marketing as occurred in the United States—e.g., the buxom doll in a hot pink jumpsuit, the palm-top game that makes the Xuxa figure look like a skimpily clad dominatrix—generally privileged Xuxa's sexual associations.[13] For all the explicit sexual representations in U.S. media culture, the hosting of a U.S. kids' TV show by a so-called blonde bombshell, however modulated for the occasion, had no precedent.

Producers and advertisers might conceivably have translated the figure of Xuxa for a largely Protestant cultural context. But doing so would have entailed somewhat recasting Xuxa in the U.S. press and otherwise educating audiences about cultural differences that are not immediately visible. Such an undertaking evidently went beyond what U.S. TV executives were willing to venture. It is ironic in this connection, and yet revealing of the contradictions within capitalist purveyance of culture, that International Family Entertainment, a corporation that ostensibly promotes traditional conservative North American values, should have undertaken through its subsidiaries first to produce Xuxa's North American English debut and subsequently to syndicate the program for continued broadcast.

Another way in which *Xuxa* deviated in possibly problematic ways from standard U.S. children's TV was in the program's distinctive "feminine" appeal. Xuxa herself stood out alone in the early 1990s for being a female children's show host. Indeed, as such she is a rare occurrence in a position that has been generally male-dominated since the popular *Shari Lewis Show* on NBC went off the air in 1963.[14] But besides the particular sex of the host, the more pointed gender dissonance of the Xuxa program lies in its explicit emotional appeal, which especially in North America counts as "feminine." As an attractive hostess of the Brazilian show, Xuxa talked to children about peace, nutrition, and self-esteem. The songs she sang on the English show made similar appeals. This affirmative educational focus stands in striking contrast to the fantasy and action orientation of the most popular children's programs—e.g., *Teenage Mutant Ninja Turtles, Power Rangers,* and *X-Men*—that played in succession on U.S. TV during the time Xuxa was reigning in Latin American children's programming.[15]

The semiotic structuring and genre positioning of Xuxa's program within U.S. children's TV programming were crucial to the program's fate. One mismatch between the Brazilian and the U.S. manifestation of Xuxa centers on her programs' very disparate lengths. U.S. TV executives were willing to invest only a one-half hour programming slot in the new venture, not the daily hour for *El Show,* let alone the full morning's schedule that she filled in Brazil. In both of those programs, Xuxa managed to deploy her already familiar star image and further build her appeal to audiences—and advertisers—by appearing as a visual and emotional center, literally and figuratively representing the "eye" in the storm of activity. Xuxa could not immediately serve as such an anchor for U.S. audiences who did not know *El Show,* and the English-language show's length compounded the problem, for it allowed the star/host no time to build connections to the children on the set or watching at home. And the "Pixies," whose analogous figures on the Portuguese and Spanish-language shows have developed their own followings as a means of building and retaining viewership, remained largely anonymous.[16]

A half-hour English-language show obviously could not duplicate the full range of the popular hour-long *El Show,* and especially not the effects of the nearly five-hour-long daily *Xou da Xuxa,* which offered a smorgasbord of cartoons, games, featured guests, songs, and commercials, interlaced with Xuxa's spectacular appearances. In the twenty-four program minutes of an English-language episode, Xuxa herself scarcely had time for a couple of songs, between the schedule of two sloppy games, an educational short, and a guest (performers as diverse as Michael Feinstein, Waylon Jennings, and Cheech Marin) who sang or juggled or otherwise entertained. Three two-minute commercial blocks filled out the half-hour with sponsors' advertisements for dolls, toys, and cereals, none of which bore any associations with the show's host.

Given that a show's duration, scheduling, and casting are organizational decisions, made largely on the basis of procuring advertising, U.S. producers could evidently find little to hook on to for an initial advertising campaign. A promotional strategy that might have built Xuxa's appeal slowly would have required U.S. producers and advertisers to educate audiences about nearly everything that even the much-shortened show offered—its format, its star, its pace—rather than just relying on familiar symbolic associations. Given the unwillingness or inability of the U.S. producers effectively to promote the series they had introduced, Xuxa faced nearly insurmountable *marketing* barriers to entry into U.S. English-language TV.

Not only Xuxa's erotic and closely related cultural encoding made her, for the U.S. context, an unfamiliar and even uncomfortable embodiment of the children's TV host: her racial identity also befuddles conventional U.S. wisdom about Latin Americans in general and Latin American women in particular. Quite bluntly, Xuxa is a blonde and blue-eyed Brazilian woman. Although there are Aryan populations scattered throughout Latin America and overrepresented in that region's quite visible power elite, the U.S. construction of a Latin American is decidedly not along these ethnic lines. The U.S. newspaper critics who initially noticed Xuxa's international stardom expressed essentialist presumptions that a blonde Brazilian is a misrepresentation, and yet generally showed little concern with the perpetuation of racism: their preoccupation with Xuxa's light-colored hair—and implicitly, skin—belie their conviction that South Americans really cannot or should not be naturally blonde and blue-eyed: read, "white."

It is scarcely coincidence that only dark-haired and -eyed Latin American and Latina women—such as Carmen Miranda, Dolores Del Río, Lupe Vélez, Rosie Perez, Jennifer Lopez, and Daisy Fuentes—have gained stardom in North America. Their particular image of Latin womanhood and beauty first fits within and then further justifies the U.S.-constructed stereotype. Xuxa thus landed in a double-bind when attempting to enter the U.S. market: she fit the local ideal of beauty, but since she was not local, she fell outside the familiar signs marking "beautiful Latin American woman"—therefore beyond ready representation. From a U.S. perspective, she remains literally, as even one fan, writing on the Internet, described her, "outlandish."

We have argued that the strictures of conventional U.S. TV and also of Anglo-American cultural expectations were key components in Xuxa's inability to gain a foothold in mainstream U.S. television, as much as personalized reasons such as language competence or even superficial economic explanations, such as inadequate marketing. Television history reveals that a show's fate often is determined in relation to sensitive political or cultural associations or longer-term economic issues, rather than necessarily to the immediate financial "bottom line."[17] Thus, Xuxa's short-term failure at cultural crossover did not necessarily result from documented ratings for her initial U.S. season, but rather arguably from the producers' and station programmers' hesitant follow-through and early withdrawal of support based as much on cultural as economic factors. Xuxa's attempted transition into U.S. TV was at once ambitious and problematic. Whereas her programs—

and her image—differed substantially and in interesting ways from formulaic U.S. TV children's fare, the very basis of her successes in Brazil and elsewhere worked against her in the Euro-Anglo U.S. context. A combination of economic and national barriers, compounded with issues of culturally specific issues of gender and ethnicity, effectively limited Xuxa's expansion into the U.S. TV market.

More than eight years after being essentially "checked" at the borders of U.S. TV programming, Xuxa continues to be a very active performer and leading icon and celebrity especially in Latin America. In addition, a North American fan base for her performances and image may yet be emerging, although not among children or young adults who might know her from Spanish-language programming or contacts with Latin America, but rather among what appears to be predominantly young men, many with Anglo names. Those new fans are finding and following Xuxa not through TV but computer screens—via the Internet. At least two unofficial but extensive and active "Xuxa Web sites" have operated over a number of years out of the United States, and at least one electronic discussion group (alt.tv.xuxa) is devoted to her. Xuxa's own flashy and constantly updated official Web site in Portuguese and English demonstrates her and her manager's continued marketing savvy and resilience and at least partial capacity to circumvent dominant global media control by identifying and developing communication channels beyond traditional TV.

The existence and content of the U.S.-run Web pages (as well as several Latin American ones) invite further study into Xuxa's possibly shifting or expanding global appeal, including in the United States. Several sites celebrate Xuxa as an unusually *nice* celebrity and smart entrepreneur; others contain predominantly "pin-up"-style pictures. For some fans Xuxa may represent primarily a sex goddess: a kind of late-twentieth-century Marilyn Monroe without her pathos or a Madonna without her brass and sass. But even such evident male construction of Xuxa as a somewhat prototypical fetishized blonde does not a priori limit nor determine her meanings for other viewers or audiences—or preclude an understanding of any broader cultural and/or political economic import she may have, from perspectives outside the United States. Consumerist, blonde, and sensual/sexy though she may be, Xuxa has constituted a creative agent and enduring indigenous resource in Latin American resistance to expanding North American financial and ideological dominance of world media.

Notes

1. Amelia Simpson (1993, 65–67, 81–82) points out that "Xou" is not only a "Xuxaspelling" of the Anglicanism "show," but also a play on Portuguese "sou," which means "I am." Thus, "Xou da Xuxa" can be understood as "I belong to Xuxa," as well as "Xuxa's Show." Simpson argues that the latter meaning soon became dominant in Brazil, in keeping with the other pro-U.S. associations Xuxa's program evoked.

2. On Globo's growth after its 1965 founding to becoming a powerful national media force and now international media presence, see Guimarães and Amaral (1988); Mattelart and Mattelart (1990); Novaes (1991); Straubhaar (1996); and Heuvel and Dennis (1995, 34–35, 104, 110–12). See also Lacan (1984); Michaels (1985a, 1985b); and Basas (1992). On Globo's current standing and recent moves in face of 1990s trends in international media monopolization, see Herman and McChesney (1997, 77, 100–01, 164–66).

3. Xuxa's 1986 Globo debut closely coincided with that corporation's international rise, which has been most evident since the mid-1980s—not just coincidentally around the time of major changes in Brazil's national government and the related shift in Globo's own dominant mandate from serving public (state) interests to concerns of private ownership. Xuxa as star and performer has surely profited through her association with Globo, for she and her long-time manager Marlene Mattos shrewdly incorporated before she joined Globo's lineup; thus her own production company retains rights to her appearances outside TV Globo, including syndication rights for her Spanish-language program. Yet TV Globo has also immensely benefited from its presentation of Xuxa, through gaining huge advertising revenues from *Xou da Xuxa* and other Xuxa spin-offs, as well as through associated publicity for her other appearances. Xuxa's well-demonstrated marketability abroad as well as at home accrues to Globo's benefit indirectly in ways that news programs, the corporation's influential and traditional highest-earning productions in the Brazilian market besides telenovelas, cannot. For specific discussion of this point, see Valdivia and Curry (1998, 34–36).

4. This position is one of Simpson's key theses, which she attributes in part to Maria Rita Kehl's essay "Eu vi um Brasil na TV," in Simões (1986).

5. Several extensive Internet Web sites devoted to Xuxa list titles of the albums she has released and the films in which she has appeared; see especially "Xuxa Web," established and maintained from 1993 to 1999 by Richard Carter Jr., a self-proclaimed Xuxa fan, but recently turned over to Don Kinney at http://www.qts1.com/xuxa/. Follow the links (in English or Portuguese) to the discography and filmography. For up-to-date (if skewed to promotional and heavily visual) information in Portuguese or English about Xuxa's productions and activities, see her official Web site at http://www.xuxa.com.br.

6. For background on Angélika, see Simpson (1993, 89, 91). For informa-

tion on Angélika's current program, see the Rede Globo web site, at http://www.redeglobo.com.br.

7. Besides Univisión's U.S. parent company, Hallmark, two Latin American companies own shares of Univisión—Televisa of Mexico and Venevisión, a private Venezuelan broadcaster. In the mid-1990s Univisión had holdings in such locales as Ecuador and was positioned to develop a comprehensive Latin American cable network. See Heuvel and Dennis (1995, 16, 34, 81, 96).

8. See, respectively, Brooke (1990); Duncan (1991); Preston (1991); Blount (1992), 9; Miller (1992); and Picker (1992).

9. Millman (1991), 301–02; also Valdivia (1998); personal correspondence with Victor Rivera and Ray Victor, (1995); and Curry, personal communication from Magali Roy-Fequiere, (1995). Reportedly, Xuxa brand cassette recorders, radios, and sunglasses were also available for a time in the United States.

10. The U.S. market is of course a particularly tough one for foreign producers to crack, given the increasing oligopolistic character of much of the economy. For example, even large U.S. corporations find it difficult to compete against Procter & Gamble in soaps and Campbell's in soups.

11. Kinder supports her argument with studies by D. S. Hayes and D. W. Birnbaum, "Pre-Schoolers' Retention of Televised Events: Is a Picture Worth a Thousand Words?" (*Developmental Psychology* 16 no. 5 [September 1980]: 410–16); and National Institute of Mental Health, *Television and Behavior: Ten Years of Scientific Progress and Implications for the Eighties,* vol. 1 (Washington, D.C.: Government Printing Office, 1982). The recent popularity of the Japanese animated *Pokéman,* in 1999–2000 the Saturday morning cartoon drawing the largest audience share, further strengthens this point. The established international success of that and previous Japanese anime hits like *Speed Racer* again suggests that children are largely indifferent to the origins of a production or the absence of well-developed dialogue: at best, anime dialogue resembles Xuxa's ad-libs in English.

12. As one published source for this argument, Simpson cites the Brazilian magazine *Manchete* (part of the multimedia conglomerate on whose TV network Xuxa had her start) from 9 May 1992.

13. Simpson (1993, 66–67) argues that Xuxa's promotion in Brazil reinforced the emphatic sexual connotations that her name has in Portuguese and Chilean Spanish (suggesting the equivalent of "pussy").

14. Although most U.S. children's shows have a female or two in their casts or in guest roles, men have dominated those programs as hosts and primary protagonists at least since the 1960s. This stricture applies to current U.S. public TV as well: besides the gentle but unmistakably male host of *Mister Rogers,* *Sesame Street* consistently features (and markets) mostly male puppets, and the warm, maternal (and rather stereotypical Latina) human Maria, interacting

with Ernie, Bert, and pals, scarcely operates as a host in the central way that Xuxa does in her programs. Shari Lewis, along with her primary puppet Lamb Chop, which is coded as female, was an exception to male dominance in U.S. children's TV programming with her revived early 1990s public TV programming. Of course the gender of the host does not necessarily entail the particular gender address of the program: in Brazil, Xuxa's programs appeal as much or more to boys as girls, and in the United States, *Barney* and *Mister Rogers* (and more recently, the British import to U.S. public TV, *Teletubbies*) all arguably have a style of "feminine" address. But much U.S. children's TV programming targets children rather older than the preschoolers who make up the audience for the shows mentioned. Xuxa's program differed from those in addressing somewhat older children, yet in a style that generally counts in the United States as "for girls."

15. These programs were targeted in the first instance at boys, although they possess a significant following among girls. U.S. advertisers and the TV industry justify what appears to have become programming dogma with research findings that supposedly show that girls will watch boy-oriented shows, but not vice versa. See Carter (1991); Seiter (1993, 147–51); and Dyson (1997).

16. An online essay by Richard Carter Jr. about Xuxa's lack of success in the United States mentions this as a possible explanation (http://www.qts1.com/xuxa/).

17. In the history of U.S. children's programming alone, we can point to at least two programs that were dropped for reasons other than low ratings. The NBC network cancelled the popular *Shari Lewis Show* in fall 1963 when word got around that Lewis had obtained an abortion in Sweden after learning of the effects of taking thalidomide. Nearly thirty years later, CBS dropped its long-running program *Pee-Wee Herman's Playhouse* (which also attracted a young adult cross-over audience) in the wake of publicity about Paul Reubens (Pee-Wee) having patronized—and been recognized in the act of self-pleasure—at a Florida X-rated movie theater.

Bibliography

Aaronson, C. S., ed. 1956. *1957 International Motion Picture Almanac.* New York: Quigley.

————. 1958. *1959 International Television Almanac.* New York: Quigley.

Acker, Joan. 1999. "Rewriting Class, Race, and Gender: Problems in Feminist Rethinking." In *Revisioning Gender,* ed. M. M. Ferree, J. Lorber, and B. Hess. Thousand Oaks: Sage. 44–69.

"Admen Don't Impress Teenagers with Brand Names." 1954. *Advertising Age* (13 September): 85.

Aguilar, T. 1999. Internet interview with Thais Aguilar, bureau chief, Servicio de Noticias de la Mujer—SEM—San Jose, Costa Rica. (With translation assistance from M. Alejandra Ferreira-Sachero). September 12.

Alarcón, Norma. 1991. "The Theoretical Subject(s) of *This Bridge Called My Back* and Anglo-American Feminism." In *Criticism in the Borderlands: Studies in Chicano Literature, Culture, and Ideology,* ed. Héctor Calderón and José David Saldívar. Durham: Duke University Press. 28–39.

Althusser, Louis. 1997. *For Marx.* London: Unwin.

Andersen, Robin. 1995. *Consumer Culture and TV Programming.* Boulder: Westview Press.

————. 2000. "Road to Ruin: The Cultural Mythology of SUVs." In *Critical Studies in Media Commercialism,* ed. R. Andersen and L. Strate. London: Oxford University Press. 158–72.

————. 2001. "Having Her Say: Tracking the Influence of the Mechanical Bride." *The Legacy of McLuhan.* New York: Fordham University Press. Forthcoming.

Anderson, Perry. 1984. *In the Tracks of Historical Materialism.* Chicago: University of Chicago Press.

Ang, Ian. 1991. *Desperately Seeking the Audience.* London: Routledge.

————. 1996. *Living Room Wars: Rethinking Media Audiences for a Postmodern World.* London: Routledge.

Ang, Ian, and Hermes Jokes. 1991. "Gender and/in Media Consumption." In *Mass Media and Society,* ed. J. Curran and M. Gurevitch. London: Edward Arnold. 307–28.

"Annual Survey." 1997. *Adweek* 38 (9): 25–26.

Appadurai, Arjun. 1996. *Modernity at Large: Cultural Dimensions of Globalization.* Minneapolis: University of Minnesota Press.

Aranda-Alvarado, Belén. 1998. "Physical Attraction." *Latina* 2 (February): 64–69.

Armstrong, Lois. 1981. "Olive's Wasn't the Only Popeye Love Story." *People* (16 March): 121.

Arnold, J. 1976. "Feminist Presses and Feminist Politics." *Quest: A Feminist Quarterly* 3: 18–26.

"The Arrival of Twiggy." 1967. *Life* (3 February): 33–38.

Arthurs, Jane. 1994. "Women and Television." In *Behind the Screens*, ed. S. Hood. London: Lawrence and Wishart. 82–101.

Astra Annual Report. 1996. Södertälje: Sweden. 1–68.

"Astra USA Fires Bildman from Top Post." 1996. *Wall Street Journal* (27 June): A3.

Atten, Michel. 1994. "At the Origins of the French Telephone Crisis." *Reseaux: The French Journal of Communication* 2(2): 237–49.

Aufderheide, P. 1999. *Communications Policy and the Public Interest: The Telecommunications Act of 1996.* New York: The Guilford Press.

Badgett, M. V. L. 1995. "The Wage Effects of Sexual Orientation Discrimination." *Industrial and Labor Relations Review.* 48(4): 726–39.

Bagdikian, Ben. 1997. *The Media Monopoly.* Boston: Beacon Press.

Baistow, Tom. 1985. *Fourth-Rate Estate: An Anatomy of Fleet Street.* London: Comedia.

Bales, Kevin. 1999. *Disposable People: New Slavery in the Global Economy.* Berkeley: University of California Press.

Balibar, Etienne. 1994. *Masses, Classes, Ideas: Studies on Politics and Philosophy Before and After Marx.* New York: Routledge.

Balka, Ellen. 1991. "Womentalk Goes On-line: The Use of Computer Networks in the Context of Feminist Social Change." Ph.D. diss. Simon Fraser University.

———. 1998. "Long Numbers and Wrong Numbers: New Technology and the Restructuring of Women's Work in Telecommunications in Atlantic Canada." Paper presented at the International Association of Media and Communication Researchers, University of Strathclyde, Glasgow, Scotland. 26–30 July. Forthcoming in *Labour/Le travail.*

Ball-Rokeach, Sandra, and Muriel Cantor, eds. 1986. *Media, Audience, and Social Structure.* Thousand Oaks: Sage.

Baltera, L. 1972. "No Gay Market Yet, Admen, Gays Agree." *Advertising Age* (28 August):3.

———. 1975. "Marketers Still in Closet Over Gays."*Advertising Age* (7 July): 3.

Barrett, Michèle. 1980. *Women's Oppression Today.* London: Verso.

———. 1985. Introduction. F. Engels, *The Origin of the Family, Private Property, and the State.* Harmondsworth: Penguin. 7–30.

——. 1991. *The Politics of Truth: From Marx to Foucault*. Cambridge: Polity Press.

——. 1992. "Words and Things: Materialism and Method in Contemporary Analysis." In M. Barrett and A. Phillips, eds., *Destabilizing Theory: Contemporary Feminist Debates*. Stanford: Stanford University Press. 201–19.

——. 1999. *Imagination in Theory: Essays on Writing and Culture*. Cambridge: Polity Press.

——, and Anne Phillips, eds. 1992. *Destabilizing Theory: Contemporary Feminist Debates*. Stanford: Stanford University Press.

Basas, Peter. 1992. "Globo Grabs the TV Jackpot in Brazil." *Variety* 23 (March): 82.

Basu, A. 1995. Introduction. *The Challenge of Local Feminisms*, ed. A. Basu. Boulder: Westview Press. 1–21.

Baxter, Janeen, and Emily Kane. 1995."Dependence and Independence: A Cross-National Analysis of Gender Inequality and Gender Attitudes." *Gender and Society* 9:193–215.

Beam, Chris. 1995. "Se Habla Ingles? Si." *Folio* 24 (12): 42–43.

——. 1996. "The Latina Link in Two Languages." *Folio* 25 (10): 23–24.

Beasley, Maureen H. 1993. "Is There a New Majority Defining the News?" In *Women and Mass Communication*, ed. P. Creedon. London: Sage. 118–33.

Beauvoir, S. de. 1952. *The Second Sex*. Trans. H. M. Parshley. New York: Knopf.

Bell, Daniel. 1973. *The Coming of the Post-Industrial Society*. New York: Basic Books.

Bensimon, Helen Frank, and Patricia A. Walker. 1992. "Associations Gain Prestige and Visibility by Serving as Expert Resources for Media." *Public Relations Journal*: 14–16.

Berger, John. 1972. *Ways of Seeing*. New York: Penguin.

Bernstein, Anita. 1994. "Law, Culture, and Harassment." *University of Pennsylvania Law Review*: 1227–311.

Biskind, Peter. 1998. *Easy Riders, Raging Bulls*. New York: Simon and Schuster.

Black, G. 1998. *Commentary: Perspective on Pinochet*. Los Angeles Times/ Times Mirror Company (wire story), 8 December.

Blau, Francine D., and Marianne A. Ferber. 1990. "Women's Work, Women's Lives: A Comparative Economic Perspective." Working Paper No. 3447. Washington D.C., National Bureau of Economic Research, Inc.

——. 1992. *The Economics of Women, Men, and Work*. Englewood Cliffs: Prentice-Hall.

Blount, Jeb. 1992. "Xuxa's Very Big Neighborhood." *Los Angles Times*, Calendar supplement 19 (April): 9–10.

Bluestone, Barry, and Bennett Harrison. 1982. *The Deindustrialization of America: Plant Closings, Community Abandonment, and the Dismantling of Basic Industries.* New York: Basic Books.

Bottomore, Thomas. 1983. *A Dictionary of Marxist Thought.* Cambridge: Harvard University Press.

Boxall, Bettina. 1996. "Opponents of Prop. 209 Target Women Voters." *Los Angeles Times* (20 August): A1.

Brabant, S. 1976. "Sex Role Stereotyping in the Sunday Comics." *Sex Roles* 2(4): 331–37.

Bradbrook, P. 1980. "The Telegraph and the Female Telegraphist in Newfoundland: A First Inquiry." Research paper prepared for History 3120, Memorial University of Newfoundland (24 pp.). Available from Centre for Newfoundland Studies, Queen Elizabeth II Library, Memorial University of Newfoundland.

Bradley, H. 1989. *Men's Work, Women's Work: A Sociological History of the Sexual Divison of Labor in Employment.* Minneapolis: University of Minnesota Press.

Brenkman, John. 1995. "Race Publics: Civic Deliberation, or Race After Reagan." *Transitions* 66: 4–36.

Bridge, Junior. 1994. "The Media Mirror: Reading Between the (News) Lines." *Quill*: 18–19.

Brock, David. 1993. "The Media and Anita Hill." *National Review* 55.

Bron-Wojciechowska, Agnieszka. 1995. "Education and Gender in Sweden: Is there Any Equality?" *Women's Studies International Forum* 18: 51–60.

Brooke, James. 1990. "Brazil's Idol is a Blonde, and Some Ask 'Why?'" *New York Times*, International Section (31 July): A4.

Brown, Carol. 1981. "Mothers, Fathers, and Children: From Private to Public Patriarchy." In *Women and Revolution*, ed. Lydia Sargent. Boston: South End Press. 239–67.

Brumberg, Joan Jacobs. 1997. *The Body Project: An Intimate History of American Girls.* New York: Random House.

Budd, Mike, Robert M. Entman, and Clay Steinman. 1990. "The Affirmative Character of U.S. Cultural Studies." *Critical Studies in Mass Communication* 7 (2): 169–84.

Burstyn, Barda, and Dorothy E. Smith. 1985. Women, Class, Family, and the State. Toronto: Garamond Press.

Busby, L. 1975. "Sex-Role Research on the Mass Media." *Journal of Communication* 25: 107–31.

Butler, Judith. 1990. *Gender Trouble: Feminism and the Subversion of Identity.* New York: Routledge.

———. 1996. "An Affirmative View." *Representations* 55: 74–83.

Butler, Ron. 1998. "Shopping for Silver Treasures Draws Tourists to Mexico." *Latina* 2 (February): 82–83.

Byars, Jackie. 1991. *All That Hollywood Allows: Re-Reading Gender in 1950s Melodrama*. Chapel Hill: University of North Carolina Press.

————, and Chad Dell. 1992. "Big Differences on the Small Screen: Race, Class, Gender, Feminine Beauty, and the Characters in *Frank's Place*." In *Women Making Meaning: New Feminist Directions in Communication*, ed. L. Rakow. New York: Routledge.

————, and Eileen R. Meehan. 1994. "Once in a Lifetime: Constructing 'The Working Woman' through Cable Narrowcasting." *Camera Obscura* 33–34: 13–41.

Byerly, Carolyn M. 1995. "News, Consciousness, and Social Participation: The Role of Women's Feature Service in World News." In *Women, Multiculturalism, and the Media*, ed. A. N. Valdivia. Thousand Oaks: Sage. 105–22.

————. 1998a. "Countdown for Women's Feature Service: Gender, News, and Development in an Era of Globalization." Paper presented at International Communication Association annual conference, Jerusalem, Israel.

————. 1998b. "Women, Media, and Structure: Feminist Research in an Era of Globalization." Paper presented to the International Association of Media and Communication Research annual conference, Glasgow.

————. 1999. "News, Feminism, and the Dialectics of Gender Relations." In *Mediated Women: Representations in Popular Culture*, ed. M. Meyers. Cresskill, N.J.: Hampton Press. 383–403.

Byerly, Carolyn M., and C. A. Warren. 1996. "At the Margins of Center: Organized Protest in the Newsroom," *Critical Studies in Mass Communication* 13 (1): 1–23.

Cabaza, Becky. 1998. "¿Habla O No Habla?" *Latina* 3 (December): 90–93.

Cahoone, Lawrence. 1996. *From Modernism to Postmodernism: An Anthology*. Malden, Mass.: Blackwell.

California Constitution, Article I, § 31(a).

Camargo, Nelly de. 1987. "Women in Media Management and Decision-Making: A Study of Radio in Ecuador." *Women and Media Decision-Making*. Paris: UNESCO. 44–62.

Canadian Press. 1991. "Anglo-phones, Franco-phones." *Vancouver Sun* (5 March): B11.

Canadian Press. 1995. "New Brunswick Entices Imperial Kool-Ray, Lands 50 More Jobs; McKenna Taunts Critics of His Scheme." *The Globe and Mail* (20 January): B3.

Cantor, Muriel G. 1977a. "Women and Public Broadcasting." *Journal of Communication* 27: 14–19.

————. 1977b. "Our Days and Our Nights on TV." *Journal of Communication* 29: 66–73

Carey, James. 1995. "Abolishing the Old Spirit World." *Critical Studies in Mass Communication* 12 (1): 82–89.

Carter, Bill. 1991. "Children's TV, Where Boys Are King." *New York Times* (1 May): A1, C18.

Carter, Cynthia. 1998. "When the 'Extraordinary' Becomes 'Ordinary': Everyday News of Sexual Violence." In *News, Gender, and Power,* ed. C. Carter, G. Branston, and S. Allan. London: Routledge. 219–32.

Carter, Cynthia, Gill Branston, and Stuart Allan. 1998. "Setting New(s) Agendas: An Introduction." In *News, Gender, and Power,* ed. C. Carter, G. Branston, and S. Allan. London: Routledge. 1–12.

"Catching the Customers at the Most Critical Age." 1957. *Business Week* (26 October): 84–88.

Cernetig, M. 1995. "CIBC Sought Tax Breaks, B.C. Alleges Rejection Costs 1,000 Jobs, Employment Minister Says." *The Globe and Mail* (13 January): A1.

Cerone, Daniel. 1992. "A Hit in L.A. Latino Homes, Xuxa Is Working on Her English." *Los Angeles Times,* Calendar supplement (19 April): 10.

Chen, M. A. 1995. "The Feminization of Poverty." In *A Commitment to the World's Women,* ed. N. Heyzer. New York: United Nations Development Fund for Women (UNIFEM). 23–37.

Chiang, Harriet. 1999. "State Appeals Court Invalidates Minority Outreach Program." *San Francisco Chronicle* (28 May): A22.

Chodorow, Nancy. 1978. *The Reproduction of Mothering.* Berkeley: University of California Press.

Christian, Barbara. 1996. "Camouflaging Race *and* Gender." *Representations* 55: 120–28.

Christmas, Linda. 1997. *Chaps of Both Sexes? Women Decision-Makers in Newspapers: Do They Make a Difference?* London: Women in Journalism.

Clark, Danea. 1991. "Commodity Lesbianism." *Camera Obscura*: 181–96.

Cobo-Hanlon, Leila. 1997. "Giselle Fernandez Has a New Attitude." *Latina* 2 (5): 46–49.

Cockburn, C. 1983. *Brothers: Male Dominance and Technological Change.* London: Pluto.

Coleman, Cynthia-Lou. 1993. "The Influence of Mass Media and Interpersonal Communication on Societal and Personal Risk Judgments." *Communication Research* 20: 611–28.

Coles, Joanna. 1997. "Boy Zone Story." *Guardian.* (28 April).

Collins, Patricia Hill. 1990. *Black Feminist Thought: Knowledge, Consciousness, and the Politics of Empowerment.* Boston: Unwin Hyman.

Compaine, Benjamin. 1982. *Who Owns the Media?* White Plains: Knowledge Industry Publications.

"Company News; Canadian Executive Named to Head Astra USA." 1996. *New York Times* (11 September): D3.

Concerned Women for America. 1991. *The Homosexual Deception: Making Sin a Civil Right*. Washington, D.C.: Concerned Women for America.

Connelly, M. P., and P. Armstrong. 1992. Introduction. *Feminism in Action: Studies in Political Economy*, ed. M. P. Connelly and P. Armstrong. Toronto: Canadian Scholars' Press.

Connerly, Ward. 1996. "Connerly Takes On Colin Powell." *Human Events* (12 July): 5–6.

Coontz, Stephanie. 1992. *The Way We Never Were: American Families and the Nostalgia Trap*. New York: Basic Books.

Cooper, S. 1995. "McKenna's Aim: Slash Business Costs to Attract More Jobs." *Times Colonist*. (20 January).

Corner, John. 1991. "Meaning, Genre, and Context: The Problematics of 'Public Knowledge' in the New Audience Studies." In *Mass Media and Society*, ed. J. Curran and M. Gurevitch. London: Edward Arnold. 267–84.

Coronel, P. 1994. "Women Leading the Paraguan Peasants' Movement." In *Companeras: Voices from the Latin American Women's Movement*, ed. G. Kuppers. Nottingham: Russell Press. 83–91.

Coward, Rosalind. 1983. *Patriarchal Precedents*. London: Routledge and Kegan Paul.

———. 1985. *Female Desires: How They Are Sought, Bought, and Packaged*. New York: Grove.

Creedon, Pamela. 1993. "The Challenge of Re-Visioning Gender Values." In *Women in Mass Communication*. 2d ed., ed. Pamela Creedon. London: Sage.

Crossette, B. 1998a. "Amnesty Finds 'Widespread Pattern' of U.S. Rights Violations," *New York Times* (5 October): A11.

———. 1998b. "For First Time, U.N. Calls Anti-Semitism Racism," *New York Times* (10 December): A10.

Curran, James. 1991. "The New Revisionism in Mass Communication Research: A Reappraisal." *European Journal of Communication* 5: 135–64.

Cyr, Diane. 1993. "The Elusive Hispanic Market." *Folio* 22 (8): 55–60.

D'Acci, Julie. 1994. *Defining Women: Television and the Case of "Cagney and Lacey."* Chapel Hill: University of North Carolina Press.

Davis, Angela. 1998/1977a. "Reflections on Race, Class, and Gender in the USA." In *The Angela Y. Davis Reader*, ed. J. James. Malden, Mass.: Blackwell. 307–25.

———. 1998/1977b. "Women and Capitalism: Dialectics of Oppression and Liberation." In *The Angela Y. Davis Reader*, ed. J. James. Malden, Mass.: Blackwell. 161–92.

Davis, J. 1962. "Sexist Bias in Eight Newspapers." *Journalism Quarterly* 59: 456–599.

Davis, Jessica. "The Middle Passage across the Dialogical Divide: Silenced Voices within 'The Other Half.'" Paper presented at the International Communication Association conference, San Francisco, May 1999.

Dent, Gina. 1992. *Black Popular Culture*. Seattle: Bay Press.

"Designed for Teen-Age Living: It's *Compact*." 1951. *Parents' Magazine* (December): 130.

"Did You Know?" *Latina* 3 (December): 30.

Dines, Gail, and Jean M. Humez, eds. 1995. *Gender, Race, and Class in Media*. Thousand Oaks: Sage.

Doherty, Thomas. 1988. *Teenagers and Teenpics: The Juvenilization of American Movies in the 1950s*. Boston: Unwin Hyman.

"Do Students Expect to Be What They Want to Be?" 1950. *Senior Scholastic* (25 October): 4–T.

Dougary, Ginny. 1994. *The Executive Tart and Other Myths: Media Women Talk Back*. London: Virago.

Douglas, Susan. 1994. *Where the Girls Are: Growing Up Female with the Mass Media*. New York: Random House.

"The Dreamy Teen-Age Market: 'It's Neat to Spend.'" 1957. *Newsweek* (16 September): 94–97.

Duncan, Amy. 1991. "Meet Brazil's Queen of Kid TV." *Christian Science Monitor* (22 January): 14.

Dyer, Gillian. 1982. *Advertising as Communication*. London: Metheun.

Dyer, Richard. 1979. *Stars*. London: British Film Institute.

———. 1981. "Entertainment and Utopia." In *Genre: The Musical: A Reader*, ed. Rick Altman. London: Routledge and Kegan Paul.

Dyson, Anne Haas. 1997. *Writing Superheroes: Contemporary Childhood, Popular Culture, and Classroom Literacy*. New York: Teachers' College Press.

Earle, Beverley H., and Gerald A. Madek. 1993. "An International Perspective on Sexual Harassment Law." *Law and Inequality* 12: 43–91.

Echols, Alice. 1989. *Daring to Be Bad: Radical Feminism in America, 1967–1975*. Minneapolis: University of Minnesota Press.

Edin, Kathryn, and Laura Lein. 1997. *Making Ends Meet: How Single Mothers Survive Welfare and Low-Wage Work*. New York: Russell Sage Foundation.

Eisenstein, Zillah R., ed. 1979. *Capitalist Patriarchy and the Case for Socialist Feminism*. New York: Monthly Review Press.

Eldridge, John, ed. 1995. *News Content, Language, and Visuals: Glasgow Media Group Reader*. Vol 1. London: Routledge.

Elliott, E. 1994. "A Sharper View of Gay Consumers." *New York Times* (9 June): D1.

Elshtain, J. B. 1981. *Public Man, Private Woman: Women in Social and Political Thought*. Princeton: Princeton University Press.

Engels, Friedrich. 1985. *The Origin of the Family, Private Property, and the State.* Harmondsworth: Penguin. (Originally published 1884).

"The English Dream." 1972. *Time* (7 February).

Equal Employment Opportunity Commission. 1995. *The Status of Equal Opportunity in the American Workforce.* Washington, D.C.: GPO.

Equal Rights Advocates. 1999. *Why Women Still Need Affirmative Action.* http://www.equalrights.org/AFFIRM/stats.html

European Commission. 1999. *Images of Women in the Media.* Luxembourg: Office for Official Publications for the European Union.

Ewen, Stuart. 1988. *All-Consuming Images: The Politics of Style in Contemporary Culture.* New York: Basic Books.

"Excerpts from the Court's Decision on Colorado's Provision for Homosexuals." 1996. *New York Times* (21 May): 20.

Fahlbeck, Reinhold. 1995. "Employee Privacy in Sweden." *Comparative Labor Law Journal* 17: 139–74.

Faludi, Susan. 1999. *Stiffed: The Betrayal of the American Man.* New York: William Morrow.

Farnham, Marynia. 1951. "The Teens Discover Themselves." *Parents' Magazine* (May): 36–37, 72–76.

Fass, Paula S. 1977. *The Damned and the Beautiful: American Youth in the 1920s.* New York: Oxford University Press.

Fejes, F., and R. Lennon. 2000. " The Lesbian/Gay Community? Market Research and the Lesbian/Gay Press." *Journal of Homosexuality* 39(1).

Feldberg, R. L., and E. N. Glenn. 1983. "Technology and Work Degradation: Effects of Office Automation on Women Clerical Workers." In *Machina Ex Dea: Feminist Perspectives on Technology,* ed. J. Rothschild. New York: Pergamon. 59–78.

Figueroa, Claudia. 1998. "A Scent of a Woman." *Estylo* (October): 58–61.

"Filmstrip Lectures!" 1950. *Senior Scholastic* (1 February): 17–T.

"First Aid in Learning: How to Be a Knockout." 1949. *Parents' Magazine* (September): 5.

Fisher, Sue, and Kathy Davis. 1993. *Negotiating at the Margins: The Gendered Discourses of Power and Resistance.* New Brunswick: Rutgers University Press.

Fiske, John. 1987. *Television Culture.* London: Methuen.

———. 1994a. *Media Matters: Everyday Culture and Political Change.* Minneapolis: University of Minnesota Press.

———.1994b. "Radical Shopping in Los Angeles: Race, Media, and the Sphere of Consumption." *Media, Culture, and Society* 16 (3): 469–86.

Folbre, Nancy. 1994. *Who Pays for the Kids? Gender and the Structures of Constraint.* London: Routledge.

Folbre, Nancy, and Heidi Hartmann. 1989. "The Persistence of Patriarchal Capitalism." *Rethinking Marxism* 2 (4): 90–96.

Franklin, Bob. 1997. *Newszak and News Media*. London: Edward Arnold.

Fraser, Nancy. 1989. *Unruly Practices: Power, Discourse, and Gender in Contemporary Social Theory*. Minneapolis: University of Minnesota Press.

Freedberg, Louis. 1997. "GOP Trying to Ban Affirmative Action." *San Francisco Chronicle* (18 June): A1.

Freeman, Mike. 1993. "Xuxa Works on U.S. Makeover." *Broadcasting and Cable* (2 August): 23–24.

Friedan, Betty. 1963. *The Feminine Mystique*. New York: Norton.

Frith, Katherine. 1997. *Undressing the Ad: Reading Culture in Advertising*. New York: Peter Lang.

Fritsch, Jane. 1999. "Not Model-Thin, but a Role Model on TV." *New York Times* (1 February): E1, E5.

Frye, Marilyn. 1983. *The Politics of Reality: Essays in Feminist Theory*. Trumansburg, N.Y.: The Crossing Press.

Gallagher, M. 1980. *Unequal Opportunities: The Case of Women and the Media*. Paris: UNESCO.

———. 1985a. "Feminism, Communication, and the Politics of Knowledge." Paper presented at the International Communication Association, Honolulu.

———. 1985b. *Unequal Opportunities: Update*. Paris: UNESCO.

———. 1987. Introduction. *Women and Media Decision-Making*. Paris: UNESCO. 11–16.

———. 1992. "Women and Men in the Media." *Communication Research Trends* 12 (1): 1–36.

———. 1995. *An Unfinished Story: Gender Patterns in Media Employment*. Paris: UNESCO.

Gallegos, Juana. 1997. "Editor's Letter." *Estylo* (fall): 7.

Gandy, Oscar. 1995a. "Colloquy: Political Economy and Cultural Studies." *Critical Studies in Mass Communication* 12(1): 60–61.

———. 1995b. "The Political Economy of Information." *Critical Studies in Mass Communication* 10: 70–97.

Garcia, Kimberly. 1998. "Spanish Playgroups: How to Keep Your Children's Cultural Identity Alive." *Moderna* (March/April): 56.

Garnham, Nicholas. 1979. "Contribution to a Political Economy of Mass-Communication." *Media, Culture, and Society* 1: 123–46.

———. 1995. "Political Economy and Cultural Studies: Reconciliation or Divorce?" *Critical Studies in Mass Communication* 12 (1): 62–71.

Gehman, Richard. 1957. "The Nine Billion Dollars in Hot Little Hands." *Cosmopolitan* (November): 72–79.

"General Mills Seeks Teen Homemakers in 'Betty' Promotion." 1954. *Advertising Age* (6 September): 57.

Gerbner, George, ed. 1983. "Ferment in the Field," *Journal of Communication* 33: 4.

Gilbert, Eugene. 1957. *Advertising and Marketing to Young People.* Pleasantville, N.Y.: Printers' Ink Books.

Gilpin, Kenneth N. 1996. "2 Top Executives Dismissed in Astra Harassment Case." *New York Times* (27 June): D2.

Giri, Ananta K. 1995. "The Dialectic between Globalization and Localization: Economic Restructuring, Women, and Strategies of Cultural Reproduction." *Dialectical Anthropology* 20: 193–216.

Glass Ceiling Commission. 1995. *Good for Business: Making Full Use of the Nation's Human Capital: A Fact Finding Report of the Federal Glass Ceiling Commission.* Washington, D.C.: GPO. http://www.ilr.cornell.edu/library/e_archive/GlassCeiling

"Glen Raven Builds Drive around Movie Tie-In." 1954. *Advertising Age* (11 October).

Glendon, M. A. 1998. "Sudan's Unpunished Atrocities," *New York Times* (8 December): A27.

Golding, Peter, and Graham Murdock. 1991. "Culture, Communications, and Political Economy." In *Mass Media and Society,* ed. J. Curran and M. Gurevitch. London: Edward Arnold. 15–32.

Goodman, Ellen. 1997. "Sexual Harassment Isn't about Sex; It's about Stereotypes." *Boston Globe* (11 December): C7.

Goodman, J. 1998. "Buried Alive: Afghan Women under the Taliban." *On the Issues* (7: 3): 26–31.

Granados, Christine. 1998. "Feminist by Degree." *Moderna* (March/April): 37–38.

Gray, Tim. 1993. "A Person Named Xuxa." *TV Guide* (9 October): 24–27.

Gregory, Jeanne. 1995. "Sexual Harassment: Making the Best Use of European Law." *The European Journal of Women's Studies* 2: 421–40.

Grewal, I., and C. Kaplan, eds. 1994. *Scattered Hegemonies: Postmodernity and Transnational Feminist Practices.* Minneapolis: University of Minnesota Press.

Grossberg, Lawrence. 1994. "Can Cultural Studies Find True Happiness in Communication?" In *Defining Media Studies: Reflections on the Future of the Field,* ed. M. Gurevitch and M. Levy. New York: Oxford University Press. 331–39.

———. 1995. "Cultural Studies vs. Political Economy: Is Anybody Else Bored with This Debate?" In *Critical Studies in Mass Communication* 12 (1): 72–81.

Grupo Televisa. 1997. Informe Anual (Annual Report). Available on-line at http://www.televisa.com.mx/info97 (accessed 1 August 1999).

"Guatemala: News in Brief." 1998. Latin American Institute (wire story). (10 December).

Guimarães, Cesar, and Roberto Amaral. 1988. "Brazilian Television: A Rapid

Conversion to the New Order." In *Media and Politics in Latin America,* ed. Elizabeth Fox. Newbury Park: Sage. 125–37.

Gurevitch, Michael, Tony Bennet, and Janet Woollacott. 1994. *Culture, Society, and the Media.* London: Routledge.

Gurevitch, Michael, and Marc Levy, eds. 1993. "The Future of the Field." *Journal of Communication* 43: 4.

———. 1994. *Defining Media Studies: Reflections on the Future of the Field.* New York: Oxford University Press.

Hagen, I. 1992. "Democratic Communication: Media and Social Participation." In *Democratic Communications in the Information Age,* ed. J. Wasko and V. Mosco. Toronto: Garamond Press. 16–27.

Haineault, Doris-Louis, and Jean-Yves Roy. 1993. *Unconscious for Sale: Advertising, Psychoanalysis, and the Public.* Minneapolis: University of Minnesota Press.

Hall, Stuart. 1985. "Authoritarian Populism: A Reply to Jessop et al." *New Left Review* 151: 115–24.

———. 1986. "Gramsci's Relevance for the Study of Race and Ethnicity." *Journal of Communication Inquiry* 10(2): 5–27.

———. 1992. "Cultural Studies and Its Theoretical Legacies." In *Cultural Studies,* ed. L. Grossberg, C. Nelson, and P. Treichler. New York: Routledge. 277–94.

Harding, Sandra. 1987. *Feminism and Methodology.* Bloomington: Indiana University Press.

———. 1991. *Whose Science? Whose Knowledge? Thinking from Women's Lives.* Ithaca: Cornell University Press.

Hardt, Hanno. 1992. *Critical Communication Studies: Communication, History, and Theory in America.* London: Routledge.

Hartley, John. 1996. *Popular Reality: Journalism, Modernity, Popular Culture.* London: Edward Arnold.

Hartmann, Heidi. 1981. "The Unhappy Marriage of Marxism and Feminism: Toward a More Progressive Union." In *Women and Revolution,* ed. Lydia Sargent. Boston: South End Press. 1–41.

———. 1996. "Who Has Benefited from Affirmative Action in Employment?" In *The Affirmative Action Debate,* ed. George Curry. Reading: Addison-Wesley. 77–96.

Hartmann, Heidi, Robert E. Kraut, and Louise A. Tilly. 1986. *Computer Chips and Paper Clips: Technology and Women's Employment.* Washington, D.C.: National Academy Press.

Haskell, Molly. 1974. *From Reverence to Rape: The Treatment of Women in the Movies.* New York: Penguin.

Hearst Corporation. 1998. "Hearst Magazines Corporate Marketing and Sales." Available online at http://www.hearstcorp.com/mag27.html (accessed 1 August 1999).

Hebdige, Dick. 1988. *Hiding in the Light: On Images and Things.* New York: Routledge.

Hegde, Radha. 1998. "A View from Elsewhere: Locating Difference and the Politics of Representation from a Transnational Feminist Perspective." *Communication Theory* 8 (3): 271–97.

Hennessy, Rosemary. 1993. *Materialist Feminism and the Politics of Discourse.* New York: Routledge.

Herbst, S. 1994. *Politics at the Margin: Historical Studies of Public Expression outside the Mainstream.* New York: Cambridge University Press.

Herdt, G., ed. 1989. *Gay and Lesbian Youth.* Binghamton: Haworth Press.

Herman, Edward S., and Noam Chomsky. 1988. *Manufacturing Consent: A Political Economy of the Mass Media.* New York: Pantheon.

Herman, Edward S., and Robert McChesney. 1997. *The Global Media: The New Missionaries of Corporate Capitalism.* London: Cassell.

Hesse-Biber, Sharlene. 1996. *Am I Thin Enough Yet? The Cult of Thinness and the Commercialization of Identity.* New York: Oxford University Press.

Heuvel, Jon Vandan, and Everette E. Dennis. 1995. *Changing Patterns in Latin America's Vital Media.* New York: Freedom Forum Media Studies Center at Columbia University.

Hill, Anita.1997. *Speaking Truth to Power.* New York: Doubleday.

Hill, Anita Faye, and Emma Coleman, eds. 1995. *Race, Gender, and Power in America (The Legacy of the Hill-Thomas Hearings).* New York: Oxford University Press.

Hobson, Dorothy. 1982. *Crossroads: The Drama of Soap Opera.* London: Methuen.

Hofstadter, D. 1979. *Goedel, Escher, Bach: Eternal Golden Braid.* New York: Vintage.

Hoge, W. 1998. "Briton Won't Free Pinochet, Ruling the Case Can Proceed," *New York Times* (10 December): A3.

Holland, P. 1977."How Straight Is Madison Avenue." *Christopher Street* (January): 26–29.

Holland, Patricia. 1987. "When a Woman Reads the News." In *Boxed In: Women and Television,* ed. H. Baehr and G. Dyer. New York: Pandora. 133–49.

———. 1998. "The Politics of the Smile: 'Soft News' and the Sexualisation of the Popular Press." In *News, Gender, and Power,* ed. C. Carter, G. Branston, and S. Allan. London: Routledge. 17–32.

Holly, S. 1979. "Women in Management of Weeklies." *Journalism Quarterly* 56: 810–15.

Honan, William. 1996. "Efforts to Bar Selection Based on Race: Moves Are Made across the Nation." *New York Times* (31 March): 14.

Honor, Elizabeth. 1957. "How to Be Young, Healthy, and Beautiful." *Cosmopolitan* (November): 81–87.

hooks, bell. 1984. *Feminist Theory from Margin to Center.* Boston: South End Press.

———. 1992. *Black Looks: Race and Representation.* Boston: South End Press.

———. 1994. *Outlaw Culture: Resisting Representation.* New York: Routledge.

———. 1997. *Cultural Criticism and Transformation* [video recording]. Northampton: Media Education Foundation.

"How Old Is Your Audience: U.S. Age Groups Shifting Fast." 1955. *Variety* (16 February): 7.

Hurgenberg, Lawrence W., et al. 1994. "International Business, Gender, and Training: Preparing for the Global Economy." Paper presented at the Meeting of the Eastern Communication Association.

Husbands, Robert. 1992. "Sexual Harassment Law in Employment: An International Perspective." *International Labour Review* 131 (6): 535–59.

International Campaign for Women's Human Rights, 1992–1993 Report. 1993. New Brunswick: Center for Women's Global Leadership, Douglass College, Rutgers.

International Institute of Communications. 1996. *Media Ownership and Control in the Age of Convergence.* Luton: University of Luton Press.

"Is It a Girl? Is It a Boy? No, It's Twiggy." 1967. *Look* (4 April): 84–90.

Ivens, Bryna, ed. 1951. *The "Seventeen" Reader: Stories and Articles from "Seventeen" Magazine.* New York: Lippincott.

Jacobs, Alexandra. 1998. "Weighty Matters." *Entertainment Weekly* (16 October): 13.

Jacobson, Michael, and Lauri Ann Mazur. 1995. *Marketing Madness: A Survival Guide for a Consumer Society.* Boulder: Westview Press.

Jaggar, Alison M. 1983. *Feminist Politics and Human Nature.* Sussex: The Harvester Press.

———. 1998. "Globalizing Feminist Ethics." *Hypatia* 13 (2): 7–31.

Jahr, Cliff. 1977. "Shelley Duvall Delivers It," *The Village Voice* (11 April): 41.

Jameson, Fredric. 1991. *Postmodernism: Or, the Cultural Logic of Late Capitalism.* Durham: Duke University Press.

———. 1993. "On 'Cultural Studies.'" *Social Text* 34: 17–52.

Janus, Noreene Z. 1978. "Research on Sex-Roles in the Mass Media: Toward a Critical Approach." In *The Uses of Literacy,* ed. Noreene Z. Janus. London: Penguin.

Jevons, W. S. 1970. *The Theory of Political Economy.* Harmondsworth: Penguin.

Jezer, Marty. 1982. *The Dark Ages: Life in the United States, 1945–1960.* Boston: South End Press.

Jhally, Sut. 1982. "Probing the Blindspot: The Audience Commodity." *Canadian Journal of Political and Social Theory* 6: 204–10.

Johannes, Laura. 1996. "Astra USA Fires Bildman from Top Post." *Wall Street Journal* (27 June): A3.

Jones, Landon Y. 1984. "1944 to 1984: A Retrospective—How Much Have Teens Changed?" *Seventeen* (September): 160–65.

Jones, Nicholas. 1996. *Soundbites and Spin Doctors: How Politicians Manipulate the Media and Vice Versa.* London: Indigo.

Jordan, Donald L. 1993. "Newspaper Effects on Policy Preferences." *Public Opinion Quarterly* 57: 191–204.

Joseph, Gloria I., and Jill Lewis. 1981. *Common Differences: Conflicts in Black and White Feminist Perspectives.* Garden City: Anchor Books.

Journal of International Communication. (Special Issue: Human Rights). 1998. (June/December) 5: 1 and 2.

Kaplan, E. Ann. 1987. "Feminist Criticism and Television." In *Channels of Discourse, Reassembled,* ed. R. C. Allen. Chapel Hill: University of North Carolina Press. 247–82.

———. 1990. "The Case of the Missing Mother. Maternal Issues in Vidor's *Stella Dallas.*" In *Issues in Feminist Film Criticism,* ed. P. Erens. Bloomington: University of Indiana Press. 126–36.

Kass, Judith M. 1978. *Robert Altman: American Innovator.* New York: Popular Library.

Kates, S. 1998. *Twenty Million New Customers: Understanding Gay Men's Consumer Behavior.* New York: Haworth.

Katz, Nancie. 1997. "How Prop. 209 Affects Claudia Ramsey's Shop." *Christian Science Monitor* (18 November): 2.

Katzenstein, Mary Fainsod, and Carol McClurg Mueller, eds. 1987. *The Women's Movements of the United States and Western Europe.* Philadephia: Temple University Press.

Kauppinen-Toropinen, Kaisa, and James E. Gruber. 1993. "Sexual Harassment of Women in Non-Traditional Jobs: Results from Five Countries." Ann Arbor: The Center for the Education of Women.

Keane, John. 1991. *The Media and Democracy.* Cambridge: Polity Press.

Kelly, Caitlin. 1997. "A Spanish 'Sleeping Giant' Looks Northward." *Folio* 26 (15): 14.

Keyssar, Helene. 1991. *Robert Altman's America.* New York: Oxford University Press.

Kinder, Marsha. 1991. *Playing with Power in Movies, Television, and Video Games: From Muppet Babies to Teenage Mutant Ninja Turtles.* Berkeley: University of California Press.

Kirby, B. 2001. "Truth in Advertising." *The Advocate* (5 June): 15.

Kirk, M., and H. Madsen. 1989. *After the Ball: How America Will Conquer Its Fear and Hatred of Gays in the 90s.* New York: Doubleday.

Klawitter, M. M., and V. Flatt. 1998. "The Effects of State and Local Anti-

Discrimination Policies for Sexual Orientation." *Journal of Policy Analysis and Management* 14(4): 658–86.

Kleinhans, Chuck. 1998. "¡Siempre Selena!" *JumpCut* 42: 28–31.

Klemesrud, Judy. 1977. "Shelley Duvall, an Unlikely Star." *New York Times* (23 March): C19.

Knight, Robert H. Family Research Council. Testimony. 1994. *Employment Non-Discrimination Act of 1994: Hearings before the Committee on Labor and Human Resources.* 103rd Cong., 2d Sess. 29: 92–96.

Knupfer, Nancy N. 1996a. "Gender Equity On-line: Messages Portrayed with and about the New Technologies." Paper presented at the conference of the International Visual Literacy Association.

———. 1996b. "Out of the Picture, Out of the Club: Technology, Mass Media, Society, and Gender." Paper presented at the Conference of the International Visual Literacy Association.

Koranteng, Juliana. 1997. "Hachette Aims for Global Ad Dollars." *Advertising Age* 68 (45): S8.

KPMG Canada. 1997. Maritime Telegraph and Telephone Company Limited. *MT&T Impact Report.* Available from http://www.mtt.ca/AboutMTT/Impact/1997.

Kraar, Louis. 1956. "Teenage Customers: Merchants Seek Teens' Dollars, Influence Now, Brand Loyalty Later." *Wall Street Journal* (6 December): 1, 11.

Kramarae, Cheris, and Jana Kramer. 1995. "Legal Snarls for Women in Cyberspace." *Internet Research Electronic Networking Applications and Policy* 5(2): 14–24.

Lacan, Jacques. 1968. *The Language of the Self.* Trans. A. Wilder. Baltimore: Johns Hopkins University Press. (Originally published 1956).

Lacan, Jean-François. 1984. "Brazil's TV Globo." *World Press Review* (excerpted and translated from *Le Monde,* 22 July 1984). (October): 60–61.

Laumann, E. O., et al. 1994. *The Social Organization of Sexuality: Sexual Practices in the United States.* Chicago: University of Chicago Press.

Lavin, Enrique. 1997a. "In Hollywood's Shadow: Latino Actors Struggle for Recognition, Work, and the Ability to Portray Themselves." *Estylo* (summer): 36–39.

———. 1997b. "Daisy in Demand." *Estylo* (summer): 40–45.

Lawton, George. 1951. "Youth . . . It's Wonderful and Fearful!" *Parents' Magazine* (August): 110–13.

Lemon, Judith L. 1977. "Women and Blacks on Primetime Television." *Journal of Communication* 27: 70–79.

Lipari, Lisbeth. 1994. "As the World Turns: Drama, Rhetoric, and Press Coverage of the Hill-Thomas Hearings." *Political Communications* 11: 299–308.

Liran-Alper, Dalia. 1994. "Media Representation of Women in Politics—Are

They Still 'Domineering Dowagers and Scheming Concubines?'" Paper presented to the International Association of Media Communication Research annual conference, Seoul.

Livant, Bill. 1979. "The Audience Commodity: On the 'Blindspot' Debate." *Canadian Journal of Political and Social Theory* 3: 91–106.

———. 1982. "Working at Watching: A Reply to Sut Jhally." *Canadian Journal of Political and Social Theory* 6: 211–15.

"Lo Ultimo." 1998. *Moderna* (March/April): 64.

López, Ana. 1995. "Are All Latins from Manhattan?" In *Mediating Two Worlds: Cinematic Encounters in the Americas*, ed. J. King, A. López, and M. Alvarado. London: British Film Institute. 67–80.

Los Angeles Times Exit Poll. 1996. http://www.acri.org/209

Lovell, Amanda. 1977. "Close Up." *Mademoiselle* (September): 190+.

Lucek, Linda E. 1995. "Women in Cyberspace." In *Eyes on the Future: Converging Images, Ideas, and Instruction.* Selected readings from the annual conference of the International Visual Literacy Association, Chicago.

Lukenbill, G. 1995. *Untold Millions: Positioning Your Business for the Gay and Lesbian Consumer Revolution.* New York: HarperCollins.

Lull, James, A. Mulac, and S. L. Rosen. 1983. "Feminism as a Predictor of Mass Media Use." *Sex Roles* 9: 165–77.

Luthra, Rashmi. 1996. "International Communication Instructions with a Focus on Women." *Journalism and Mass Communication Educator* 50(4): 42–51.

Macdonald, Dwight. 1958a. "A Caste, a Culture, a Market—I." *The New Yorker* (22 November): 57–94.

———. 1958b. "A Caste, a Culture, a Market—II." *The New Yorker* (29 November): 57–107.

Machlup, F. 1962. *The Production and Distribution of Knowledge in the United States.* Princeton: Princeton University Press.

Malson, Helen. 1998. *The Thin Woman: Feminism, Psychoanalysis, and the Social Psychology of Anorexia.* London: Routledge.

Mangan, Jennifer. 1993. "Brazilian No-No." *Chicago Tribune*, sec. 5 (13 September): 7.

Manheim, Camryn. 1999. *Wake Up, I'm Fat.* New York: Broadway Books.

Mann, Patricia. 1994. *Micro-Politics: Agency in a Postfeminist Era.* Minneapolis: University of Minnesota Press.

Marchand, Marianne H. 1996. "Reconceptualizing 'Gender Development' in an Era of Globalization." *Millennium* 25(3): 577–603.

Marchand, Roland. 1982. "Visions of Classlessness, Quests for Dominion: American Popular Culture, 1945–1960." In *Reshaping America: Society and Institutions, 1945–1960*, ed. R. H. Bremner and G. W. Reichard. Columbus: Ohio State University Press. 163–82.

Maremont, Mark. 1996. "Abuse of Power: The Astonishing Tale of Sexual Harassment at Astra." *Business Week* (13 May): 86–98.

Marin, Allan, ed. 1980. *Fifty Years of Advertising as Seen through the Eyes of "Advertising Age" 1930–1980.* Chicago: Crain Communications, Inc.

Maritime Telegraph and Telephone Company Limited. 1997. *1996 Annual Report, MT&T.* "Message to Shareholders." Available from http://www.mtt.ca/AboutMTT/Profile/Message/.

Maritime Telegraph and Telephone Company Limited. 1998. *1997 Annual Report, MT&T.* Available from http://www.mtt.ca/MTTInvestors/AnnualReport/.

Martin, Michéle. 1988. "Communication as Circulation: The political Economy of Systems of Communication." Paper presented at the International Communication Association, Montreal.

———. 1991. *Hello, Central? Gender, Technology, and Culture in the Formation of Telephone Systems.* Montreal: McGill-Queen's University Press.

———. 1998. "Help! What Feminist Theory in International Communication?" Paper presented at the international conference on Questioning International Communication: Discrepancies in Theories and Research. Carleton University, Ottawa.

———. 1999. "La Culture Québécoise Mise aux Enchères?" In *Usages et Services des Télécommunications,* conference proceedings, ed. ADERA, 215–25, Paris: Télécom.

Martin, Stana. 1997a. "The Formation of the Global Office: Women and the Globalization of Information Labor." *Women, Work, and Computerization: Spinning a Web from Past to Future.* Proceedings of the IFIP WG 9.1 Conference on Women, Work, and Computerization, Bonn, 22–24 May.

———. 1997b. Information Technologies and Information Employment 1970–1995: Gender, Technology, and Work in the Information Society. Ph.D. diss. University of Texas at Austin.

———. 1998. "Information Technology, Employment, and the Information Sector: Trends in Information Employment 1970–1995." *Journal of the American Society for Information Science* 49, no. 12: 1053–69.

Marvin, Carolyn. 1988. *When Old Technologies Were New.* New York: Oxford University Press.

Marx, Karl. 1963. *The Eighteenth Brumaire of Louis Bonaparte.* New York: International Publishers.

———. 1973. *Gundrisse.* New York: Vintage.

———. 1976. *Capital: A Critique of Political Economy.* London: Penguin.

———. 1979. "The Mystery of the Fetishistic Character of Commodities." In *Communication and Class Struggle.* Vol. 1., ed. A. Mattelart and S. Siegelaub. New York: International General. 80–84.

Marx, Karl, and Friedrich Engels. 1968. *The German Ideology.* Moscow: Progress.

Marzolf, M., R. B. Rush, and D. Stern. 1974–1975. "The Literature of Women in Journalism History." *Journalism History* 1 (4): 117–28.

Mattelart, Armand, and Michèle Mattelart. 1990. *Carnival of Images: Brazilian Television Fiction.* Trans. David Buxton. New York: Bergin and Garvey.

McAllister, Matthew. 1996. *The Commercialization of American Culture: New Advertising, Control, and Democracy.* Thousand Oaks: Sage.

McChesney, Robert W. 1994. "Critical Communications Research at the Crossroads." In *Defining Media Studies: Reflections on the Future of the Field,* ed. M. Gurevitch and M. Levy. New York: Oxford University Press. 340–46.

———. 1996. "The Internet and U.S. Communication Policy-Making in Historical and Critical Perspective." *Critical Studies in Mass Communication* 46(1): 98–124.

McCormack, T. 1983. "The Political Content and the Press of Canada." *Canadian Journal of Political Science* 16: 451–72.

McCracken, Ellen. 1993. *Decoding Women's Magazines: From Mademoiselle to Ms.* New York: St. Martin's Press.

McFarland, J., and R. Buchanan. 1998. "The Political Economy of New Brunswick's 'Call Center' Industry: Old Wine in New Bottles." *Socialist Studies Bulletin* 17.

McLaughlin, Lisa. 1993. "Feminism and the Public Sphere." *Media, Culture, and Society* 15(4): 599–620.

———. 1995. "Feminist Communication Scholarship and 'The Woman Question' in the Academy." *Communication Theory* (May): 144–62.

———. 1997. "Class Difference and Indifference in Feminist Media Studies." *The Public* 4 (3): 27–40.

———1998. "Gender, Privacy, and Publicity in 'Media Event Space.'" In *News, Gender, and Power,* ed. C. Carter, G. Branston, and S. Allan. London: Routledge. 71–90.

———. 1999. "Beyond 'Separate Spheres': Feminism and the Cultural Studies/Political Economy Debate." *Journal of Communication Inquiry* 23 (4): 327–54.

McLuhan, Marshall. 1967. *The Mechanical Bride: Folklore of Industrial Man.* Boston: Beacon. (Originally published in 1951 by Vanguard Press, New York).

McRobbie, Angela. 1978a. *Jackie: An Ideology of Adolescent Femininity.* Birmingham: The Centre for Contemporary Cultural Studies.

———. 1978b. "Working-Class Girls and the Culture of Femininity." In *Women Take Issue,* ed. Women's Studies Group. London: Hutchinson. 96–108.

———. 1980. "Settling Accounts with Subcultures: A Feminist Critique." *Screen Education* 34: 37–49.

———. 1982. "The Politics of Feminist Research: Between Talk, Text, and Action." *Feminist Review* 12: 46–57.

———. 1984. "Dance and Social Fantasy." In *Gender and Generation*, ed. A. McRobbie and M. Nava. New York: Macmillan. 130–62.

———. 1994. *Postmodernism and Popular Culture*. London: Routledge.

Meehan, Eileen R. 1984. "Ratings and the Institutional Approach." *Critical Studies in Mass Communication* 1: 216–25.

———. 1986. "Between Political Economy and Cultural Studies: Towards a Refinement of American Critical Communication Research." *Journal of Communication Inquiry* 10 (3): 86–94.

———. 1990."Why We Don't Count." In *Logics of Television*, ed. P. Mellencamp. Bloomington: Indiana University Press. 117–37.

———. 1991. "Holy Commodity Fetish, Batman!: The Political Economy of a Commercial Intertext." In *The Many Lives of Batman: Critical Approaches to a Superhero and His Media*, ed. W. Uricchio and R. Pearson. New York: Routledge. 47–65.

———. 1994. "Heads of Household and Ladies of the House: Gender, Genre, and Broadcast Ratings, 1929–1990." In *Ruthless Criticism: New Perspectives in Communication History*, ed. W. S. Solomon and R. W. McChesney. Minneapolis: University of Minnesota Press. 204–21.

———. 1999. "Commodity, Culture, Common Sense: Media Research and Paradigm Dialogue." *Journal of Media Economics* 12(2): 149–63.

Meehan, Eileen R., Vincent Mosco, and Janet Wasko. 1994. "Rethinking Political Economy: Change and Continuity." In *Defining Media Studies: Reflections on the Future of the Field*, ed. M. Gurevitch and M. Levy. New York: Oxford University Press. 347–58.

Meehan, Eileen, and Jackie Byars. 2000. "Telefeminism: The Case of the Lifetime Cable Channel." *Telvision and New Media* 1(February): 33–51.

Meehan, Johanna. 1995. Introduction. *Feminists Read Habermas: Gendering the Subject of Discourse*, ed. J. Meehan. New York: Routledge.

Melin-Higgins, Margareta, and Madeline Djerf Pierre. 1998. "Networking in Newsrooms: Journalist and Gender Cultures." Paper presented to the International Association of Media and Communication Research annual conference, Glasgow.

Mellencamp, Patricia. 1995. *A Fine Romance: Five Ages of Film Feminism*. Philadelphia: Temple University Press.

Menard, Valerie. 1998a. "Blonde Ambition: Cristina Saralegui Reveals Her True Self in a New Autobiography." *Moderna* (summer): 26–28.

———. 1998b. "Mayan Gateway." *Moderna* (fall): 60–61.

Menzies, Heather. 1996. *Whose Brave New World*. Toronto: Between the Lines.

Mercer, Kobena. 1994. *Welcome to the Jungle: New Positions in Black Cultural Studies*. New York: Routledge.

Merret, M. 1988. "A Gay Look at Advertising." *The Advocate* (5 December): 42–45.

Merry, Sally Engle. 1996. Review of *Crime Talk: How Citizens Construct a Social Problem* in *The Law and Politics Book Review* 6: 90.

Messaris, Paul. 1996. *Visual Persuasion: The Role of Images in Advertising*. Thousand Oaks: Sage.

Michaels, Julia. 1985a. "Big Brazil TV Network Plans Major European Expansion." *Advertising Age* (16 September): 70.

———. 1985b. "Latins Take TV Battles Global." *Advertising Age* (2 December): 54, 59.

Michener, Charles. 1977. "Year of the Actress." *Newsweek* (14 February): 55–66.

Michielsens, Magda. 1991. *Women in View: How Does BRTN Portray Women? An Audience Survey*. Brussels: BRTN/Commission of European Communities.

Miller, C. 1992. "Mainstream Marketers Decide Time is Right to Target Gays." *Marketing News* (20 July): 8.

Miller, Rick. 1992. "Xuxa's Newest Neighborhood." *Boston Globe* (25 November): 35.

Millman, Joel. 1991. "Shoe-Shoe, Buy, Buy." *Forbes* (9 December): 300–02.

Mills, Kay. 1990. *A Place in the News: From the Women 's Pages to the Front Page*. New York: Columbia University Press.

———1997." What Difference Do Women Journalists Make?" In *Women, Media, and Politics,* ed. P. Norris. New York: Oxford University Press. 41–56.

Moen, Phyllis. 1989. *Working Parents: Transformations in Gender Roles and Public Policies in Sweden*. Madison: University of Wisconsin Press.

Moghadam, Valentine M. 1999. "Gender and the Global Economy." In *Revisioning Gender,* ed. M. M. Ferree, J. Lorber, and B. B. Hess. Thousand Oaks: Sage. 128–60.

Mohanty, Chandra T. 1991a. "Introduction: Cartographies of Struggle: Third World Women and the Politics of Feminism." In *Third World Women and the Politics of Feminism,* ed. C. T. Mohanty, A. Russo, and L. Torres. Bloomington: Indiana University Press. 1–47.

———. 1991b. "Under Western Eyes: Feminist Scholarship and Colonial Discourses." In *Third World Women and the Politics of Feminism,* ed. C. T. Mohanty, A. Russo, and L. Torres. Bloomington: Indiana University Press. 51–80.

Moraga, Cherríe, and Gloria Anzaldúa, eds. 1983. *This Bridge Called My Back: Writings by Radical Women of Color* 2d. ed. New York: Kitchen Table/Women of Color Press.

Morley, David. 1992. *Television, Audiences, and Cultural Studies.* London: Routledge.

Morris, M. B. 1973. "Newspapers and the New Feminists: Blackout as Social Control?" *Journalism Quarterly* 50: 37–42.

Morritt, Hope. 1996. "Women and Computer-Based Technologies: A Feminist Perspective." Paper presented at the meeting of the American Educational Research Association.

———. 1997. *Women and Computer-Based Technology.* Lanham: University Press of America.

Mosco, Vincent. 1996. *The Political Economy of Communication.* London: Sage.

———. 1998. "Location, Location, Location! States, Regions, and High Technology." Paper presented at the international conference on Questioning International Communication. Carleton University, Ottawa.

Mueller, Charles W., et al. 1994. "Swedish Professionals and Gender Inequalities." *Social Forces* 73(2):555–73.

Mukherjee, Roopali. 2000. "Regulating Race in the California Civil Rights Initiative: Enemies, Allies, and Alibis." *Journal of Communication* 50(2): 27–47.

Mulvey, Laura. 1975. "Visual Pleasure and Narrative Cinema." *Screen* 16: 6–18.

Murdock, Graham. 1978. "Blindspots about Western Marxism: A Reply to Dallas Smythe." *Canadian Journal of Political and Social Theory* 2: 109–19.

———. 1982. "Large Corporations and the Control of the Communications Industries." In *Culture, Society, and the Media,* ed. M. Gurevitch et al. London: Routledge. 118–50.

———. 1995. "Across the Great Divide: Cultural Analysis and the Condition of Democracy." *Critical Studies in Mass Communication* 12 (1): 89–95.

Murdock, Graham, and Peter Golding. 1997. "For a Political Economy of Mass Communications." In *The Political Economy of the Media.* Vol. 1. Ed. P. Golding and G. Murdock. Cheltenham: Edward Elgar Publishing Limited.

Myers, M. 1992. "Reporters and Beats: The Making of Oppositional News." *Critical Studies in Mass Communication* 9: 75–90.

NBTel. (1998). *Annual Report.*

Negrine, Ralph. 1998. *Parliament and the Media.* London: Cassell.

Negrón-Muntaner, Frances. 1997. "Jennifer's Butt." *Aztlán* 22 (2): 181–94.

Negt, Oskar, and Alexander Kluge. 1993. *Public Sphere and Experience: Toward an Analysis of the Bourgeois and Proletariat Public Sphere.* Trans. P. Labanyi, J. O. Daniel, and A. Oksiloff. Minneapolis: University of Minnesota Press.

Nelson, Barbara J., and Najima Chowdhury, eds. 1994. *Women and Politics Worldwide*. New Haven: Yale University Press.

Nelson, Cary, and Lawrence Grossberg. 1998. *Marxism and the Interpretation of Culture*. Urbana: University of Illinois Press.

Neves, Helena. 1994. Speech to the Prix Niki Conference. Lisbon.

NewTel Enterprises Limited. 1994. *1993 Annual Report*. St. John's: NewTel Enterprises Limited.

NewTel Enterprises Limited. 1995. *1994 Annual Report*. St. John's: NewTel Enterprises Limited.

NewTel Enterprises Limited. 1996. *1995 Annual Report*. St. John's: NewTel Enterprises Limited.

NewTel Enterprises Limited. 1998. "NewTel Re-organization Sets Agenda for Growth" [press release]. 3 July 1998. St. John's: NewTel. 4p. Available from http://www.newtel.com.

"A New, $10–Billion Power: The U.S. Teen-Age Consumer." 1959. *Life* (31 August): 78–85.

Nichols, Elizabeth. 1951. "The Pre-Teen Look." *Parents' Magazine* (September): 92.

Nicholson, Daniel R. 1997. "The Diesel Jeans and Workwear Advertising Campaign and the Commodification of Resistance." In *Undressing the Ad: Reading Culture in Advertising*, ed. K. Frith. New York: Peter Lang. 175–96.

Nightingale, Virginia. 1996. *Studying Audiences: The Shock of the Real*. London: Routledge.

Nogales, Ana, and Laura Golden Bellotti. 1998. "Latino Lovers under the Sabanas." *Latina* 2 (February): 32–35.

Norris, Pippa, ed. 1997. *Women, Media, and Politics*. New York: Oxford University Press.

Novaes, Adauto, ed. 1991. *Rede Imaginária: Televisão e Democracia*. São Paolo: Companhia das Letras.

Nuiry, Octavio. 1996. "Magazine Mania: Whose Media Is This, Anyway?" *Hispanic* 9 (December): 53–56.

OECD. 1986. *Trends in the Information Economy*. Information, Computers, and Communication Policy Section (ICCP).

Ogan, C., and D. Weaver. 1978–79. "Job Satisfaction in Selected U.S. Daily Newspapers: A Study of Male and Female Top Managers." *Mass Communications Review* 6: 20–26.

Orbach, Suzie. 1997. *Fat Is a Feminist Issue*. New York: Budget Book Services.

Owen, Diana, and Jack Dennis. 1992. "Sex Differences in Politicization: The Influence of Mass Media." *Women and Politics* 12(4): 19–37.

Palladino, Grace. 1996. *Teenagers: An American History*. New York: Basic Books.

Parker, Beth. 1998. *The Impact of Proposition 209 on Education, Employ-ment, and Contracting: Opportunities for Women in California*. Equal Rights Advocates. http://www.equalright.org/AFFIRM/Full209.html.

Penaloza, L. 1996. "We're Here, We're Queer, and We're Going Shopping: A Critical Perspective on the Accommodation of Gays and Lesbians in the U.S. Marketplace." *Journal of Homosexuality* 31(1/2): 9–41.

Pendakur, M. 1993. "Political Economy and Ethnography: Transformations in an Indian Village." In *Illuminating the Blindspots: Essays Honoring Dallas W. Symthe*, ed. J. Wasko, V. Mosco, and M. Pendakur. Norwood, N.J.: Ablex. 82–108.

Pendleton, J. 1980. "National Marketers Beginning to Recognize Gays." *Advertising Age* (6 October): 84–85.

"Perfect Magazine Gifts for Teen-Agers." 1949. *Parents' Magazine* (November): 139.

Peterson, V. Spike. 1996. "The Politics of Identification in the Context of Globalization." *Women's Studies International Forum* 19(1–2): 5–15.

Petrazzini, Ben A. 1995. *The Political Economy of Telecommunications Reform in Developing Countries*. London: Praeger.

Phillips, Reed. 1994. "Mexico through the Eyes of NAFTA." *Folio* 23 (6): 39.

Picker, Lauren. 1992. "The Brazilian Bombshell's Neighborhood." *New York* (9 March): 23.

Pingree, Suzanne, and Rosemary P. Hawkins. 1978. "News Definitions and Their Effects on Women." In *Women and the News*, ed. L. K. Epstein. Mamaroneck N.Y.: Hasting House.

Pipes, Sally, and Michael Lynch. 1996. *Women Don't Need Affirmative Action*. Heritage Foundation. http://www.heritage.org/commentary/op-sp1.html.

Poe, A. 1976. "Active Women in Ads." *Journal of Communication* 26: 185–92.

Pogrebin, Robin. 1996. "Lesbian Publications Struggle for Survival in a Mar-ket Dominated by Gay Males." *New York Times* (23 December): D7.

———. 1997a. "Success and the Black Magazine: As Readers Prosper, Advertising Still Eludes Publishers." *New York Times* (25 October): B1.

———. 1997b. "Ousted Editor Sees Bias at Gay-Lesbian Monthly." *New York Times* (8 December): D12.

———. 1998a. "Once a Renegade, Hachette Magazines Chief Gains Respect." *New York Times* (6 April): D1.

———. 1998b. "Magazine Marketing Raises Question of Editorial Independ-ence." *New York Times* (4 May): D1.

Pollert, A. 1996. "Gender and Class Revisited: Or the Poverty of Patriarchy." *Sociology* 30 (4): 639–59.

Poole, Ithiel de Sola, and Herbert I. Schiller. 1981. "Perspectives on Commu-nications Research: An Exchange." *Journal of Communication* 31: 15–23.

Porat, Marc Uri. 1977. *The Information Economy.* Washington, D.C.: Department of Commerce.

Porges, Irwin. 1958. "Your Teenager Is Big Business." *American Mercury* (July): 94–96.

Press, Andrea. 1991. *Women Watching Television: Gender, Class, and Generation in the American Television Experience.* Philadelphia: University of Pennsylvania Press.

Preston, Julia. 1991. "Brazil's Tot-to-Teen Idol." *Washington Post* (2 December): B1, B4.

Raboy, M. 1998. "Global Communication Policy and the Realisation of Human Rights." *Journal of International Communication* (June/December) 5: 1 and 2, 83–104.

Radner, Hilary. 1995. *Shopping Around: Feminine Culture and the Pursuit of Pleasure.* New York: Routledge.

Radway, Janice. 1984. *Reading the Romance: Women, Patriarchy, and Popular Culture.* Chapel Hill: University of North Carolina Press.

———. 1989. "Ethnography among Elites: Comparing Discourses of Power." *Journal of Communication Inquiry* 13(2): 3–11.

Rakow, Lana. 1986. "Rethinking Gender Research in Communication." *Journal of Communication* 36(4): 11–26.

———. 1998. "Feminist Approaches to Popular Culture: Giving Patriarchy Its Due." In *Cultural Theory and Popular Culture: A Reader.* 2d ed. Ed. J. Storey. Athens: The University of Georgia Press. 275–91.

Rapping, Elayne. 1995. "Daytime Enquiries." In *Gender, Race, and Class in Media,* ed. G. Dines and J. M. Humez. Thousand Oaks: Sage. 377–82.

Remmers, Hermann H., and Don H. Radler. 1957. *The American Teenager.* Indianapolis: Bobbs-Merrill.

"Results of Recent I.S.O. Poll." 1951. *Senior Scholastic* (16 May).

Riesman, David, with Reuel Denney and Nathan Glazer. 1950. *The Lonely Crowd: A Study of the Changing American Character.* New Haven: Yale University Press.

Roach, Colleen. 1993. "Feminist Peace Researchers, Culture, and Communication." In *Communication and Culture in War and Peace,* ed. Colleen Roach. Newbury Park: Sage. 175–91.

Robinson, Gertrude. (forthcoming). "Theorizing the Impact of Gender in Canadian Journalism." In *Gender, Culture, and Journalism: A Study of Industrialized Nations,* ed. R. Froelich and S. A. Lalky. The Edwin Mellin Press.

Robinson, Gertrude, and Armande Saint-Jean. 1997. *Women's Participation in the Canadian News Media: Progress since the 1970s.* Unpublished report. Montreal: McGill University.

Rodriguez, América. 1996. "Objectivity and Ethnicity in the Production of the *Noticiero Univisión.*" *Critical Studies in Mass Communication* 13 (1): 59–81.

Roediger, David. 1997. "White Workers, New Democrats, and Affirmative Action." In *The House That Race Built,* ed. Wahneema Lubiano. New York: Vintage. 48–65.

Rondon, Nayda. 1997. "Couture Queen." *Moderna* (winter): 22–24.

Root, Jane. 1986. *Open the Box: About Television.* London: Channel 4 and Comedia series no. 34

Rosen, J. 1994. "*Out* Magazine's National Reach." *New York Times* (7 March): D6.

Ross, Karen. 1995a. *Women and the News Agenda: Media-ted Reality and Jane Public.* Discussion paper no. MC95/1. Centre for Mass Communication Research, Leicester University.

———. 1995b. "Gender and Party Politics: How the Press Reported the Labor Leadership Campaign, 1994." *Media, Culture, and Society* 17 (3): 499–509.

———. 1996. *Black and White Media: Black Images in Popular Film and Television.* London: Polity Press.

———. 1998. "Making Race Matter: An Overview." In *Making the Local News,* ed. B. Franklin and D. Murphy. London: Routledge. 228–40.

Ross, Karen, and Annabelle Sreberny-Mohammadi. 1997. "Playing House—Gender, Politics, and the News Media in Britain." *Media, Culture, and Society* 19(1): 101–09.

Rowe, Kathleen. 1995. *The Unruly Woman: Gender and the Genres of Laughter.* Austin: University of Texas Press.

Roy-Fequiere, Magali. 1996. Personal communication to Ramona Curry.

Rubin, M. 1986. *The Knowledge Industry in the United States, 1960–1980.* Princeton: Princeton University Press.

Saffioti, Heleieth I. B. 1978. *Women in Class Society.* New York: Monthly Review Press.

Sainsbury, Diane. 1996. *Gender, Equality, and Welfare State.* Cambridge: Cambridge University Press.

Salwen, Michael, and Bruce Garrison. 1991. *Latin American Journalism.* Hillsdale, N.J.: Lawrence Erlbaum Associates.

Sancho-Aldridge, Jane. 1997. *Election '97.* London: Independent Television Commission.

Sargent, Lydia, ed. 1981. *Women and Revolution.* Boston: South End Press.

Savan, Leslie. 1994. *The Sponsored Life: Ads, TV, and American Culture.* Philadelphia: Temple University Press.

Savin-Williams, R. C. 1990. *Gay and Lesbian Youth: Expressions of Identity.* New York: Hemisphere.

Scanlon, Jennifer. 1995. *Inarticulate Longings: The Ladies' Home Journal, Gender, and the Promises of Consumer Culture.* London: Routledge.

Scherman, Tony. 1980. "Shelley Duvall: The Sailor Man's Lady." *Mademoiselle* (December): 168–69.

Schiller, Dan. 1994. "Back to the Future: Prospects for Study of Communication as a Social Force." In *Defining Media Studies: Reflections on the Future of the Field*, ed. M. Gurevitch and M. Levy. New York: Oxford University Press. 359–66.

Schiller, Herbert I. 1971. *Mass Communications and American Empire.* Boston: Beacon Press.

———. 1976. *Communication and Cultural Domination.* White Plains: Sharpe.

Schulman, S. 1998. *Stage Struck: Theater, AIDS, and the Marketing of Gay America.* Durham: Duke University Press.

Seager, J. 1997. *The State of Women in the World Atlas.* New Edition. London: Penguin.

Seiter, Ellen. 1993. *Sold Separately: Parents and Children in Consumer Culture.* New Brunswick: Rutgers University Press.

Self, Robert. 2002. *Robert Altman's Subliminal Reality.* Minneapolis: University of Minnesota Press.

Sender, K. 1999. "Selling Subjectivities: Audiences Respond to Gay Window Advertising." *Critical Studies in Mass Communication* 16: 172–96.

Senjen, Rye, and Jane Guthrey. 1996. *The Internet for Women.* Melbourne: Spinifex Press.

"*Seventeen*'s Treasure Chest for Your Happy Future." 1956. *Seventeen* (May): 126–29.

Shade, Leslie. 1996. "The Digital Women." womens-studies-www@mit.edu.

———. 1998. "A Gendered Perspective on Access to the Information Structure." *The Information Society* 14(1): 33–44.

Shalit, Gene. 1977. "What's Happening." *Ladies' Home Journal* (August): 8.

Sharar, S. A. 1998. "Life Behind Closed Doors: Case of Battered Women." *The Star.* World Sources, Inc. (wire story). (10 December).

Sharkey, Jacqueline. 1993. "When Pictures Drive Foreign Policy." *American Journalism Review*: 15–19.

Sheiman, Bruce. 1994. "Make Your Circ Plan Match Your Goals." *Folio* 23 (20): 130.

Shiach, Morag. 1998. "Feminism and Popular Culture." In *Cultural Theory and Popular Culture: A Reader.* 2d ed. Ed. J. Storey. Athens: University of Georgia Press. 333–41.

Shultz, Vicki. 1992. "Women 'Before' the Law: Judicial Stories about Women, Work, and Sex Segregation on the Job." In *Feminists Theorize the Political,* ed. J. Butler and J. Scott. New York: Routledge. 297–338.

Siltanen, J., and Stanworth, M. 1984. Introduction. In *Women and the Public Sphere,* ed. J. Siltanen and M. Stanworth. New York: St. Martin's Press. 19–36.

Simões, Inimá F., et. al., eds. 1986. *Um país no ar: História da TV Brasileira em Três Canais.* São Paulo: Brasiliense.

Simpson, Amelia. 1993. *Xuxa: The Mega-Marketing of Gender, Race, and Modernity.* Philadelphia: Temple University Press.

Sinclair, John. 1996. "Mexico, Brazil, and the Latin World." In *Peripheral Vision: New Patterns in Global Television,* ed. J. Sinclair, E. Jacka, and S. Cunningham. New York: Oxford University Press. 33–66.

Skelton, George. 1996. "Capitol Journal: The Risks of Wooing Strange Bedfellows." *Los Angeles Times* (28 October): A3.

Skidmore, Paula. 1995. "Telling Tales: Media Power, Ideology, and the Reporting of Child Sexual Abuse." In *Crime and Media: The Postmodern Spectacle,* ed. D. Kidd-Hewitt and R. Osborne. London: Pluto. 78–106.

———. 1998. "Gender and the Agenda: News Reporting of Child Sexual Abuse." In *News, Gender, and Power,* ed. C. Carter, G. Branston, and S. Allan. London: Routledge. 204–19.

Smith, Adam. 1924. *An Inquiry into the Nature and Causes of the Wealth of Nations.* London: J. M. Dent. (Originally published 1776).

Smith, Dorothy E. 1987. *The Everyday World as Problematic: A Feminist Sociology.* Toronto: University of Toronto Press.

———. 1990a. *The Conceptual Practices of Power: A Feminist Sociology of Knowledge.* Boston: Northeastern University Press.

———. 1990b. *Texts, Facts, and Femininity: Exploring the Relations of Ruling.* London: Routledge.

Smythe, Dallas W. 1960. "The Political Economy of Communication." *Journalism Quarterly.*

———. 1977. "Communications: Blindspot of Western Marxism." *Canadian Journal of Political and Social Theory* 1: 1–27.

———. 1978. "Rejoinder to Graham Murdock." *Canadian Journal of Political and Social Theory* 2: 120–29.

Soothill, Keith, and Sylvia Walby. 1991. *Sex Crime in the News.* London: Routledge.

Spakes, Patricia. 1995. "Women, Work, and Babies: Family-Labor Market Policies in Three European Countries." *AFFILIA* 10(4): 369–97.

Spigel, Lynn. 1989. "The Domestic Economy of Television Viewing in Postwar America." *Critical Studies in Mass Communication* 6 (4): 337–54.

Spivak, Gayatri C. 1996. "Diasporas Old and New: Women in the Transnational World." *Textual Practice* 10(2): 245–69.

———. 1999. *A Critique of Postcolonial Reason.* Cambridge: Harvard University Press.

Sreberny-Mohammadi, Annabelle. 1994. "Women Talking Politics." In *Perspectives on Women in Television.* Broadcasting Standards Council. Research Working Paper 9, London: BSC. 60–79.

Sreberny-Mohammadi, Annabelle, and Karen Ross. 1996. "Women MPs and the Media: Representing the Body Politic. In *Women and Politics*, ed. J. Lovenduski and P. Norris. Oxford: Oxford University Press. 105–17.

St. John, J. D. 1978. "Sex Role Stereotyping in Early Broadcast History: The Career of Mary Margaret McBride."*Frontiers: Journal of Women's Studies* 3: 31–38.

Stabile, Carole A. 1995. "Resistance, Recuperation, and Reflexivity: The Limits of a Paradigm." *Critical Studies in Mass Communication* 12: 403–22.

Stabiner, K. 1982. "Tapping the Homosexual Market." *New York Times Magazine* (2 May): 34.

Star, Susan L. 1996. "From Hestia to Home Page: Feminism and the Concept of Home in Cyberspace." In *Between Monsters, Goddesses, and Cyborgs: Feminist Confrontation with Science, Medicine, and Cyberspace*, ed. N. Lykke and R. Braidotti. London: Zed Books. 30–46.

Steeves, H. Leslie. 1987. "Feminist Theories and Media Studies." *Critical Studies in Mass Communication* 4(2): 95–135.

———. 1988. "What Distinguishes Feminist Scholarship in Communication Studies?" *Women's Studies in Communication* 11: 12–17.

———. 1993. "Creating Imagined Communities: Development Communication and the Challenge of Feminism." *Journal of Communication* 43 (3): 218–29.

Steeves, H. Leslie, Sam Becker, and Hyeon Choi. 1988. "The Context of Employed Women's Media Use." *Women's Studies in Communication* 11: 21–43.

Steinberg, Stephen. 1995. *Turning Back: The Retreat from Racial Justice in American Thought and Policy.* Boston: Beacon Press.

Steiner, Linda. 1998. "Newsroom Accounts of Power at Work." In *News, Gender, and Power,* ed. C. Carter, G. Branston, and S. Allan. London: Routledge. 145–59.

Stephenson, Mary-Ann. 1998. *The Glass Trapdoor.* London: Fawcett Society.

Stith, Anthony. 1996. *Breaking the Glass Ceiling: Racism and Sexism in Corporate America: The Myths, the Realities, and the Solutions.* Orange, N.J.: Bryant and Dillon.

Stockdale, Margaret S., ed. 1996. *Sexual Harassment in the Workplace.* Thousand Oaks: Sage.

Straubhaar, Joseph D. 1996. "The Electronic Media in Brazil." In *Communication in Latin America: Journalism, Mass Media, and Society,* ed. Richard Cole. Washington, D.C.: Scholarly Resources. 217–43.

Streicher, Helen White. 1974. "The Girls in the Cartoons." *Journal of Communication* 24: 125–29.

Streitmatter, Rodger. 1995. *Unspeakable: The Rise of the Gay and Lesbian Press in America.* Boston: Faber and Faber.

Strinati, Dominic. 1995. *An Introduction to Theories of Popular Culture.* London: Routledge.

Stucker, Jan Collins. 1991. "The Missing Questions." *Nieman-Reports* 45(4): 21.

Studlar, Gaylyn. 1991. "Midnight S/Excess: Cult Configurations of 'Femininity' and the Perverse." *The Cult Film Experience: Beyond All Reason,* ed. J. P. Telotte. Austin: University of Texas Press. 138–55.

Subervi-Vélez, Federico, et al. 1997. "Hispanic-Oriented Media." In *Latin Looks,* ed. Clara Rodríguez. Boulder: Westview Press. 225–37.

Switzer, M. 1998. "Doing Right by Aboriginals." *The Ottawa Citizen* (10 December): 13.

Takaki, Ronald. 1993. *A Different Mirror: A History of Multicultural America.* Boston: Little, Brown.

Taylor, Jeanie, Cheris Kramarae, and Maureen Ebben, eds. 1993. *Women, Information Technology, and Scholarship.* Urbana: WITS.

"Teen-Age Consumers." 1957. *Consumer Reports* (March): 139–42.

"Teen-Agers' Refusal to Wear Hose Upsets Hosiery Industry." 1950. *Advertising Age* (11 September): 11.

Tester, Keith. 1994. *Media, Culture, and Morality.* London: Routledge.

Tewkesbury, Joan. 1976. *Nashville.* New York: Bantam Books.

Thomas, Richard. 1996. "Blair's Bad Hair Day." *Guardian* (7 November).

Tierney, J. 1998. "America: The World's Cop is a Cop-Out." *On the Issues* (7: 4): 20–22.

Tobenkin, David. 1994. "'Xuxa' Resurfaces on Family Channel." *Broadcasting and Cable* (16 May): 39.

Tomasevski, K. 1995. *Women and Human Rights.* London: Zed Books.

Tong, Rosemarie. 1997. *Feminist Thought: A Comprehensive Introduction.* London: Routledge.

Traube, Elizabeth. 1992. *Dreaming Identities: Class, Gender, and Generation in 1980s Hollywood Movies.* Boulder: Westview.

Tuana, Nancy, and Rosemarie Tong. 1995. *Feminism and Philosophy: Essential Readings in Theory, Reinterpretation, and Application.* Boulder: Westview Press.

Tuchman, Gaye. 1978a. *Making News: A Study in the Construction of Reality.* New York: The Free Press.

———. 1978b. "The Symbolic Annihilation of Women by the Mass Media." In *Hearth and Home: Images of Women in the Mass Media,* ed. G. Tuchman et al. New York: Oxford University Press.

Tuchman, Gaye, Arlene Kaplan Daniels, and James Benet, eds. 1978. *Hearth and Home: Images of Women in the Mass Media.* New York: Oxford University Press.

Turow, Joseph. 1997. *Breaking Up America: Advertising and the New Media World.* Chicago: University of Chicago Press.

Tunstall, Jeremy. 1977. *The Media Are American*. London: Constable

"TV . . . Caught in Its Own Network." 1951. *Senior Scholastic* (10 October): 13–14.

"Twiggy Makes U.S. Styles Swing Too." 1967. *Life* (14 April): 99–100.

"Twiggy: Click! Click!" 1967. *Newsweek* (10 April): 62–66.

United Nations. 1995a. *The World's Women 1995: Trends and Statistics*. New York: United Nations.

United Nations. 1995b. *The United Nations and the Advancement of Women, 1945–1995*. New York: United Nations.

United Nations Development Programme (UNDP). 1997. Human Development Report, 1997. New York: Oxford University Press.

United Nations Development Programme (UNDP). 1998. Human Development Report, 1998. New York: Oxford University Press.

University of Loughborough. 1992. *Election Study for the Guardian*. Loughborough: University of Loughborough.

University of Loughborough. 1997. "Election Study for the Guardian, Post Election Review." *Guardian* (2 May).

U.S. Bureau of the Census. 1975. *Historical Statistics of the United States, Colonial Times to 1970, Bicentennial Edition*. Washington, D.C..

Ussher, Jane M. 1997. *Fantasies of Femininity: Reframing the Boundaries of Sex*. New Brunswick: Rutgers University Press.

Vaid, U. 1995. *Virtual Equality: The Mainstreaming of Gay and Lesbian Liberation*. New York: Anchor Books.

Valdivia, Angharad, and Ramona Curry. 1998. "Xuxa at the Borders of Global TV: The Institutionalization and Marginalization of Brazil's Blonde Ambition." *Camera Obscura* 38: 31–59.

van Zoonen, Liesbet. 1989. "Professional Socialization of Feminist Journalists in the Netherlands." *Women's Studies in Communication* 12(3): 1–23.

———. 1994. *Feminist Media Studies*. London: Sage.

———. 1998. " One of the Girls? The Changing Gender of Journalism." In *News, Gender, and Power*, ed. C. Carter, G. Branston, and S. Allan. London: Routledge. 33–46.

Vatter, Harold G. 1963. *The U.S. Economy in the 1950s: An Economic History*. New York: Norton.

Vedel, Thierry. 1991. "Telematics and the Configuration of Actors: A European Perspective." In *European Telematics*, ed. Josiane Jouët and Patrice Flichy. New York: Elsevier Science. 91–105.

"Victims of Violence Not Best Served under One Umbrella." 1998. Canadian Corporate News Inc. (wire story) (8 December).

Volokh, Eugene. 1997. "The California Civil Rights Initiative: An Interpretive Guide." *UCLA Law Review* 44(5): 1335–404.

Wahl, Anna, ed. 1995. *Men's Perceptions of Women and Management*. Stockholm: Ministry of Health and Social Affairs.

Walby, Sylvia. 1986. *Patriarchy at Work: Patriarchal and Capitalist Relations in Employment.* Minneapolis: University of Minnesota Press.

———. 1990. *Theorizing Patriarchy.* Oxford: Basil Blackwell.

———. 1992. "Post-Post-Modernism? Theorizing Social Complexity." In *Destabilizing Theory: Contemporary Feminist Debates,* ed. M. Barrett and A. Phillips. Cambridge: Polity Press. 31–52.

Walker, John F., and Harold G. Vatter. 1996. "Why Has the United States Operated below Potential since World War II?" In *History of the U.S. Economy since World War II,* ed. H. G. Vatter and J. F. Walker. Armonk, N.Y.: M. E. Sharpe. 481–92.

Walt Disney Company. 1998. Annual Report. Anaheim, Calif.

Wambold, Kay. "Good Grooming for Two." 1949. *Parents' Magazine* (April): 91.

Waring, Marilyn. 1988. *If Women Counted.* San Francisco, Harper and Row.

———. 1999. *Counting for Nothing: What Men Value and What Women Are Worth.* Toronto: University of Toronto Press.

Warnke, Georgia. 1995. "Discourse Ethics and Feminist Dilemmas of Difference." In *Feminists Read Habermas: Gendering the Subject of Discourse,* ed. J. Meehan. New York: Routledge. 247–61.

Warren, Jenifer, and Kenneth Weiss. 1997. "Agencies Left to Sort Out How to Obey." *Los Angeles Times* (9 April): A1.

Wasko, Janet. 1992. Introduction. *Democratic Communications in the Information Age,* ed. J. Wasko and V. Mosco. Toronto: Garamond Press.

———. 1994. *Hollywood in the Information Age.* Austin: University of Texas Press.

———. 2000. "Political Economy of Film." In R. Stam and T. Miller, *Film and Theory: An Anthology.* Malden: Blackwell. 221–33.

Wasko, Janet, Vincent Mosco, and Manjunath Pendakur, eds. 1993. *Illuminating the Blindspots: Essays Honoring Dallas W. Smythe.* Norwood: Ablex.

Weaver, Carolyn. 1992. "A Secret No More." *Washington Journalism Review* 25.

Webster, Frank, and Kevin Robbins. 1986. *Information Technology: A Luddite Analysis.* Norwood: Ablex.

Weibel, Kathryn. 1977. *Mirror, Mirror: Images of Women Reflected in Popular Culture.* Garden City: Anchor Books.

Weir, Allison. 1995. "Toward a Model of Self-Identity: Habermas and Kristeva." In *Feminists Read Habermas: Gendering the Subject of Discourse,* ed. J. Meehan. New York: Routledge. 263–82.

Whitworth, Sandra. 1994. *Feminism and International Relations: Towards a Political Economy of Gender in Interstate and Non-governmental Institutions.* New York: St. Martin's Press.

Wilke, M. 1996. "Simmons Plans a Definitive Survey of Gay Consumers." *Advertising Age* (19 February): 39.

————. 1997a. "Data Shows Affluence of Gay Market." *Advertising Age* (3 February): 58.

————. 1997b. "Big Advertisers Join Move to Embrace Gay Market." *Advertising Age* (4 August): 1.

————. 1998. "Fewer Gays are Wealthy, Data Says." *Advertising Age* (19 October): 58.

Wilkins, K. G. 1997. "Gender, Power, and Development." *Journal of International Communication.* Special issue: Communication and Development: Beyond Panaceas. (December) 4: 2: 102–20.

Williams, Linda. 1988. "Feminist Film Theory: *Mildred Pierce* and the Second World War." In *Female Spectators: Looking at Film and Television,* ed. E. D. Pribram. London: Verso. 12–30.

————. 1990. "'Something Else Besides a Mother': *Stella Dallas* and the Maternal Melodrama." In *Issues in Feminist Film Criticism,* ed. Patricia Erens. Bloomington: University of Indiana Press. 137–62.

Williams Crenshaw, Kimberlé. 1997. "Color Blindness, History, and the Law." In *The House that Race Built,* ed. W. Lubiano. New York: Vintage. 280–88.

Williamson, Judith. 1978. *Decoding Advertisements.* London: Marion Boyars.

Wolf, Naomi. 1991. *The Beauty Myth: How Images of Beauty Are Used against Women.* New York: Anchor Books.

Wolfus, Daniel. 1998. "Publisher's Note." *Estylo* (August): 10.

Wollstonecraft, Mary. 1995. *Vindication of the Rights of Women.* Cambridge: Cambridge University Press. Originally published 1891.

Women and Media Decision-Making. 1987. Paris: UNESCO.

"Women Helped Push Through 209." 1996. *Fresno Bee* (12 November): A3.

Women's Broadcasting Committee. 1993. *Her Point of View.* London: WBC and Bectu.

Women's Communication Centre. 1996. *What Women Want.* London: WCC.

Wood, Abbott. 1993. "Hispanic Ratings Get Real; Buyers' Suspicions of Ratings Inflation in Spanish TV Are Confirmed by NHTI." *Mediaweek* 3 (16): 16.

Wood, Ellen Meiksins. 1988. "Capitalism and Human Emancipation." *New Left Review* 167 (January/February): 1–20.

World Bank. 1999. *World Development Report: Knowledge for Development.* New York: Oxford University Press.

World Investment Report on Transnational Corporations and Competitiveness, 1995. 1996. New York: UN Conference on Trade and Development (UNCTAD).

Wright, Erik Olin, et al. 1995. "The Gender Gap in Workplace Authority: A Cross-National Study." *American Sociological Review* 60: 407–35.

Wyatt, Justin. 1996. "Economic Constraints/Economic Opportunities: Robert Altman as Auteur." *The Velvet Light Trap* 38 (fall): 51–67.

Wykes, Maggie. 1998. "A Family Affair: The British Press, Sex, and the Wests." In *News, Gender, and Power,* ed. C. Carter, G. Branston, and S. Allan. London: Routledge. 233–47.

Yacowar, Maurice. 1980. "Actors as Conventions in the Films of Robert Altman," *Cinema Journal* 20.1 (fall): 14–27.

Young, Iris Marion. 1990. *Justice and the Politics of Gender.* Princeton: Princeton University Press.

Contributors

Robin Andersen is associate professor of communication and media studies and director of the Peace and Justice Studies Program at Fordham University. She is author of *Consumer Culture and TV Programming* and editor (with Lance Strate) of *Critical Studies in Media Commercialism*. She edits the book series Media Studies, published by Fordham University Press.

Ellen Balka is associate professor in the School of Communication at Simon Fraser University. Her research examines women's interactions with information technology, ranging from the politics of technology design to policy issues that influence use. She is the author of *Computer Networking: Spinsters on the Web* and coeditor of *Women, Work, and Computerization: Charting a Course to the Future*.

Amy Beer holds a Ph.D. in radio/television/film from Northwestern University and a law degree from New York University. She teaches media studies and worked for many years with Latino human rights organizations in the United States and Central America.

Carolyn M. Byerly holds a doctorate in communications from the School of Communications, University of Washington. She conducts research on women's relationship to international news industries, political economy of news, alternative media, and the impact of social movements on the news. She has served on the journalism and women's studies faculties of Ithaca College in New York and Radford University in Virginia. She presently lives in Hyattsville, Maryland.

Ramona Curry is associate professor in the Department of English at the University of Illinois in Urbana-Champaign. She is author of *Too Much of a Good Thing: Mae West as Cultural Icon* (Minnesota, 1996). Her research focuses on critical theory, film history, and cultural studies.

Fred Fejes is professor of media studies at Florida Atlantic University. His areas of interest include sexualities and the media, sociology of news, and gay/lesbian history. He is currently working on a study of the campaign led by Anita Bryant in 1977 to repeal Dade County's ordinance banning discrimination against gays and lesbians.

Nancy Hauserman is Williams Teaching Professor of Management and Organization, and associate dean of undergraduate programs, at the Tippie College of Business, University of Iowa. Her research focuses on sexual harassment, media portrayals of family and work issues, and ethics.

Michèle Martin is professor at the School of Journalism and Communication of Carleton University, Canada. Her books include *Hello Central? Gender, Technology, and Culture in the Formation of Telephone Systems* and *Communication and Mass Media*; both focus on feminism and communications.

Stana Martin is assistant professor of communication at Central Missouri State University. Her research examines how gender mediates the impact of information technology on work; she also works with elementary and junior-high school teachers to incorporate technology into their curricula.

Lisa McLaughlin is assistant professor of mass communication and women's studies at Miami University in Oxford, Ohio. Her articles on feminism, political economy, and the public sphere have appeared in such journals as *Media, Culture, and Society* and *Journal of Communication Inquiry*. She coedits the international journal *Feminist Media Studies*.

Eileen R. Meehan is associate professor of media arts at the University of Arizona. Her research examines the political economy of culture and processes of commodification.

Roopali Mukherjee is assistant professor in the Department of Communication and Culture at Indiana University, Bloomington. She has been a postdoctoral fellow at the Center for African American Studies at UCLA. Her research interests include critical policy studies and race/ethnicity.

Angela R. Record is a doctoral candidate at the Institute of Communications Research, University of Illinois at Urbana-Champaign. Her research focuses on gender and the dynamics of the teenage market in the post–World War II era.

Ellen Riordan is assistant professor of communication at Miami University, Ohio. Her research focuses on political economy, feminist theory, and popular culture.

Karen Ross is director of the Centre for Communication, Culture, and Media Studies at Coventry University. Her research examines women's participation in politics, the representation of women, and women's employment in British news media.

H. Leslie Steeves is professor at the School of Journalism and Communication, University of Oregon. Her research examines communication and gender issues in developing countries, especially in Africa. She is author of *Gender Violence and the Press: The St. Kizito Story* and co-author of *Communication for Development in the Third World: Theory and Practice for Empowerment*.

Angharad N. Valdivia is research associate professor at the Institute of Communications Research, University of Illinois at Urbana-Champaign. Her books include *Geographies of Latinidad: Latina/o Studies into the Twentieth Century, Media Studies Companion, A Latina in the Land of Hollywood,* and *Feminism, Multiculturalism, and the Media.* Her research focuses on issues of gender, multiculturalism, and popular culture especially as they pertain to Latin American and U.S. Latina/o Studies.

Janet Wasko is professor in the School of Journalism and Communication at the University of Oregon. She is author of *Movies and Money* and *Hollywood in the Information Age.* Her research focuses on political economy of communication.

Justin Wyatt is executive director consultant at the media research and consulting firm Frank N. Magid Associates in Sherman Oaks, California. He is the editor of the Commerce and Mass Culture Series at the University of Minnesota Press.

Index